Land Campaigns of the Civil War

PAUL CALORE

McFarland & Company, Inc., Publishers
Jefferson, North Carolina, and London

The present work is a reprint of the library bound edition of Land Campaigns of the Civil War, *first published in 2000 by McFarland.*

All maps are by Paul Calore.

LIBRARY OF CONGRESS CATALOGUING-IN-PUBLICATION DATA

Land campaigns of the Civil War / Paul Calore.
p. cm.
Includes bibliographical references and index.

ISBN 978-0-7864-7399-1
softcover : acid free paper ∞

1. United States — History — Civil War, 1861–1865 — Campaigns. 2. United States — History — Civil War, 1861–1865 — Campaigns — Chronology. I. Title.

E470.C16 2012 99-52495
973.7'3 — dc21

BRITISH LIBRARY CATALOGUING DATA ARE AVAILABLE

On the cover: Bird's-eye view of Gettysburg battlefield, showing positions of Union and Confederate armies during the Civil War, W. Endicott & Co., Lithographer, N.Y., ca. 1863 (Library of Congress)

Manufactured in the United States of America

McFarland & Company, Inc., Publishers
Box 611, Jefferson, North Carolina 28640
www.mcfarlandpub.com

Land Campaigns of the Civil War

Also by Paul Calore
and from McFarland

The Causes of the Civil War: The Political, Cultural, Economic and Territorial Disputes between North and South (2008)

Naval Campaigns of the Civil War (2002)

Acknowledgments

Special thanks to my daughter Cheryl Calore for enduring my endless demands on her time and especially for the tremendously helpful books she bought for me on publishing this, my first book. I owe her a debt of gratitude for all her assistance. Also, many thanks to my daughter Vickie and my son, Stephen. Their enthusiasm and excitement was always welcome and gratefully received. Thanks also to Christopher Abatecola for being my personal computer engineer and for the software that made writing this book a bit easier. And finally, a very heartfelt thanks of appreciation goes to my wife, "Beal," for her patience and understanding throughout this project.

Contents

List of Maps

Preface

The American Civil War is perhaps the most significant single event ever experienced by the people of the United States. In terms of its human misery, physical destruction, and the loss of life and property, the war resulted in enormous suffering.

The causes of the war were rooted in a divided political and social ideology of a young and troubled nation. The loss of more than a half million American lives over four terrible years was presumed to have settled those divisive issues, but even during the Reconstruction years that followed, it was necessary to continue addressing the civil rights and racial equality disputes that contributed so significantly to the onset of the war. In an attempt to clear up the disillusionment following emancipation, additional federal action was necessary, including constitutional amendments, the Freedmen's Bureau, and various civil rights laws.

The Civil War has been over since 1865, yet there is still a residue of those same problems confronting our nation today. Traceable to those chaotic years, civil rights issues are still being fought over, albeit in the more subtle battlefields of the American courtroom, state governments, and the U.S. Congress.

In that sense, the Civil War is a continuing conflict, and the struggle to relieve these remaining social tensions goes on. There is a clear connection between our present-day racial problems and the racial problems of the Civil War years. This connection is one of the sub-liminal motivations that drives the student of American history on his or her search for additional knowledge of this period. The reader seeks an understanding of those times, both to become better informed about the history of today's sensitive social ills and to understand the mechanics of the conflict. The Civil War materials on the shelves of today's bookstores are "specialty books" on specific topics or personalities associated with the conflict. There are books on a great number of particular battles, both large and small. One is also never at a loss to find books dealing exclusively with any number of Civil War generals, both Union and Confederate. Likewise on the shelves are Civil War source books, battlefield guides, photographic histories, question-and-answer books, the memoirs of soldiers, books on memorabilia, spies, accounts of heroes, and works on many other Civil War topics.

There is no question that the reading public benefits tremendously from this proliferation and diversity of subject matter. No matter what level of expertise or interest the Civil War reader has, there is almost always a book to fill his or her need.

However, for the person looking for a first volume on the Civil War, the above books may not serve adequately. A first-time researcher looking for a book on the history of the Civil War itself will discover that the books available seem to be written mostly for the more advanced reader. Learned and respected historians write the majority of these books. Their styles commingle United States political history, in-depth social commentary, and everything else connected to that period with the fighting of the war. For a comprehensive understanding of those turbulent years, this kind of analysis is necessary. But not everyone is looking for a deep analytical study of those times. Without a basic understanding of Civil War events, the reader may not be able to fully enjoy the benefits of these in-depth works, no matter how well they are written. I suspect that many readers may become confused after reading page after page of sometimes tedious detail. Such encounters may result in a loss of interest.

It is my opinion that a definite need exists for a Civil War history that is simplified, understandable and easily readable. I think this book will fill that need. Simply written, *Land Campaigns of the Civil War* is an ideal book for students, teachers, Civil War aficionados, and partisans of American history. It is succinct but complete, accurate and to the point.

In writing this book, I endeavored to accomplish several goals. The first was to provide a brief background of the political events that set the stage for war, the events that many historians believe had a significant contribution to the outbreak of hostilities. And, second, I wanted to present a complete account of the Civil War land campaigns that could be easily understood without relying on an abundance of extraneous detail and commentary.

My challenge was to describe the events of those four terrible years in a compressed and simplified format without compromising the facts. Despite the fact that the war was fought on three different fronts, sometimes at the same time, I tried to offer the reader a seamless flow of events in order to provide a better grasp of the war's chronology. Understanding the sequence of events is fundamental for the reader to capture the whole picture. I hoped to reduce the complexity in this area, and to clarify the relationships among the various armies.

This book is for those wanting a baseline or foundation of Civil War knowledge. I hope that by providing this foundation, I have also provided an impetus for further study. With this book in the reader's "tool kit," an understanding of specialized and highly detailed works on the Civil War will certainly be easier—and as a consequence, a much more enjoyable reading experience.

Introduction

The United States in the mid–19th century were in reality two Americas with two distinct cultural, political and economic philosophies, struggling to coexist peacefully.

The Northern states were relatively advanced economically, and flaunted their success as a thriving and dynamic region of industrial progress. The North was also the center for banking, education, railroads, commerce, the arts and politics. Fueling this progress was the endless stream of immigrants entering major cities such as New York, Boston and Philadelphia.

A lack of urbanization in the South was one of the region's characteristics that made it unable to keep pace with the mostly urban North. The economy of the South suffered, slipping further and further behind. This mattered little to the wealthy planters who controlled the region's political and economic power. For the elite aristocratic classes, the Southern lifestyle was especially grand. They enjoyed lavish dinner parties, gala balls, imported clothing and the finest food and drink. They took pride in their relatively genteel life, one they considered superior to that of the North. There, they believed, factory "wage slaves" toiled in conditions that sometimes seemed to make those experienced by Southern slaves positively humane. Northern criticism of Southern ways impressed most Southerners as hypocritical.

Over time, this profound clash of fundamental principles culminated in intense social, economic and political differences that strained the very ideals of the Founding Fathers and set in motion a chain of events leading to war. Of these differences, unquestionably the greatest separating North from South was the institution of slavery.

The importation of Africans was primarily designed to alleviate critical labor shortages on the plantations of wealthy colonial-era planters. Their need for a huge labor force was based on production forecasts to satisfy the tremendous demand for tobacco, rice, sugar and cotton by the English. Because the sparse population of the times did not supply enough hands to work the fields, farm owners resorted to buying workers from slave-traders. Following the invention of the cotton gin in 1793, cotton production and the cotton industry itself exploded in importance. The ability to process raw cotton faster and more easily meant that the planters needed more and more slaves to work the crop. As a result, the cotton-growing states began importing tens of thousands of additional slaves. Slave importation was especially vigorous in the years just before 1808, when Congress outlawed the practice. Despite the ban, a high birthrate among the slave population led to a tremendous growth in numbers. By the mid–19th century, slaves accounted for about a third of the Southern population; the cash crops exported to Europe, grown largely by these slaves, enhanced the pocketbooks of their masters, who in turn became even more politically influential.

To many Northerners, America was the land of freedom, where men were created equal, with liberty and justice for all. At the same time the United States was the world's largest slave-holding country. This glaring conflict was the epitome of hypocrisy and a shocking embarrassment to many Northerners.

The psychological character of the South was rooted in its dependence on a class-based society. To the antebellum aristocrat, the cultural alliance of a class structure was responsible for the progress and superiority of the Southern way of life. One class had to perform the servile toils to enable the other class to lead the way to prosperity for all. Perceived by the South as a natural requisite for a thriving society, slavery to the Northerner was immoral, degrading, and stifling to growth — economically, culturally, and socially.

Angered by this political and social inconsistency, in October of 1859, John Brown, a staunch abolitionist, took matters into his own hands. With his four sons and fourteen supporters, Brown traveled to Harpers Ferry, Virginia, and seized the federal arsenal, the armory and the engine house. Armed with over 200 rifles and pistols and a thousand pikes, he intended to incite the blacks to follow his movement. From Harpers Ferry they would continue through the South, gaining strength and destroying slavery. The plan soon unraveled. Within a matter of hours the group was surrounded by the local militia, who killed ten of Brown's men, including two of his sons. The next day, government troops under the command of Col. Robert E. Lee and Lieut. J.E.B. Stuart arrived and stormed the fire-engine house where Brown and his men were trapped. They captured Brown after a brief encounter. That December, following his trial at Charles Town, Virginia (now West Virginia), Brown was hanged for treason and murder.

John Brown's raid at Harpers Ferry in 1859 not only brought the slavery issue to the fore, but also exacerbated the growing division that was tearing the country apart. Brown's attempt to fight the institution by force was unsuccessful, but unquestionably, it set the stage and focused the nation's conflicting views for the four years of war to come. Slavery was rejected in the North as an abomination, but the South prized it as the mainstay of its economy and even wanted to extend it to other parts of the country.

As it is to this day, the federal government in Washington was empowered to enact legislation governing all states, under one union and one flag. The cotton-growing states were not happy with this arrangement. The South felt victimized because a vast majority of federal laws, regulations and tariffs, especially those influencing their economy and their "states' rights," were passed by a Congress or administrative body that was dominated by Northerners. Because free states outnumbered slave states 20 to 11, and because population in the free states (22 million) far exceeded that of the South (6 million whites), the congressional representation and the electoral vote would always favor the Northern point of view. In the Southern mind that point of view was mostly anti–Southern and anti-slavery.

To correct this perceived inequity, the South needed to expand. It needed more territory. It would populate new states with new Southerners and in turn increase its congressional representation. In this way the South hoped to balance the power in Washington. The territories stretching from the Mississippi River to the California border were prime targets. To promote their expansionist ideals, Southern Democrats believed that their only hope for success depended on a victory in the presidential election of 1860.

Expansion of slavery into the territories was the most significant issue of the presidential campaign. There were three clear and distinct positions on this single political issue. The Republican Party, represented by Abraham Lincoln, held the "Northern" point of view that slavery was wrong but that it could be tolerated by restricting it to its present borders. The Democrats held two entirely different opinions on this matter. This difference would split the Democratic Party and result in the nomination of two Democratic presidential candidates. One was Sen. John C. Breckinridge of Kentucky, who represented the Southerners' presumed right to extend slavery to the territories. The other was Sen. Stephen A. Douglas of Illinois, who believed in popular sovereignty, the right of the people of the territory to decide for themselves the question of slavery within their borders.

During the campaign, some Southern leaders vigorously preached the dire consequences to all slave states in the event the Republicans won the election. In this political climate the first serious threat of secession was heard.

When the votes were counted, Abraham Lincoln, the young Republican lawyer from Illinois, won the election. Southern politicians were incensed, but still they searched for some political compromise over the slavery question.

As President-elect Lincoln was preparing for his inauguration, he was asked to consider a last-resort compromise proposal drawn up by Sen. John J. Crittenden of Kentucky. In 1820, the "Missouri Compromise" had granted statehood to Missouri as a slave state with the proviso that in the remaining area of the Louisiana purchase, a line roughly consistent with Missouri's Southern border would mark the separation of slave states from free states. The "Crittenden Compromise," an attempt to cool the threat of secession, requested that this imaginary line be extended from its current position all the way across the territories to California. All land above this line would be reserved for free states; all land below would be open to slavery. Not surprisingly, Lincoln flatly rejected this proposal by reiterating his well-known position: tolerating slavery within its current borders but refusing to accept, on any condition, an expansion of slavery to the territories. Lincoln believed that slavery, if contained, would eventually cease to exist.

To the Southern politicians bent on preserving their way of life, seceding from the Union now seemed the only solution to their problem. With Lincoln in the White House and Southern views castigated in Congress, control of Southern interests and principles would be forever lost to outsiders. Southerners sincerely believed that the right of each state to govern itself under its state constitution and laws had to be upheld.

In December of 1860, the South Carolina state convention, meeting in Charleston, ran out of options, ran out of patience and ran out of loyalty to the country. The convention delegates voted to secede from the Union.

At first, this act of defiance was not taken very seriously by Lincoln or by most Northerners. By Lincoln's inauguration day in March, however, six more Southern states had joined South Carolina: Mississippi, Florida, Alabama, Georgia, Louisiana and Texas. In February, Jefferson Davis was sworn in as president of the new Confederate States of America.

Lincoln did not recognize secession under the Constitution and believed the seceding states would all eventually return to the fold. Despite this belief, in his inaugural address Lincoln made a veiled threat to the rebellious Southerners by reminding them that as president, he was sworn to protect all federal property within the nation's borders. Lincoln would soon have to back these words with action because of events to come in Charleston Harbor, South Carolina, site of Fort Sumter.

A Note on Battle Nomenclature

Union and Confederate sources sometimes referred to certain battles by different names. For example, the battle that the Union army came to call Antietam was known by the Confederates as Sharpsburg. The following list of differing battle names is offered to clarify any references to these battles.

Union	*Confederate*
Antietam	Sharpsburg
First Bull Run	First Manassas
Second Bull Run	Second Manassas
Pea Ridge	Elkhorn Tavern
Shiloh	Pittsburg Landing
Logan's Cross Roads	Mill Springs
Stones River	Murfreesboro
Opequon Creek	Winchester
Wilson's Creek	Oak Hills

I
The War Begins: Fort Sumter to Bull Run
(April–July 1861)

On April 12, four months after South Carolina seceded from the Union, Fort Sumter, still under construction on a small island in Charleston Harbor, was occupied by 65 Union militiamen. Their commander was Maj. Robert Anderson, a 56-year-old Southerner from Kentucky. Major Anderson, a graduate of the U.S. Military Academy where he taught classes in gunnery, was married to a Georgia woman, and supported slavery and states' rights. Yet his loyalty to the Union and the welfare of his men were paramount.

The Union troops seized the island fortress on the night of December 26, having moved from Fort Moultrie, a small Revolutionary-era sea battery just across the bay. While at Fort Moultrie, Anderson and his men were constantly subjected to threats from neighboring townspeople. Fears for the safety of their families grew each day. Anderson considered the fort extremely vulnerable, particularly from the rear, which lay entirely exposed to the surrounding heights of the city.

Misinterpreting an order that he believed gave him authority to move his men when in imminent danger, Anderson ordered his troops to evacuate the fort. After making arrangements for the safekeeping of their families at Fort Johnson, opposite Charleston, the men destroyed the artillery at Fort Moultrie and then quietly rowed the one mile across the bay in the cold darkness of that winter night.

Unknown to Anderson, on December 10 President Buchanan arranged a deal with South Carolina congressmen over the future of the government facilities in the Charleston area, namely Fort Sumter, Fort Moultrie, Castle Pinckney and the U.S. arsenal. To delay a confrontation on this matter until Lincoln was sworn in, the lame-duck Buchanan agreed to open negotiations on the transfer of these properties and also agreed not to reinforce, resupply or change their military status during the negotiating process.

In the morning, when Anderson's whereabouts was discovered, the new Confederate government as well as the people of Charleston grew extremely agitated, considered the move a hostile act in light of the agreement, and vowed to take "their" fort back, by force if necessary.

In Washington, Southern members of Buchanan's cabinet, furious over what they considered a breach of political ethics, submitted their resignations. The cabinet vacancies were immediately filled with loyal Unionists. With General-in-Chief Winfield Scott, the president's 76-year-old military advisor, the cabinet convinced Buchanan that he must at least make an attempt to assist the Union garrison. As a result, a secret mission was devised to resupply Fort Sumter using an unarmed steamer, the *Star of the West.* When the ship tried to enter Charleston Harbor on January 9, Confederate batteries on Morris Island, tipped off beforehand of her departure, fired one shot across her bow, effectively terminating her mission.

For three-and-a-half months, Anderson and his men mounted guns, bricked up embrasures, stacked sandbags, secured the approaches, and set up wire traps to tighten the defenses against the expected assault. The besieged fort, running out of rations and threatened by an arc of coastal artillery, prepared for the worst.

In Washington, the recently sworn-in President Lincoln was compelled to act. General-in-Chief Scott told the president that reinforcing Fort Sumter at this stage of the crisis was impossible without the necessary fleet of ships and 25,000 troops. The majority of Lincoln's cabinet agreed with the general and even recommended recalling the garrison and abandoning the fort. The president's dilemma required that he either evacuate Fort Sumter, as the majority of his cabinet advised, or adhere to his principles and his constitutional responsibilities so eloquently communicated in his inaugural address. At a March 28 meeting, Lincoln convinced the cabinet that General Scott's recommendation was flawed, that his statements were in fact politically motivated. The astonished cabinet, now suspicious of General Scott's credibility, reversed its opinion and voted to support the president. Notwithstanding his newly found support, Lincoln decided he must resupply the garrison and at the same time avoid provoking an incident.

On April 6, Lincoln assured Gov. Francis Pickens that a supply ship enroute to the island fortress was carrying only needed provisions. The president's message read, "an attempt will be made to supply Fort Sumter with provisions only; and that, if such attempt be not resisted, no effort to throw in men, arms, or ammunition, will be made, without further notice, [except] in case of an attack on the Fort." Three days later, despite Lincoln's pledge, the Confederate secretary of war, Leroy P. Walker, acting under orders from President Davis, issued instructions to deliver an ultimatum to Major Anderson before the relief ship arrived. If the garrison did not surrender by 4 A.M., April 12, shelling from Confederate batteries would commence.

The ultimatum was delivered by aides-de-camp of Gen. Pierre Gustave Toutant Beauregard, a former major in the U.S. Engineers and once a student in Major Anderson's gunnery class at West Point. Beauregard now commanded 6,000 South Carolinians. The goals were to demonstrate South Carolina's commitment to her sovereignty, and thus possibly lure Virginia into the Confederacy.

Major Anderson refused to surrender, saying, "Gentlemen, if you do not batter the fort to pieces about us, we shall be starved out in a few days."

At 3:20 A.M. on April 12, two Confederate officials delivered a final message to Anderson. "By authority of Brigadier General Beauregard, commanding the Provisional Forces of the Confederate States, we have the honor to notify you that we will open the fire of his batteries on Fort Sumter in one hour from this time."

At 4:30 A.M. on April 12, General Beauregard began a bombardment of Fort Sumter. The artillery barrage lasted for some 33 hours. Shells and hot-shot rained down on the fort from Morris, James and Sullivan Islands, Fort Moultrie, Stevens' Point floating battery (artillery mounted on a floating platform), the floating battery in Charleston Harbor and from Cumming's Point battery. The fiery spectacle created an Independence Day mood for the civilian spectators who crowded the rooftops to witness the show.

With the few guns previously mounted, the garrison made a

valiant attempt to fight back, but Major Anderson's firepower was no match for the Rebel assault. The Union position was desperate. There was no food to eat, fires threatened the main powder magazine, Lincoln's supply ship had stalled in the harbor, and the fort was being destroyed by over 3,000 shells.

Finally, on April 13, Major Anderson surrendered the fort. The next day, following a 50-gun salute to the Stars and Stripes, he marched his troops out and sailed to New York City, a hero. Miraculously, no one died on either side as a result of the artillery barrage. During the salute, however, one private was killed instantly when sparks entered the muzzle of one of the guns, causing it to explode.

The president responded almost immediately to the Southern aggression and loss of Fort Sumter. The day after Major Anderson surrendered, Lincoln called for 75,000 men to be recruited by the governors of the states and territories. Believing that the impending conflict would prove brief, authorities set the term of enlistment at only 90 days.

Northern states responded to Lincoln's call with unparalleled enthusiasm and patriotism. In some states, whole towns signed up to defend the Union. Washington soon resembled one huge training camp as thousands of men eagerly prepared for what they perceived as one grand confrontation to save the Union.

Lincoln's call for thousands of troops was considered a serious threat by pro-secessionists. In fact, they considered it the president's declaration of war against the South. The mere suggestion of sending troops against their sister states was abhorrent to Southern governors.

On April 17, the remaining uncommitted Southern states, Arkansas, North Carolina, Tennessee and Virginia, seceded as well.

The secession of Virginia and its significant impact on the balance of power was not overlooked by either side. Virginia brought critical resources to the Confederacy. Not only was she the most populous but also the most advanced industrial state in the South. Tredegar Iron Works in Richmond became the production leader, supplying armaments to the Southern military for the duration of the war. Norfolk's Gosport Navy Yard was the largest shipbuilding and repair facility in the South. In May, Richmond was declared the Confederate capital. It lay a mere hundred miles from Washington, D.C. This act secured Virginia's role in the new Southern Confederacy.

Another significant benefit gained from the inclusion of Virginia into the Confederacy was the South's inheritance of many outstanding military officers from the Regular Union Army. Virginia was home to such men as Gen. Robert E. Lee, Gen. Thomas J. "Stonewall" Jackson, and Gen. Joseph E. Johnston. Loyalty to their home state and strong commitment to family was persuasion enough for them to resign their Union commissions. After considering an offer by President Lincoln to command all Union forces, Robert E. Lee chose instead to support his native state and his Southern heritage. This loss would prove quite damaging to the Union Army over the next four years.

Four days after Lincoln's call to arms, four members of the 6th Massachusetts Infantry Regiment and 12 civilians were killed in Baltimore, a city infected with political resentment and hatred. As the Union troops marched through the city streets between the train stations en route to Washington, a pro-secession crowd of onlookers became increasingly angry over the presence of Union soldiers in their city. Within moments, an uncontrollable mob formed and attacked the Union troops. This incident resulted in the first casualties of the Civil War. It also persuaded the mayor and police chief to order the destruction of the railroad bridges into the city from Harrisburg and Philadelphia to prevent the Union from entering Baltimore again. This in turn forced the Union army to open a new circuitous route from Annapolis for transporting the thousands of troops from the North to Washington.

The war continued to escalate. On April 19, President Lincoln issued a proclamation announcing that all Southern ports would be blockaded. Shortly thereafter, the South responded by withholding exports, confident that England and France, whose financial interests lay in the South's continued exportation of cotton, would enter the conflict on the Southern side.

Confederate President Jefferson Davis reacted to the growing crisis. He positioned 15,000 Confederate volunteers within range of Alexandria, Virginia, just across the Potomac River from Washington. On April 18, he ordered his commander, Gen. Joseph E. Johnston, to seize Harpers Ferry, the vital northern entrance to the Shenandoah Valley, and to take control of the Gosport Navy Yard on April 20.

Born in Kentucky in 1808, Davis was a graduate of the West Point class of 1828, but had been forced to resign his commission from ill health seven years later. Finding himself back in civilian life, Davis settled in Mississippi where he found his niche as a planter until 1845, when he was elected to the U.S. House of Representatives. However, after serving only one year of his term, he left Congress to fight in the Mexican War. Following his short stint in Mexico, Davis won a three-year term in the U.S. Senate in 1847, was appointed secretary of war under President Franklin Pierce, and married Varina Howell. In 1857, Davis returned to the Senate, where he remained until 1861.

Believing the expected confrontation to be one glorious battle to settle all, thousands of southerners, not wanting to be left out, raced to join the army. There was no shortage of volunteers for the 12-month term of enlistment.

When the Virginia legislature voted to secede from the Union, the farmers in the remote western sections of the state adamantly opposed secession but were powerless to prevent it. The Lincoln administration was fully aware of their anti-secession sentiments, and also knew that the farmers' interests attached them more to Ohio than to eastern Virginia. The Lincoln administration persuaded Gov. William Dennison of Ohio to help organize a government in Virginia that would repudiate the existing administration in favor of one loyal to the Union. Consequently, Governor Dennison urged Maj. Gen. George B. McClellan, a 35-year-old graduate of West Point and commander of the Department of Ohio, to cross into Virginia to encourage the anti-secession farmers to join the Union cause.

When a small army of Confederates burned several vital bridges of the Baltimore & Ohio Railroad at Grafton, 60 miles south of Wheeling on May 26, communications from Washington to the west were cut off. This provocative act triggered Union military forces into action for the first time in the war. The next day, McClellan ordered two Union regiments stationed at Wheeling to protect the railroads at Grafton, but as the regiments approached, the Rebel forces broke camp and immediately fled to Philippi, about 30 miles farther south.

After the bridges were rebuilt, the Union force, now numbering about 3,000 men, mostly Ohio and Indiana volunteers, was assigned to Gen. Thomas A. Morris, who approved a plan for a June 3, nighttime assault on Philippi. The night of the attack was stormy and the Southern army, caught by surprise, retreated again, this time to the nearby town of Beverly, 35 miles to the southeast. This minor skirmish, "The Philippi Races," gave the Union its first taste of victory.

More significantly, the newspapers were eager for the chance to print exciting front-line battle reports. In their zeal to out-sell the competition, they highly exaggerated the battles and made Gen. McClellan a Lincoln favorite.

In July, as a result of Union successes in Western Virginia, a Confederate contingent commanded by Gen. Robert S. Garnett was ordered to withdraw from Harpers Ferry. As he traveled south, Gen. Garnett's orders were to assume command of the defeated and disorganized units camped in Beverly. As Gen. McClellan's Union army moved closer, Garnett divided his command between two defensive positions near Rich Mountain and Laurel Mountain. McClellan, now personally in command, also divided his forces between Gen. William S. Rosecrans and Gen. Morris, and on July 9 assaulted the two Confederate positions. Following sporadic fighting, both of Garnett's units quietly evacuated their positions under the cover of night and escaped into the mountain woods. In the course of this maneuver, Gen. Garnett was killed in a Union skirmish with his rear guard on July 13. Garnett was the first general officer killed in the Civil War.

As a result of this campaign, Confederate forces fled from northwestern Virginia. This cleared the way for counties in the western sector of the state to eventually secede from Virginia and to join the Union as the state of West Virginia in 1863.

McClellan's successes, although small, were the talk of Washington. His reports and dispatches on the battle, however exaggerated and self-serving, created much excitement for the people, who believed them true. On July 22, McClellan was summoned to the White House to be honored with a new command.

A debatable result of the Union victories in Western Virginia was that it probably helped whet the appetites of Northern hawks straining for an escalating war. Consequently, with mounting pressure from public opinion and with newspapers demanding offensive action on Richmond, Lincoln had little choice but to order the Union field commander, Brig. Gen. Irvin McDowell and his 35,000 minimally trained, 90-day volunteers southward. Forward "to Richmond" was the cry of the day.

A former officer on Gen. Scott's staff, the 43-year-old McDowell enjoyed the confidence of the president and Secretary of War Edwin M. Stanton, and came highly recommended for his first field command. Born in Ohio, the rotund general neither drank nor smoked, but made up for the abstinence with his huge appetite.

General McDowell and his new army began their march to Richmond on the bright and hot summer afternoon of July 16. With the regimental band playing "Yankee Doodle," and with flags waving and much cheering, the new recruits, dressed in brilliant new uniforms of various styles and colors, filed out of Alexandria. A government policy on standardized uniforms did not exist at this time, so many units dressed in the uniforms of their local militia. Some dressed in red baggy trousers with yellow sashes in the French Zouaves style, others, like the Guthrie Grays from Cincinnati dressed in smart gray uniforms with large white plumes in their hats, and yet others wore varying shades of blue.

Lack of military discipline became quickly apparent as the fierce heat took its toll on the young men unaccustomed to long journeys on foot. Over the next two days their main concern was the lack of water, not the life-threatening danger that may have lurked just over the next hill. In one letter to his folks back home, a Union soldier wrote, "I never suffered so much from thirst before. When we came to a brook or spring the soldiers would break their ranks and run for the water, but it was mostly so muddy and rily that it was hardly fit to drink, but yet it was water!" For food, the Northerners each carried three days' rations, consisting mostly of hardtack, salt pork, and coffee. To supplement their meager diet many troops periodically abandoned the march to pick blackberries, peaches and potatoes. Although these forays proved rewarding in a culinary sense, they also glaringly illustrated the lack of discipline instilled in the young soldiers, as well as the officers' inability to control their men.

On July 18, McDowell's army finally reached Centreville, a small town about 20 miles from Washington and only six from Bull Run Creek where General Beauregard and his Confederate army were camped. The Union army at Centreville was organized into five divisions of 12 brigades, but because his army lacked combat experience, McDowell immediately ruled out any chance for success from a frontal attack. Instead he reconnoitered the left side of the Run to test the possibility of turning Beauregard's right flank. Finding the terrain in this quarter unsatisfactory for this purpose, McDowell ordered his troops into bivouac. During this time he studied the layout of the surrounding countryside and tried to decide on a new plan of attack. Since the men's rations were nearly gone, this delay also gave the supply wagons a chance to catch up.

Meanwhile, near Harpers Ferry, 69-year-old Union Gen. Robert Patterson was directed to move his Pennsylvania Militia into the

Shenandoah Valley to contain Confederate Gen. Joseph E. Johnston's Army of the Shenandoah, and to prevent them from reinforcing Beauregard. Patterson failed in this critical assignment and most of the Southerners slipped out of the valley by rail to join Beauregard at Manassas Junction.

On the Southern side, Gen. Pierre G.T. Beauregard, the Confederate hero of Fort Sumter, took command of the Rebel army at Manassas Junction on June 2. His army of eight brigades was concentrated along eight miles of Bull Run Creek. Their mission was to defend Richmond against the expected Union invasion.

Beauregard was regularly briefed on Union troop strengths and battle plans through his small network of spies in Washington. When the decision was made for McDowell to march south to Richmond, Beauregard had the ciphered message in his tent that very night.

The approximately 29,000 troops under Beauregard's command included a brigade under Gen. Theophilus H. Holmes just arriving from Aquia Creek, and brigades under Gens. Milledge C. Bonham, Nathan Evans, Richard S. Ewell, D.R. Jones and James Longstreet, and Cols. Philip St. George Cocke and Jubal Early.

Also on hand were 8,000 soldiers of General Johnston's Army of the Shenandoah, recently arrived by train after successfully evading Gen. Patterson's Union forces. Johnston's army consisted of brigades under Gen. Thomas J. Jackson, Gen. Barnard E. Bee, Col. Francis S. Bartow and Gen. Kirby Smith, who arrived from the Shenandoah Valley on July 20 while McDowell sat in his tent trying to figure out what to do next. Although Johnston was the ranking officer on the field, he was not particularly familiar with this area or with Beauregard's battle plans. For these reasons he deferred authority as well as all responsibility to Beauregard.

The Confederate line of defense, the Alexandria Line, was more or less the line of Bull Run Creek. The Confederate army was located on the south side of the creek, in the vicinity of Manassas Junction, the vital railroad depot of the Orange & Alexandria Railroad and the Manassas Gap Railroad. The Union troops were just across the creek at Centreville. In addition to a number of fords, the most direct path to the Confederate army from Centreville ran straight down the Warrenton Turnpike, a distance of only five miles. This included the distance across two small bridges, the Cub Run Bridge and the Stone Bridge spanning Bull Run Creek.

The Battle of Bull Run (Manassas)

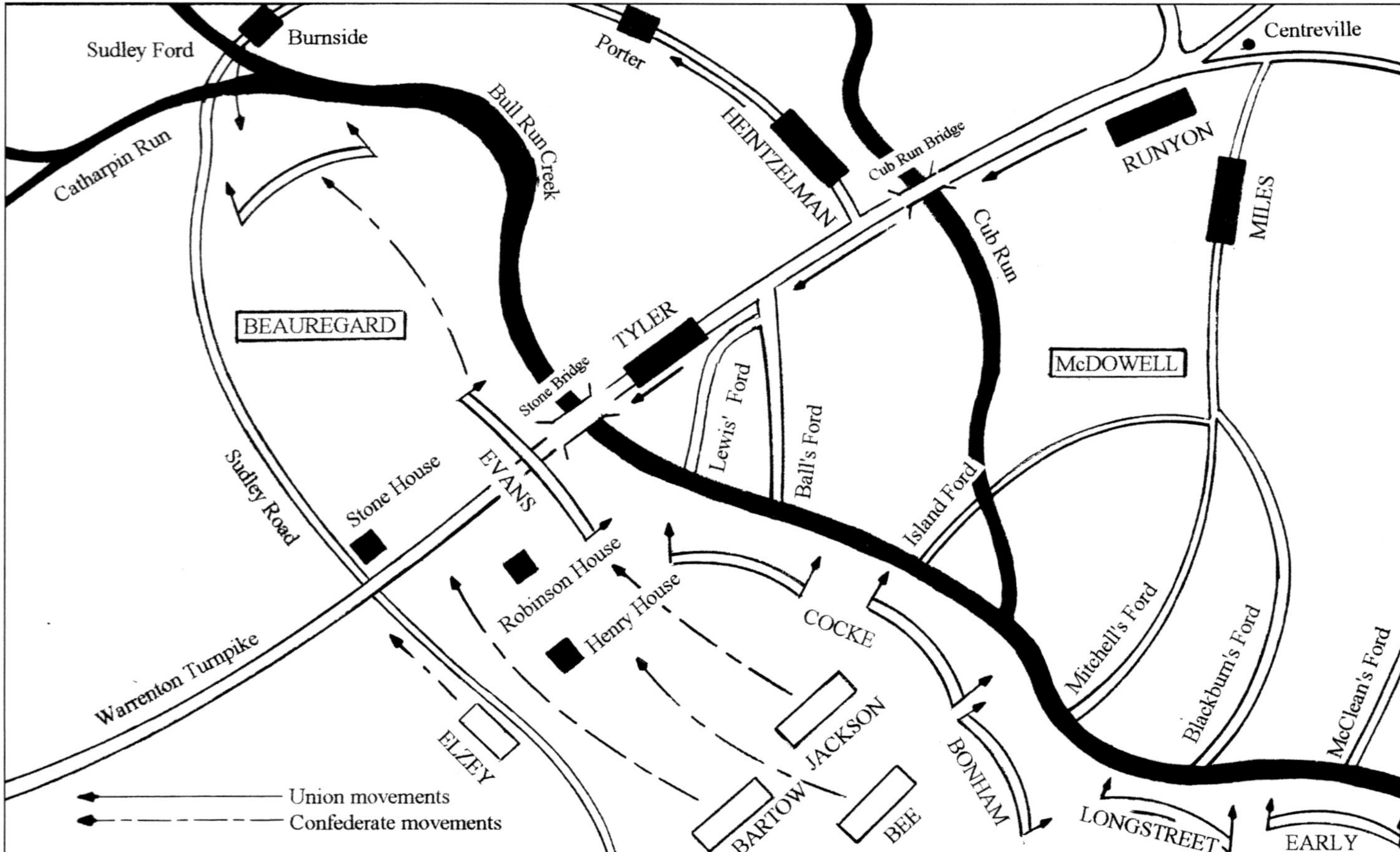

Beauregard dispersed his army along the Bull Run, strategically positioning each brigade to cover the many fords which crossed the creek. Union Mills Ford was protected by Generals Ewell and Holmes; McLean's Ford, by General Jones and Colonel Early; Blackburn's Ford by General Longstreet; Mitchell's Ford by General Benham; and Lewis' Island and Ball's Fords by Colonel Cocke. The Stone Bridge was defended by Gen. Nathan B. Evans. Generals Bee, Bartow and Jackson were held as reserves.

During the 19th and the 20th of July, the atmosphere of the Union camp at Centreville stood in stark contrast in its military decorum to the Confederate camp at Manassas. The Federal camp was inundated with crowds of visitors arriving in carriages, wagons and on horseback to watch the great event. Politicians, socialites and ordinary citizens flocked to the battlefield with baskets of food and drink. With no restrictions imposed on their movements, the Union camp looked like a holiday picnic.

McDowell's army of some 35,000 troops consisted of five divisions commanded by Gens. David Hunter, Samuel P. Heintzelman and Theodore Runyon, and Cols. Daniel Tyler and Dixon S. Miles. These five divisions in turn were made up of 11 brigades, with support from seven companies of cavalry and 10 artillery batteries. It was indeed an impressive force.

The great battle to settle all scores, the Battle of Bull Run began on July 21. (In the Southern vernacular, the battle is called the Battle of Manassas. The Confederates usually named their battles after the towns that served as their bases, the Battle of Shiloh being the only exception. On the other hand, the Union selected a landmark, such as a river or stream. See the Note on Battle Nomenclature, page 11, for battles known by two names.) After two days, General McDowell decided on a plan that would turn the enemy's left flank. At 2:30 in the morning, the advance force, Colonel Tyler's division, would go forward, straight down the Warrenton Turnpike directly toward the Stone Bridge. About two miles from the bridge, two brigades under the command of Gen. Ambrose Burnside would veer to the right along a side road. This road crossed Bull Run Creek at the unguarded Sudley Ford, about three miles upriver from the Stone Bridge at a point where the Confederates did not expect the Yankees to appear. Once across the creek, Burnside's men would come down on the left flank and rear of Evans' and Cocke's troops, forcing them to open the way for Tyler's division to cross the bridge and attack from that side. Tyler would first need to create a diversion at the Stone Bridge to direct attention away from Burnside's turning column.

The problems began when Tyler, moving slowly down the Turnpike, caused Burnside's flanking movement to fall over two hours behind schedule. This extra time gave Evans the opportunity to surmise McDowell's plan, especially when he saw Burnside's lengthening dust cloud above the trees. As the first diversionary shots were fired from the Stone Bridge, Gen. Beauregard immediately sent his reserves, Jackson, Bee and Bartow, to the Turnpike to support Evans and Cocke, who were receiving the brunt of the Union attack opposite the Stone Bridge. Evans, aware that the shooting was a cover for a flanking movement in his sector, shifted six companies to the Sudley Ford area and waited for the unsuspecting Federals.

At 10 A.M., Burnside's brigades came charging through the woods. The waiting Confederates could not contain themselves as they let loose their first volley and immediately scattered the surprised Yankees. Again the Union ranks charged and again they were repulsed. Union reinforcements were sent in and the fighting continued with neither side able to provide the fatal blow.

Meanwhile, the Confederate reserve brigades and batteries under Bee and Bartow moved behind Evans and Cocke along the Turnpike on Henry House Hill, opposite the Stone Bridge. The reinforcements were located in the vicinity of Widow Henry's house, the Stone House and the Robinson House. Responding to an urgent call for more direct support, Bee moved his brigade farther down the hill and joined forces with General Evans. When Union Col. William T. Sherman's forces entered the fray at the Stone Bridge, the now overwhelming Union numbers forced Bee's troops to retreat back up the hill. As Bee's men broke in complete chaos, he tried to stop them by exclaiming, "Look at Jackson's brigade! It stands there like a stone wall." These words immortalized General Jackson and his brigade, which became known as the "Stonewall Brigade." Bee's forces rallied around their colors, but as Bee's troops retreated, Burnside's men saw their opportunity and charged forward up Henry House Hill, seizing the Robinson and Henry houses in the process. Advancing with Burnside's men came the heavy artillery support commanded by Capts. Charles Griffin and James B. Ricketts. The two Yankee batteries were soon the key irritants in the Union front as they severely pounded the Confederate lines.

A growing concern for both sides was that each army lacked standardized uniforms, which at times resulted in death by "friendly fire." During the course of the battle, in the confusion of the fighting, Union soldiers dressed in gray and Confederates in blue were easily mistaken for the enemy and were shot and killed by their own sides. Conversely, the enemy was sometimes not recognized as such owing to the color confusion. This is what happened to the artillery batteries on Henry House Hill. Many of Griffin's and Ricketts' men were killed when they mistakenly identified an approaching regiment, dressed in blue, as Union troops. Ignoring their advance, the Union batteries were wiped out at point blank range by the 33rd Virginia, demoralizing the young Federal troops who witnessed the slaughter.

General Beauregard, now on the battlefield in person, redirected his forces from his right flank to the left and called for an all-out charge, reserves included. The suddenness of the entire Confederate line charging at once swept the already discouraged Federals back toward the Stone Bridge. In this headlong charge, both General Bartow and General Bee were killed.

As Beauregard prepared for a second charge, around 3 P.M., 1,700 more Confederate troops, the balance of Johnston's army, arrived from the Shenandoah Valley. The fresh reinforcements, commanded by Col. Arnold Elzey, charged onto the field and attacked the remaining Northerners, General Oliver O. Howard's brigade, regrouping on the far left. The sight of fresh troops energizing a new Confederate assault created a severe case of anxiety in the Northerners and forced the young soldiers to flee from the field of combat.

At first the Union retreat was somewhat orderly. Panic set in when civilian spectators on wagons and carriages caught sight of the retreating soldiers. People made a dash for the small Stone Bridge on horseback, competing with carriages and with those on foot. Sheer pandemonium broke out when a Confederate shell upset a carriage and blocked Cub Run Bridge. In no time at all, the retreat turned into a scramble for survival as the civilians panicked along with the green Union soldiers, who retreated from the battlefield in a 25-mile rout across Bull Run Creek back to Washington, defeated and humiliated. Confederate President Jefferson Davis was at Manassas when the Union forces left the field. Satisfied with the South's smashing victory, Davis chose not to chase the fleeing Federals.

The Confederate losses numbered about 2,000 killed, wounded

and missing. For the Union, the number was about 2,900. For both sides there was a lesson learned: that the realities of war were obvious.

As the 90-day volunteers left the ranks, President Lincoln asked for an additional 100,000 or more men to serve three-year terms. These men would fill the ranks of a newly-formed army, the Army of the Potomac. Impressed by his success in Western Virginia, Lincoln appointed General McClellan commander of the new army on July 22, the day after the defeat at Bull Run Creek.

His responsibility was not a small one. McClellan needed to organize, train, and equip over 100,000 raw recruits into a new striking force. At the same time, he needed to rekindle the fighting spirit and aggressiveness lost in the Bull Run fiasco. This effort would continue for the rest of 1861.

II
The Border States to Ball's Bluff (May–December 1861)

As General McClellan began building and training the Army of the Potomac in Washington, Lincoln's attention turned to the uncommitted border states of Missouri and Kentucky. Missouri, a slave state admitted to the Union as a result of the Missouri Compromise of 1820, chose not to secede with the rest of the South. Despite the urgings of secessionist leaders to join the Confederacy, the state convention representatives, who were heavily pro–Union, decided otherwise. This decision proved unpopular and provoked bitter fighting between pro-secessionist and pro–Unionist groups within its borders. The secessionist movement gained its momentum from its leading spokesman, Democratic Gov. Claiborne Fox Jackson. Taking on the Union cause was Brig. Gen. Nathaniel Lyon, a red bearded, 20 year veteran and fanatical "free-soiler," who felt it was his duty to fight the secessionist movement in Missouri. General Lyon served as the commander of the Federal arsenal in St. Louis, the largest U.S. arsenal in Rebel territory.

Learning of a plot by Governor Jackson to seize the arsenal, Lyon quickly transferred most of the arms to Illinois and distributed the rest to the Missouri Home Guard. During this same time, Lyon also mustered into service several regiments of German-American Unionists, and together with a regiment raised by U.S. Rep. Francis P. Blair, Jr., a Union leader in Missouri, Lyon now commanded some 7,000 troops.

Determined to act decisively, on May 10 Lyon led his men in the capture of Camp Jackson on the outskirts of St. Louis. The Rebel camp was a training facility for the pro-secessionist militia and a storage site for Confederate arms imported from the South. The sudden overwhelming invasion of Union troops left the 700 secessionists with little choice but to surrender without firing a shot. However, while the prisoners marched through the streets to the arsenal, shooting broke out from Lyon's army and 28 civilian men, women and children were killed. This bloody incident enraged the state legislature to such an extent that now a pro–Confederate Missouri State Guard was organized and former governor Sterling Price, a Jackson ally, was selected as its commander.

In an attempt to stem the escalating tensions, approximately a month later a conference took place among General Price, Governor Jackson and Lyon to discuss a truce. About two hours into the meeting Jackson and Price tried to take control of Union troop movements within Missouri. Lyon, incensed over their audacity, promptly ended the meeting, telling Jackson, "This means war."

Three days later, on June 14, General Lyon backed up his threat with action. The combative redhead and 2,000 troops took control of the state capital, Jefferson City, forcing Jackson and his followers to flee to Boonville. On the 17th, Lyon's forces again attacked Jackson and his 1,300 militia and routed them from the town, scattering the Rebels south.

General Lyon's small army had severely weakened the secessionist movement in two bold strikes. By capturing Camp Jackson, Lyon eliminated the weapons necessary for the "Southern-rights" men of Missouri to carry out their campaigns. By evicting the state government from its seat of power and dispersing its followers, Lyon had also removed the authority that provided the impetus behind the movement. Flushed with success, Lyon was eager to continue his campaign to rid Missouri of Confederate secessionists. Needing reinforcements, Lyon urgently requested additional troops from Gen. John C. Frémont, commander of the Western Department, but to no avail. The troops were needed elsewhere.

Undaunted, the Union commander would not be denied. With his 5,500 men, now called the Army of the Union, Lyon marched 200 miles south to stop the bloody warfare being waged along the Missouri-Kansas border. General Price, leading the Missouri State Guard, joined Rebel forces under Gen. Benjamin McCulloch, the Confederate commander from northwest Arkansas. On August 10, this combined army, now twice the size of the Union force, clashed with General Lyon at Wilson's Creek (Oak Hills), 10 miles from Springfield. Tragically, Lyon, waving his hat in the air for his men to follow, was shot through the heart and killed and his small Union army driven back to St. Louis.

Although Generals Price and McCulloch went on to take Springfield and Lexington, Missouri's allegiance to the Union was not settled until March 7, 1862, at the Battle of Pea Ridge (Elkhorn Tavern), on the Missouri-Arkansas border. The Confederate army at Pea Ridge, now under a new commander, Gen. Earl Van Dorn, was severely routed and General McCulloch was killed. The Union force was led by Gen. Samuel R. Curtis, whose victory finally eliminated the last vestiges of organized resistance to Missouri's anti-secession campaign.

Meanwhile, Kentucky, ironically the home state to both Lincoln and Jefferson Davis, was so divided between Union and Confederate supporters that on May 20 the state legislature decided not to secede. Instead, the delegates voted to remain neutral. Aware that their neutrality would not last very long, proponents from both sides began establishing training camps, acquiring weapons and recruiting armies to support their own causes.

Owing to Kentucky's neutrality, both Lincoln and Davis were reluctant to cross her borders. They feared an invasion would drive Kentucky to the other side, yet both desired to strike. Poised to advance from Cairo, Illinois, Union army and naval forces were ready to move into Kentucky at a moment's notice. Likewise, Confederate troops under the command of Gen. Leonidas Polk, Confederate commander on the central Mississippi, and a bishop in the Episcopal Church, bivouacked nearby in northwest Tennessee. Despite the hesitancy of President Davis to act, General Polk elected to invade Kentucky. Far from helping the Confederate cause, Polk's decision was in direct violation of the very principle of states' rights that the Confederacy was sworn to uphold.

On September 3, Polk seized Columbus, a small town about 20 miles from Cairo strategically located at the junction of the Ohio and Mississippi rivers. The Confederate general believed the occupation of Columbus necessary to prevent Union naval forces from launching an anticipated advance down the Mississippi River from Cairo.

Within a few weeks of the Confederate invasion of Columbus, the state of Kentucky elected a new Unionist legislature, which voted to end the state's neutrality and to side with the Northern flag. (Although only 11 Southern states seceded, the Confederate battle flag carried 13 stars. The extra two stars represented Kentucky and Missouri, which were voted into the Confederacy at Richmond but chose to remain loyal to the North.)

With Columbus securely entrenched, and defended with over 130 guns, Polk ordered his troops to occupy Paducah, Kentucky, approximately 40 miles to the northeast. Fully cognizant of Paducah's strategic importance, Gen. Ulysses S. Grant, when informed of Polk's maneuver, reacted immediately. From his headquarters in Cairo, the newly commissioned brigadier general boarded two regiments of the 21st Illinois Infantry on steamboats that very night and reached Paducah first, occupying the city on September 6. Taking Paducah, located at the mouths of the Tennessee and Cumberland rivers, created a huge tactical advantage for the North. The rivers represented two superhighways running through Kentucky and Tennessee. The Tennessee River allowed command of passage in a north-south direction through western Tennessee and into Mississippi. The Cumberland provided an east-west route through Tennessee which then swung back up into the eastern half of Kentucky. What the West lacked in roads and rail systems was more than made up in the many navigable rivers in that section of the country. By occupying Paducah, the North now controlled the mouths of both rivers.

With Union forces occupying Paducah and the northern two-thirds of Kentucky, the Confederate army spent the remainder of 1861 positioning troops in the southwestern half of the state and in Tennessee. In Kentucky, Gen. Felix K. Zollicoffer, commanding four regiments, advanced to the banks of the Cumberland River, and Gen. Simon Buckner was ordered to Bowling Green with his 5,000 troops. Completing their defensive line were the two forts built and garrisoned in northern Tennessee, Fort Henry and Fort Donelson.

To coordinate the movements of these scattered Southern armies, President Davis commissioned Gen. Albert Sidney Johnston to the post of commander of Confederate forces in the West, with headquarters in Nashville. Davis thought very highly of General Johnston, and in fact praised him as the best soldier in either army, North or South. The 58-year-old Kentuckian, a classmate of Davis at the U.S.

Military Academy, served as a brigadier general in the Republic of Texas army and as the Republic's secretary of war.

While Southern forces established their defensive line in Kentucky and Tennessee, General Grant was preoccupied with going on the offensive. Grant was concerned that his men were idle and growing more restless each day. He believed they needed to engage the enemy they had volunteered to fight. Therefore, under the pretense of preventing the Confederates from reinforcing Gen. Sterling Price in Missouri, on November 7 Grant took 3,000 men and two companies of cavalry by steamboats from Cairo to within six miles of Columbus. Fully aware of the strong fortifications defending Columbus and the numerical inferiority of his army, Grant prudently changed his original plans. He would attack a small Confederate camp at Belmont, Missouri, just across the Mississippi River from Columbus.

Disembarking three miles upriver from the Confederate camp, Grant's flotilla of five steamers and two gunboats was quickly spotted by the Columbus batteries. Artillery fire opened from both sides, and soon the opposing armies were engaged in a fierce battle. After four hours of trading gunfire with the Rebel forces, Grant and his men barely escaped from the reinforced Belmont troops. Pushing off at the last moment, the Union men steamed away from Belmont, their boats riddled in a hail of bullets. Although this escapade drew severe criticism at home as an unnecessary loss of 500 men, Grant believed that it was an excellent confidence builder for his troops fighting in their first battle and considered it not only necessary but also quite successful.

That same week, as a result of issuing policy beyond his authority, an act which also proved embarrassing to President Lincoln, General Frèmont, the Union commander in the western theater, was reassigned. His replacement was Gen. Henry W. Halleck, a 47-year-old former attorney nicknamed "Old Brains."

General Halleck was convinced that now was the time for Union forces in Kentucky to march south into eastern Tennessee, but the Union commander in Kentucky, Gen. William T. Sherman, would not consider an advance without 200,000 men to carry it out. Concerned about Sherman's unrealistic demands, General McClellan relieved him of his command and Halleck sent him to Missouri. In Sherman's place, McClellan selected Gen. Don Carlos Buell to command what now would be called the Army of the Ohio.

Not surprisingly, one of Buell's first orders directed Gen. George H.

Thomas, bivouacked with a small army in the northeastern sector of Kentucky, to head south toward the Tennessee border. Learning of Buell's order, Confederate General Zollicoffer abandoned his defensive position on the Cumberland River and marched to the vicinity of Mill Springs, Kentucky, not far from the Tennessee border. Zollicoffer intended to head off the Union attempt to invade Tennessee, and as a result extended the Confederate defensive line across all of southern Kentucky.

In October, the Confederate government at Richmond organized a Department of Northern Virginia, appointing the 54-year-old West Pointer, Gen. Joseph E. Johnston, as its commander. The new command comprised three districts: the Valley District, commanded by Gen. Thomas J. Jackson; the Potomac District under Gen. P.G.T. Beauregard, and the Aquia District headed by Gen. Theophilus H. Holmes.

Shortly after his victory at Fort Sumter, President Jefferson Davis had stationed some 15,000 Confederate troops in Alexandria, Virginia, just across the Potomac River from Washington. Suspecting these Rebel troops were responsible for obstructing navigation on the Potomac, General McClellan sent a new brigade of his largely untrained and untested troops to attack and dislodge Rebel forces at Leesburg, Virginia, about 40 miles upriver from Washington. On October 21, while other northern units distracted the Rebels from the Maryland side, several Union regiments crossed the Potomac downriver at Ball's Bluff to attack the Confederate flank. A contingent of Southern soldiers, watching the crossing from the woods, attacked first. The advancing Union regiment was severely defeated. Scores of men in blue were shot and killed or drowned in a mass rout back across the river. More than half of the 1,700 Union men were killed, wounded or captured. This second humiliating loss for the Lincoln administration provoked much anger and disappointment in Washington and led to Congress establishing a Joint Committee on the Conduct of the War to investigate the defeats at Ball's Bluff and Bull Run.

As 1861 came to a close, the border states were for the most part considered safely on the Union side and the maneuvering in western Kentucky and Tennessee by Northern and Southern armies was nearly complete. Gen. Albert Johnston's line of defense extended from Columbus, Kentucky, on his left, through Fort Henry, Fort Donelson, Bowling Green and to Mill Springs on his far right. Union battlefield encampments, stretching from Cairo, Illinois, to Lebanon, Kentucky, were preparing to move south. Gen. U.S. Grant's and Gen. John Pope's forces were in Paducah and Cairo; Gen. Don Carlos Buell, in Louisville, had his sights on the Confederate-held city of Nashville, and Gen. George H. Thomas was preparing to move into Tennessee.

Over the next several months, the Union offensive strategy would evolve into moving these four separate armies south in parallel with each other, each with a clearly defined mission.

One initiative was to gain control of the Mississippi River from the mouth of the Ohio River south, while Flag Officer David G. Farragut, commanding 14 gunboats and 19 mortar schooners, tried to capture New Orleans and control the river north. To do this, General Pope and his Army of the Mississippi first needed to attack Polk's Confederate stronghold at Columbus, just a few miles south of Pope's forces outside Cairo. General Grant's mission would be to capture Fort Henry and Fort Donelson. That accomplished, Grant would then transport his Army of the Tennessee down the Tennessee River to a point close to the Mississippi border, where he would join General Buell's Army of the Ohio, which would be marching down from Kentucky. The three combined armies would then advance into Mississippi.

To impede these Union troop movements, Confederate forces were entrenched in five defensive positions. To counter Pope on the Mississippi, General Polk dug in at Columbus. To prevent Grant's advancement, Confederate soldiers and batteries waited at two strategic positions in northern Tennessee: Fort Henry on the Tennessee River and Fort Donelson on the Cumberland River. Meanwhile, General Zollicoffer occupied the vicinity of Logan's Cross Roads, Kentucky, to block Thomas, as General Buckner at Bowling Green kept Buell in check at Louisville.

In Washington, on November 1, Gen. Winfield Scott retired as general-in-chief, the Union's highest command position. At 74, his age and poor health degraded his ability to perform effectively the myriad of duties in this most critical of times. That, at least, was the way McClellan portrayed Scott to President Lincoln. To replace Scott, Lincoln selected none other than Gen. George B. McClellan. With this appointment, Lincoln demonstrated complete confidence in his new general. Now, as both general-in-chief and commander of the Army of the Potomac, McClellan stood at the pinnacle of his military career.

III
The War Moves West: Logan's Cross Roads to Corinth
(January–July 1862)

As the new year began, President Lincoln's growing frustration was evident. He was unable to establish a momentum, a drive to set the machinery of war in motion. His field commanders, Halleck, Buell and McClellan, were reluctant to move out. They all pleaded for more time to get their armies ready.

Gen. Henry W. Halleck, serving as commander of the Department of the West, was in St. Louis, Missouri. In the central theater, Gen. Don Carlos Buell commanded the Army of the Ohio at Louisville, Kentucky, and in Washington was Gen. George B. McClellan. McClellan served in a dual role as commander of the Army of the Potomac in the East, as well as general-in-chief of all Union forces. McClellan's hesitancy to move his new army out was compounded by his recovering at home from typhoid fever.

To force his commanders, particularly McClellan, to cooperate, in January Lincoln issued his first General War Order. In this order Lincoln demanded that all land and naval forces begin operations by February 22, Washington's birthday.

General McClellan, however, received specific instructions to move out immediately. McClellan's orders were to march the Army of the Potomac overland toward Richmond. In this march, he was to advance against Gen. Pierre G.T. Beauregard, still bivouacked on the battlefield at Manassas from the previous July.

By this time, Lincoln was well aware of McClellan's reputation as a paranoid procrastinator. The general's insecurity over enemy troop strength was legend, and in this regard Lincoln's general order may very well have been meant for McClellan alone. Characteristically McClellan begged off and refused to move his army. He would not clash head-on with an enemy that, at least in his mind, far outnumbered his own. Lincoln was mystified and depressed. Overheard discussing the situation with his quartermaster, Lincoln lamented, "General, what shall I do?"

Meanwhile, in the west and central theaters, the maneuvering for position had played itself out and the armies were ready for action. Ironically, Kentucky, the state that voted to remain neutral from the start, would now be the first major battlefield of 1862.

The stage was set when Gen. Felix K. Zollicoffer and his Confederate army set up camp in the vicinity of Logan's Cross Roads, in the southeast quarter of Kentucky, near Mill Springs. Zollicoffer's mission was to prevent the Union force in Lebanon under Gen. George H. Thomas from advancing south into Tennessee. Interpreting General Zollicoffer's defensive tactic as a bold attempt to challenge his drive into eastern Tennessee, General Buell ordered Thomas to prepare his forces for an attack on the enemy. Consequently, in early January General Thomas led his 4,000 men south toward Logan's Cross Roads, only 10 miles north of Zollicoffer's camp.

The weather was not kind to Thomas. Rain fell almost every day, and the muddy roads hindered the troops and bogged down the artillery and wagons. By January 17, only a part of the Union army had reached Logan's Cross Roads, the rest of the troops remaining farther back struggling in the mud.

In mid–January, Gen. Albert S. Johnston, the highest-ranking Confederate officer and commander of all western forces, replaced Zollicoffer with Maj. Gen. George B. Crittenden. Despite losing overall command, General Zollicoffer agreed to remain with the unit to lead one of the two brigades.

Within a few days, a decision was reached to go on the offensive and attack Thomas' smaller army before it regrouped. On January 18, with 5,000 men in seven regiments, two companies of cavalry and two

THE WAR MOVES WEST

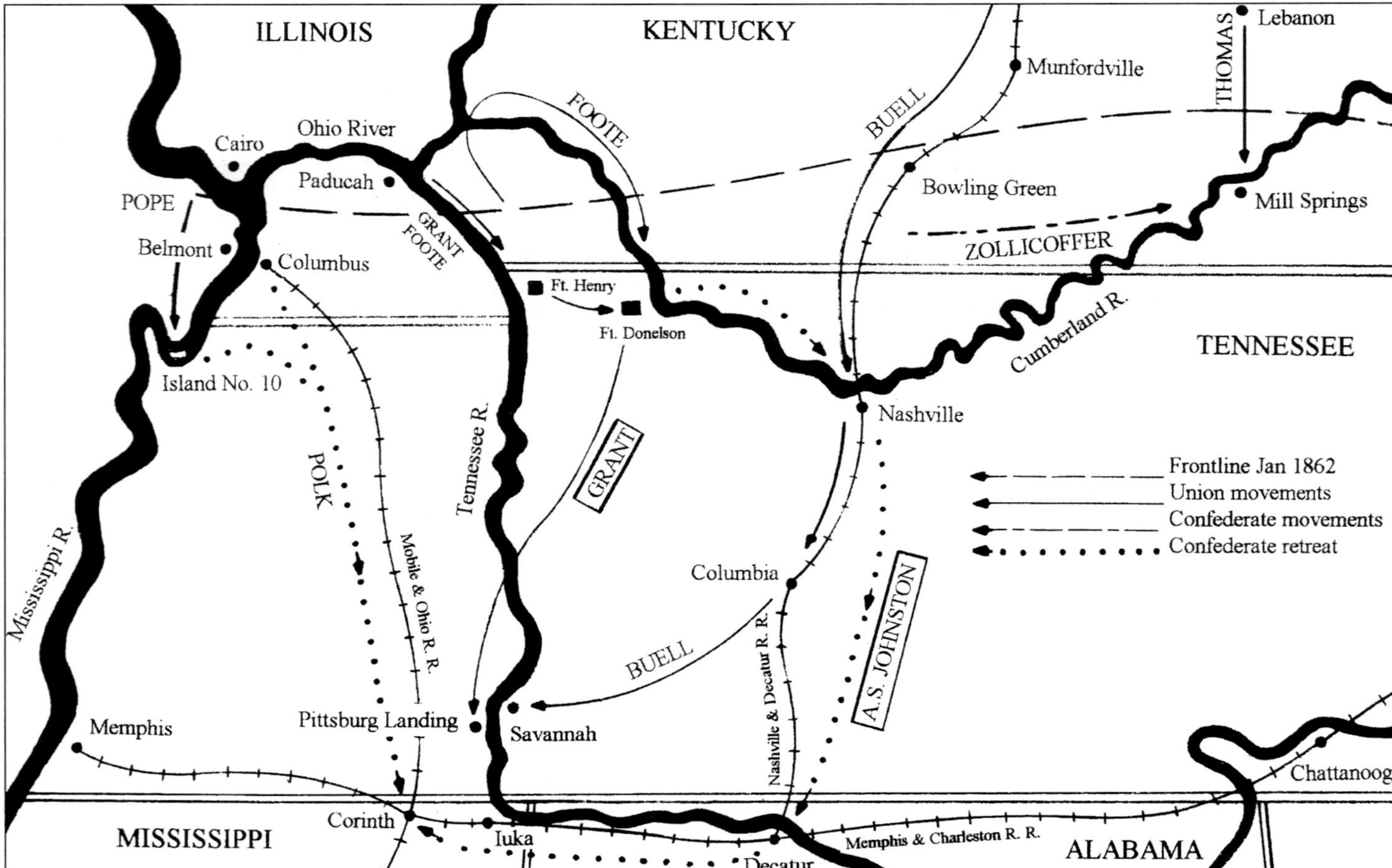

units of artillery, Crittenden made a surprise attack on the smaller Union force. The Battle of Logan's Cross Roads (Mill Springs) was the first combat action of 1862.

Caught off guard by the unexpected attack, Thomas' men were initially driven back. When General Zollicoffer was shot and killed, the loss of their beloved commander demoralized the Rebel soldiers, and their gritty fighting spirit dissipated. From that moment on, the Union troops were able to steadily push the Rebels farther and farther back. Suddenly, the Union's 9th Ohio infantry broke from the pack in a headlong bayonet charge. Crittenden's troops, already demoralized from the loss of their commander, quickly retreated, falling back in disorder. The Union troops were spurred on by the sight of the fleeing Confederates and pursued even more vigorously. In turn, the Confederate retreat quickly degraded into a rout and then into desertion as a run-for-your-life mentality overtook the Confederate army. On stolen horses and mules, both officers and enlisted men abandoned the field and fled to the safety of the Tennessee border. In spite of the Confederate flight to Tennessee, Thomas did not continue his advance south. Because of severe supply problems, he was ordered to join Buell's main column, still in Louisville.

With the Union left wing secure in eastern Kentucky, General Halleck turned to General Grant, at Cairo, Illinois. Grant, a 40-year-old native Ohioian, was educated at the U.S. Military Academy, graduating 21st in a class of 39 in 1843. After serving in the Mexican War from 1845 to 1848, and on the West Coast from 1851, he resigned from the Army in 1854. Grant complained that he wasn't able to support his family on the wages of a captain, although boredom, which contributed to his drinking problem, may have been closer to the reason for his resignation. Following unsuccessful attempts at farming and a real estate business, Grant worked as a clerk in his father's leather-goods store in Galena, Illinois. Because of Grant's army experience, at the outbreak of the war Gov. Richard Yates appointed him a colonel in the Illinois Militia. In August of 1861 he was commissioned by the U.S. government as a brigadier general in the Illinois Volunteers. Known for his unkempt appearance, he was an avid cigar smoker who spent hours relaxing by whittling big sticks into little sticks.

On February 1, approximately one month after presenting his plan to Halleck, Grant received approval for a joint Army-Navy operation. Grant and his army, now officially called the Army of the

Tennessee, joined Flag Officer Andrew Foote and his fleet of seven iron-clad gunboats for an assault on Fort Henry.

After ferrying the Northern troops down the Tennessee River on February 5, the fleet delivered the Union army to within 10 miles of the fort. To support Grant, his two division commanders, Gen. Charles F. Smith and Gen. John A. McClernand, and about 15,000 men took part in the operation.

According to their plan, on February 6 Grant would march his men through the woods to the small fort and attack from the rear while Foote delivered his shells from the gunboats in his fleet. At the designated rendezvous time, Grant's ground troops were late. Constant rains and thick woods impeded their mobility through the high water and muddy terrain. The gunboats arrived first, and after a short wait, Foote decided to press the attack alone. He ordered his ships to open fire and easily battered the Fort Henry garrison into surrendering.

Fortunately for Admiral Foote, the fort's defenses had been drastically reduced. The commander, Brig. Gen. Lloyd Tilghman, knowing his fortification was outgunned, had ordered his 2,500 men overland to Fort Donelson, 12 miles to the east on the Cumberland River. As a result, only one artillery company of about 75 men guarded Fort Henry. Kept behind only to delay the Union forces, the Rebel company quickly fell before Grant's ground forces arrived to assist in the attack. When Grant's forces finally reached the fort, General Smith and two brigades of about 5,500 men also found that a smaller earthworks on the opposite bank known as Fort Heiman had been evacuated.

Promptly following his arrival at Fort Henry, General Grant ordered his army to resume their advance. Fearing that Fort Donelson would soon be heavily reinforced, Grant marched his men to Fort Donelson, while Flag Officer Foote steamed back up the Tennessee and down the Cumberland to rendezvous with the Union army outside the fort.

Fulfilling Grant's worst fears, General Johnston moved to counter the Union threat by reinforcing Fort Donelson. On February 11, Gen. Simon Buckner and his 12,000 men were transferred from Bowling Green to help defend the fort. To Johnston, a great deal was at stake. The possession of Kentucky and Tennessee as well as the survival of the present Confederate line depended entirely on a Southern victory at Fort Donelson. Of General Johnston's 35,000 men, 14,000 were still in Nashville keeping a watchful eye on Buell; 21,000 occupied Fort Donelson.

For the Union attackers, Fort Donelson would be a tougher challenge. There were three brigade commanders at the fort: Gen. John B. Floyd, who because of his seniority assumed overall command, arrived on the 13th; Gideon J. Pillow arrived on February 9; and Simon Buckner on the 11th. All told, the Confederate force consisted of 28 regiments, artillery and a cavalry regiment under Col. Nathan B. Forrest. Grant's army of 27,000 men, on the other hand, was about equal in strength to 25 Southern regiments, although with Foote's fleet of gunboats, the Union had a formidable army matched against a formidable foe.

Generals McClernand and Smith reached the vicinity of Fort Donelson on February 12, and immediately took up their positions. McClernand's line stretched out on the Union right and Smith's to the left. Arriving on the 14th from Fort Henry, Gen. Lew Wallace was given command of a third division composed of newly-arrived reinforcements. This third division was inserted in the Union center and extended McClernand's line farther to the right. By the morning of the 14th, Union ground forces were in place along a three-mile front; the fleet, having arrived the night before, was ready to go.

At three P.M., Foote ordered his four gunboats into action. The new iron-clads steamed ahead and came to within 400 yards of the fort. The Confederate artillery, consisting of two floating batteries, 11 32-pounders and one 10" Columbiad (a large siege gun), opened fire and disabled two of the gunboats very quickly, killing or wounding 54 men. The other two boats were forced into defensive roles as protectors as the current slowly spun the disabled craft downriver, out of range.

Because of Foote's failure to damage Donelson's defenses, Grant decided against sending in his troops at this point. Instead, they bedded down in the midwinter snow yet another night and suffered terribly. The nights proved an extreme test of stamina and tenacity for the Union soldiers. Not only did they endure sleeping each night in the cold snow without campfires and tents, but also most lacked blankets and coats, and used wet leaves for protection from the bitter cold.

In the morning mist of February 15, sensing their situation desperate, a column of Confederate troops charged from the fort and attempted to cut an escape route through the Union lines. Almost immediately, the Union soldiers were roused from their "beds" and formed into defensive positions. The Confederate assault concentrated on the Union right, McClernand's division. To make matters worse, in the midst of the fighting McClernand's division ran out of ammunition. With Confederate reinforcements continuing to stream from the fort, the battle proved too much for McClernand's men to handle. The Union right broke and very soon the Northerners were in full retreat. By 11 o'clock, the Rebels held the ground previously occupied by the Union right. Strangely enough, at this point came a sudden lull in the fighting, leaving the Confederates under the impression that the entire Union army was fleeing to their boats.

As the Union right was being decimated, General Grant was five miles away conferring with Foote on his flagship. Riding out to the battle when told of the attack, Grant coolly instructed Wallace and McClernand, "Gentleman, the position on the right must be retaken." With that said, Grant rode off to confer with General Smith on the Union left. Inspired by Grant's apparent vote of confidence, Wallace ordered his men to resume their attack and the battle was renewed. The tide began to shift as Wallace's men drove the Confederates back into their fortifications. This was the moment Grant believed most critical. Since the Confederates had attacked in force and had just returned to the fort, Grant surmised it highly unlikely that the Rebel commanders had the time to regroup their defenses within their works. Consequently, now was the best time to commence an attack from the left using a full division, with the likelihood of little or no opposition from the enemy. General Smith was given this responsibility while the Union center and right launched diversionary attacks and Foote resumed his shelling from the river. General Smith's mission was a roaring success; that night his men bedded down within the enemy's lines.

In the fort that night, the Confederate commanders assembled to decide the fate of their men. In the end, they decided to surrender the fort. The following morning, Grant received word that the Confederates would capitulate and desired terms. Grant's response: "Sir: Yours of this date, proposing armistice and appointment of Commissioners to settle terms of capitulation, is just received. No terms except an unconditional and immediate surrender can be accepted. I propose to move immediately upon your work."

The Northern newspapers had a field day with this victory and

Grant's name became a household word. He drew great publicity not only by capturing some 15,000 troops, a large number of prisoners by anyone's standards, but also through his insistence on an unconditional surrender, which added new meaning to the first two initials of his name.

One footnote to the Rebel capitulation is that not everyone at the fort surrendered. Col. Nathan B. Forrest, whose future battlefield exploits would earn him the rank of general, refused to surrender himself or his men. The night before, he led all 700 of his cavalrymen on horseback out of the fort, through the icy woods and 75 miles to Nashville. Not surrendering as well was General Floyd, who was President Buchanan's secretary of war and was now under federal indictment. In anticipation of the secession, Floyd used his powers as secretary of war and scattered Union forces thinly around the country, and transferred arms from Northern to Southern arsenals. Fearful of the treatment he might receive as a prisoner of war, Floyd and his men boarded two steamers during the night, and they too left for the safety of Nashville. General Pillow also elected not to give himself up and left with his staff. Only General Buckner remained. As the junior commander, he decided it was his duty to stay with the troops even in this hour of despair.

Practically ignoring Grant's role in the victories at Forts Henry and Donelson, General Halleck, as Western Department commander, took full credit for Grant's success and was promptly promoted to the command all Union forces west of the Alleghenies. Notwithstanding Halleck's self-serving maneuvers, Grant was also promoted to the rank of major general, along with all three of his division commanders.

Only a month before, Confederate forces in the West had enjoyed a defensive line that extended from Columbus, Kentucky, on the left to Fort Henry and Fort Donelson in the center, to Bowling Green and Logan's Cross Roads on the right. With the loss of his extreme right and center positions, General Johnston had little choice but to order General Polk to abandon Columbus, which became extremely vulnerable. Johnston also evacuated Nashville on February 23, and retreated with the remaining Confederate troops to Corinth, Mississippi. Union General Buell seized this opportunity and marched his Army of the Ohio south to occupy Nashville.

The loss of Fort Donelson caused an instant furor in Richmond. The Southern newspapers were unmerciful in their criticism of Johnston, and several Confederate congressmen even called for Davis to remove him from command, but to no avail.

Rebel forces began evacuating Columbus on February 20, and by March 2, troops, artillery and supplies were in place on Island Number 10, so called because it was the tenth island south of the Mississippi and Ohio River junction. This island fortress, about 30 miles south of Columbus, commanded the river in both directions and was considered an extremely formidable target for the North to penetrate. Because the Union had so many state-of-the-art ironclads on the Mississippi, the Confederate government found it imperative to erect strong batteries at Columbus, Island Number 10, Memphis and Vicksburg.

On March 16, a fleet of 17 union gunboats opened fire on the Confederate defenses protecting Island Number 10. The fleet was under the command of Flag Officer Andrew Foote, recently arrived following his victories at Fort Henry and Fort Donelson. On April 1, as Foote continued his bombardment from the north side, Gen. John Pope, commander of the Army of the Mississippi, made an amphibious landing on the south end. For the Confederates, escape was impossible. On April 7, the garrison on Island Number 10 surrendered,with 7,000 taken prisoner. With this victory, Pope's popularity in the White House soared. Without much time to celebrate, Pope and his men were ordered to Pittsburg Landing, Tennessee, to consolidate with the armies of Grant and Buell.

After the fall of Fort Donelson, Gen. Albert S. Johnston ordered all Confederate forces to regroup at Corinth, Mississippi, a border town significant because it was the junction of the Confederates' main north-south and east-west railroads in the Mississippi Valley, specifically the Mobile and Ohio Railroad and the Memphis & Charleston respectively. At Corinth, Johnston pondered the next move for his 40,300 troops.

The Northern government knew well that the Confederate army was massing at Corinth. With Kentucky and western Tennessee securely in Union hands, General Halleck ordered Grant and Buell south to challenge the enemy at Corinth and to capture this all-important railroad junction. To carry out this order, Grant transported his 45,000 men down the Tennessee River, and Buell marched his 40,000 troops south from Nashville. Their destination was Pittsburg Landing, Tennessee, the staging area for their assault on Corinth, only 20 miles away.

Grant's forces began arriving on March 18. Over the next two weeks the Army of the Tennessee swelled to 67,000 men in six divisions, commanded by Gens. John A. McClernand, W.H.L. Wallace, (replacing Grant's premier division commander C.F. Smith, who was fatally ill), Stephen A. Hurlbut, Benjamin M. Prentiss, and William T. Sherman. Lew Wallace's division bivouacked at Crump's Landing only five miles away. Tent cities sprang up overnight as thousands of soldiers settled in to the pleasures and pains of military life in camp. General Grant saw no point in fortifying the camp because in his mind, the Confederates were the defenders, entrenched in Corinth fully expecting an attack from the Union army.

Leaving Columbia, just south of Nashville on April 5, Buell's army began marching the 82 miles to Savannah, Tennessee, a small river town where they would board transports for the nine-mile ride to Pittsburg Landing. With the combined forces of both armies, Grant would then advance on General Johnston's Army of Mississippi.

Johnston was not to be underestimated. He anticipated this maneuver and was not about to sit and wait for Grant and Buell to combine and overwhelm his smaller army. In addition, Johnston was stung by the criticism of his losses and subsequent retreats. He felt he must seize this moment to vindicate himself. Accordingly, he ordered his corps commanders to strike the first blow in a surprise attack before Buell and Grant could combine their forces.

On hand to assist Johnston as second in command was General P.G.T. Beauregard, moved westward from the Manassas battlefield victory of the previous July. Also present to lead the 40,000 Confederate soldiers were Johnston's corps commanders: Gen. Leonidas Polk, just arriving from Columbus; Gen. Braxton Bragg, a Mexican War veteran arriving from Mobile; Gen. William J. Hardee, author of Hardee's *Tactics*, a training manual used extensively by both sides, and Gen. John C. Breckinridge, who ran as one of the two Democratic candidates in the presidential election of 1860. Johnston planned to attack the Union army head-on with three infantry lines, each composed of one corps. Hardee's line would go in first, followed by Bragg and then Polk, with Breckinridge in reserve.

"Tonight we will water our horses in the Tennessee River," Johnston told his staff on the morning of the attack.

On April 6, the Confederates attacked in the Battle of Shiloh (Pittsburg Landing), and what a surprise it was. With the exception

The Battle of Shiloh (first day)

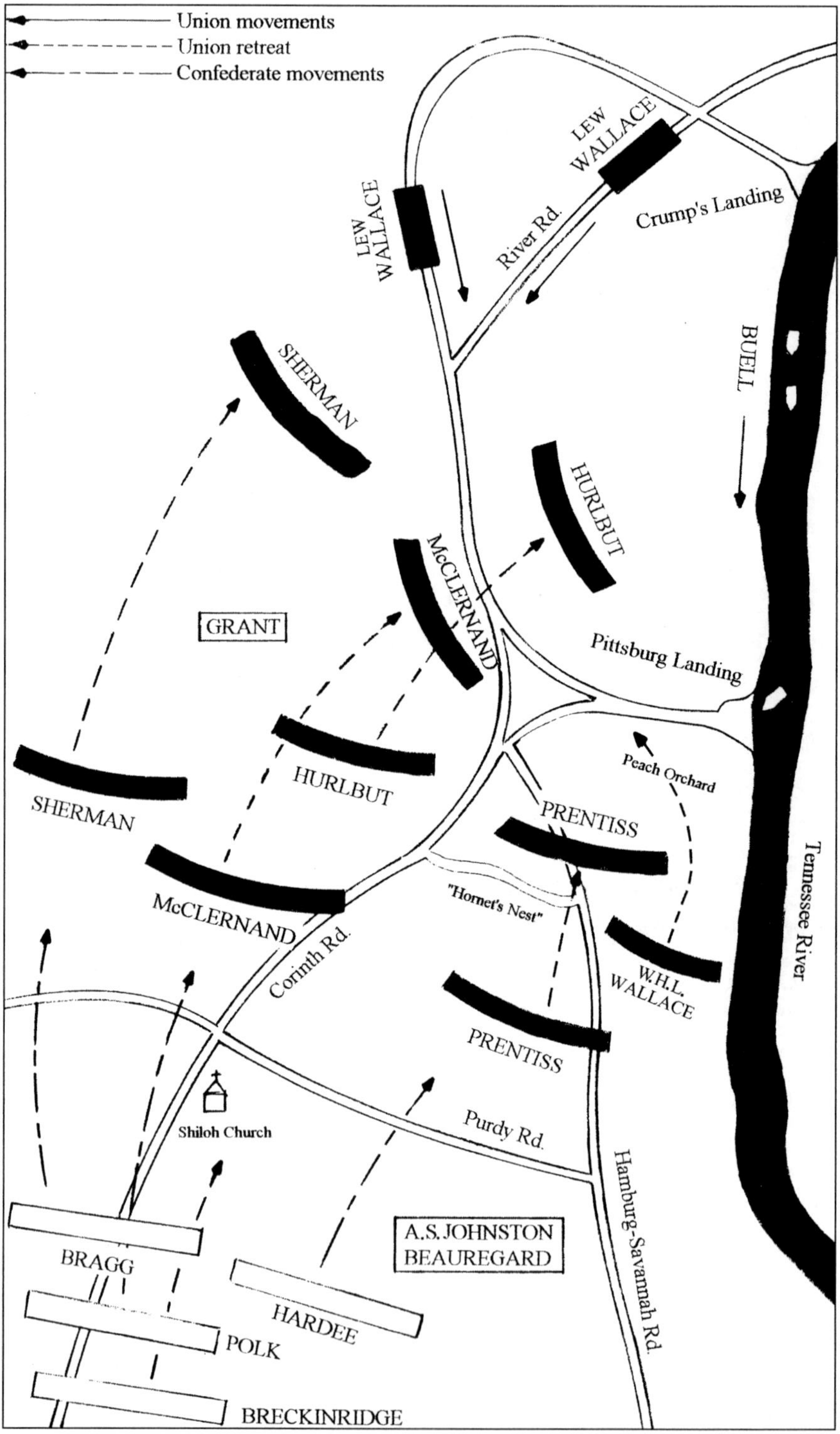

of several companies of advance guard, the Union troops were oblivious to the approaching enemy. Bivouacked on the outer perimeter of the Union camp, General Prentiss was on the Union left, Sherman on the right, with McClernan and the reserves behind them. The 61st Illinois Infantry, on the extreme left of Prentiss, was peacefully preparing for a Sunday morning inspection. The Union men were busy cleaning shoes, polishing rifles and tending to the myriad of other details soldiers occupied themselves with getting ready for this longstanding military tradition. Unfortunately, raw recruits filled the ranks of about half of the Union army. In an instant, the charging, screaming and yelling Rebels overran General Prentiss' camp, attacking from the vicinity of Shiloh Church. Confederate colors flooded the Union camp as the men in blue, most still half dressed, quickly formed into their defensive positions. The troops under McClernand and Prentiss were pressed back, step by step, shocked and bewildered by this sudden turn of events. By 7 A.M., all three Confederate corps were fully engaged and advancing steadily through the Yankee camps. Also one who dismissed the possibility of a Confederate attack, General Sherman believed this to be a Confederate demonstration until he saw the Rebels charging out of the woods into his ranks. In a short time Sherman's camp was also overcome as the Confederate advance proceeded to the front lines of the reserves, led by generals Hurlbut and W.H.L. Wallace.

As the Battle of Shiloh heated up, many of the young Union soldiers decided they would rather be somewhere else and abandoned the field. Unable to use fully the cavalry on the front lines, Grant employed the horsemen to round up these stragglers. When sufficient numbers were brought back, they were sent to any commander needing additional men to fill his depleted ranks.

Johnston's strategy was to make a strong effort on the Union left, Prentiss' Division, to drive it back and away from Pittsburg Landing, thereby cutting off escape. With no escape Grant's army would be compelled to surrender. On the extreme Union left was a peach orchard defended by a small brigade. Strangely enough, the brigade's gallant fighting without the benefit of artillery, along with their stubborn resistance and their varying line formations, fooled the Confederate commander into thinking he was being set up for a ruse. When the Union brigade ran out of ammunition and retreated, the Rebel commander refused to pursue for fear of falling into what he thought was a trap of hidden artillery.

By the end of the day, as the sun began to set, Grant's entire front line was in full retreat. General Prentiss' line, the division taking the first hit, fell back to a sunken road, later called the "Hornet's Nest." As the Union line moved back, Prentiss did not follow. This break in the Union line exposed Prentiss on both flanks and he was quickly surrounded. Beginning at 9 A.M., the raging battle between Prentiss' division and Johnston's soldiers mercilessly devoured human lives. On both sides, line after line was repulsed, and rallied anew only to fall again. The men in blue could not hold out. At 5 P.M., trapped, with no escape, no ammunition and no hope, General Prentiss surrendered his 3,000 valiant soldiers.

Back on the extreme Union left, as Confederate soldiers approached the peach orchard, the first of Buell's troops began to disembark at the river's edge. With musical accompaniment from their ever-present band, Buell's advance regiments filed up the bluff overlooking Pittsburg Landing and fell into formation on the battlefield. In the waning hours of daylight, the retreating soldiers of Grant's army were overjoyed at the sight of fresh troops lining up for action, fully equipped for the battle ahead. One young Union onlooker wrote, "Never was the sight of reinforcing legions so precious and so welcome as on that Sunday evening"

By this time soldiers from both sides were fatigued and fighting had noticeably slackened. General Johnston was not so fortunate as to benefit from the lull. He was killed at 2:30 P.M.: he bled to death from a severed artery after taking a single round in the leg.

As the sun set and the sky grew darker, General Beauregard, now in control of the army and the field, ordered his troops to hold their fire. It was a very successful day for the Army of Mississippi, so much so that Beauregard telegraphed President Davis, exulting over his excellent field position and confident of ultimate victory the following morning. Fate dictated otherwise, for during the night General Buell's army continued to arrive, with the additional 5,000 men in General Lew Wallace's division from Crump's Landing.

That night the weather changed for the worse when a thunderstorm swept the area bringing with it torrential rain. Adding to the misery of the moment, the Union soldiers were forced to sleep in the outdoors, lying in the mud and water, while their counterparts enjoyed the shelter of their captured tents. Even Grant, hobbling around on crutches from a riding accident, spent the night under a tree with his men. Despite their hardships, these Union troops had a better night than the thousands of wounded soldiers, both Union and Confederate, who spent the night suffering on the battlefield unattended, screaming in agony and left to die in the rain and mud.

In the morning, General Buell's Army of the Ohio, with the exception of General Thomas' division, was on the battlefield ready to go. Buell's command at Shiloh consisted of four divisions under Gens. Alexander M. McCook, Thomas L. Crittenden, William Nelson, and S.A.M. Wood. Completely exhausted from lack of food and rest, Grant's army took the field on the right wing and the Army of the Ohio, the left. With Grant's order to counterattack, the Federals were now the attacking army, and this time the Rebels were surprised. Pushed back initially, the Confederate soldiers recovered and stiffened their resolve to fight. For both sides, the sight of their fallen comrades on the field from the day before was a grotesque reminder of the terrible carnage that war not only expects but demands. On this day, along with the thousands of other casualties, General Smith's replacement, Gen. W.H.L. Wallace, was killed in the line of duty. The battle raged on until 3 P.M., when the Confederates found themselves back at Shiloh Church and the road to Corinth where they had started from the previous day. Considering the heavy casualties suffered by his army, with no reinforcements at his disposal and knowing his victory gone, General Beauregard led his defeated army limping back to Corinth. Too exhausted to make a serious pursuit, the Union soldiers retired to their camps.

Shiloh was the bloodiest battle fought in the western theater. For both sides the number of killed and wounded was staggering. One open field was "so covered with dead that it would have been possible to walk across the clearing, in any direction, stepping on dead bodies without a foot touching the ground" (*Personal Memoirs of U.S. Grant* 185). Killed, wounded, and missing numbered close to 13,000 for the Blue and 10,700 for the Gray. To many in Washington, the exorbitant number of casualties was a national disgrace.

After the battle, Grant came under heavy criticism from armchair generals for not pursuing and destroying Beauregard's defeated army and for failing to fortify his camp. Grant answered to his critics by saying he didn't have the heart to subject his exhausted troops to more fighting, and would have requested the Army of the Ohio to continue but by the time he spoke to General Buell, it was too late. As for the lack of perimeter security, Grant had sincerely believed that fighting would never take place at Pittsburg Landing, since he had considered the Union the aggressor, and it would have been the Union doing the attacking. He also reminded his critics that his troops were so raw, they needed discipline and drill experience more than pick-and-shovel experience.

Years later, Beauregard wrote that on the morning of the second day, he suspected that Buell's army had arrived and he knew his troops would not be victorious. As he related, "To indulge a hope of success with these fearful odds against me would have been to show a lack of judgment." Beauregard went on to admit he planned the retreat from the beginning, "The only plan left, I thought, was to fight so as to deceive the enemy as to my real intentions, and to effect an orderly, safe and honorable retreat."

The Confederate president was incensed over this defeat. His forces whipped by an army that was beaten only hours before, Davis was unforgiving. For failing to continue his assault to a final surrender on April 6, Beauregard was relieved from command. The Army of Mississippi was split into a new Army of Tennessee with Gen. Braxton Bragg commissioned as its commander.

Taking his usual opportunistic slant on the current state of affairs, Halleck seized this occasion to discredit Grant and at the same time enhance his own image. Instead of supporting Grant, Halleck not only joined the criticism but also spread false rumors of Grant being drunk during the battle. In reality, Halleck envied Grant's success and fame and tried to take credit for the Shiloh victory by discrediting the competence of General Grant. To drive this point home, Halleck left his headquarters at St. Louis on April 11 and travelled to Pittsburg Landing to personally take over the battlefield operations.

On April 21, Gen. John Pope and his 21,000-man Army of the Mississippi, fresh from their victory at Island Number 10, reached the Landing and added even more firepower to the growing army. Now at Halleck's disposal was an awe-inspiring force of 120,000 troops. His army consisted of the Army of the Mississippi, under Pope, and now designated as the right wing; the Army of the Ohio, under Buell, in the center; and the Army of the Tennessee, as the right wing and the reserves, now under General Thomas. Grant was Halleck's second in command.

Completely ignoring Grant in his assault plans, Halleck marched from camp on April 30 to take care of matters in Corinth himself. The troops quickly discovered that Halleck was better suited for a desk job than a field command. After every skirmish Halleck ordered his men to corduroy or rebuild the roads, and to entrench at every forward movement. As a result, it took the Union army a month to march the 20 miles to Corinth. When they finally reached Corinth on May 30, the Union forces found the town completely abandoned — no army, no artillery, nothing. Halleck also found himself with thousands of sick Union soldiers dying of fever and diarrhea. He failed as well to pursue the Confederates now in Tupelo, Mississippi, only 50 miles down the Mobile and Ohio Railroad line.

In Corinth, General Halleck encamped his huge army of over 100,000 men, the largest body of Union fighting power ever assembled in the western theater. Faced with myriad demands for their services, "Old Brains" initiated a number of organizational changes to his army that in his judgement served the country's best interests. His modifications pleased very few people and brought instant attacks from his harshest critics.

Instead of maintaining this highly successful fighting machine as one gigantic sledge hammer against Vicksburg, as many would have liked, Halleck split it up. General Buell's Army of the Ohio was ordered to move on Chattanooga, and General Grant's Army of the Tennessee was downsized, with a portion sent to Jackson, Tennessee, to maintain the peace in that sector, and the remainder going to repair railroad tracks or to reinforce General Buell. Halleck also sent entire divisions from the Army of the Mississippi to other parts of the West where he considered their presence necessary, even to repair rail lines as far north as Columbus.

As for General Grant, since the fall of Donelson he and Halleck had not enjoyed a good relationship. Halleck's powerplay after Shiloh, his accusations of Grant's drinking, and his shabby treatment of Grant during the march to Corinth forced Grant to consider resigning from the military. His best friend, Gen. William T. Sherman, persuaded him to apply for a transfer. Consequently, on June 21, Grant and his staff arrived at his new headquarters in Memphis to supervise railroad repairs and to maintain the peace. General Grant's tenure in Memphis proved short-lived.

President Lincoln was very impressed and highly gratified with the performance of the western armies and the western commanders.

To demonstrate his satisfaction, Lincoln reorganized the highest levels of the military command structure, and in so doing, promoted three commanders serving in the western army: Halleck, Grant, and Pope.

General Halleck was promoted to general-in-chief, filling the vacancy left by McClellan's removal in March, and was called to Washington to begin his new duties. Since Grant was second in rank, he was immediately recalled to Corinth on July 15 and was promoted to fill Halleck's prior position as commander of the Western Department. General Pope was also called to Washington, to command the newly-formed Army of Virginia.

In the East however, Lincoln had his hands full dealing with General McClellan.

IV
The Peninsula and Shenandoah Campaigns (February–June 1862)

In February, while General Grant and his Army of the Tennessee won battles at Fort Henry and Fort Donelson, President Lincoln had problems merely getting General McClellan to agree on a logistic plan for his drive on Richmond.

Lincoln wanted McClellan to march the Army of the Potomac from Washington overland to the old Bull Run battlefield. Once in place he would confront Gen. Joseph E. Johnston's army, under Beauregard, still camped out at Manassas from the previous July. General McClellan disliked this plan for several reasons. It would force him to march his huge army over 100 miles. The route would entail dealing with the problems involved in crossing several rivers with over 100,000 men, wagons, artillery and animals. McClellan would also have to depend on the railroad to get his supplies to him on time, where he needed them.

McClellan wanted to transport his men and supplies by boat down the Chesapeake Bay to Urbanna, a small port on the Rappahannock River, about 80 miles southeast of Manassas. All the difficulties he would face from Lincoln's plan, McClellan insisted, would be avoided through this approach. In addition, he would enjoy tactical superiority by positioning his troops between Johnston's army and Richmond. McClellan surmised that Richmond was there for the taking; even if Johnston moved to fight, it would be on McClellan's terms.

Lincoln thought his general's plan much too risky for the safety of the capital. As the president reasoned, with McClellan between Johnston and Richmond, who would stand between Johnston and Washington?

General Johnston himself settled the issue on March 9 by moving his 40,000 troops closer to Richmond. This maneuver not only assured Johnston a better defensive position to protect the Confederate capital, but also allowed the Confederate commander the opportunity to select the field for a counterattack.

Not to be deterred, McClellan offered another plan to Lincoln. Still refusing to march directly south, McClellan proposed to ship his entire army of 150,000 men and supplies down the Potomac River to Fort Monroe, on the tip of the peninsula formed by the James and York rivers. With the fort as a staging area, he would launch a land campaign up the Peninsula and capture Richmond. This route featured only two rivers to cross over a mere 70 miles of flat terrain, with no need for railroads, and would avoid Johnston's army altogether.

Lincoln, unimpressed, agreed only out of frustration and his desire to get on with the campaign. He imposed one condition: Enough troops would have to be left behind to satisfy Lincoln that Washington was adequately defended. Over McClellan's objections, Lincoln withheld General McDowell and his 34,000 troops to guard the Washington perimeter. Lincoln worried that Confederate Gen. "Stonewall" Jackson, then in the Shenandoah Valley in northern Virginia, might have his sights on the Union capital.

Besides keeping McDowell's army for himself, Lincoln also depended on Gen. Nathaniel Banks, who replaced the inept General Patterson after the battle of Bull Run. Banks, a staunch anti-slavery proponent, was a political general, rewarded for supporting Lincoln's views in the presidential campaign. Banks' army was also in the Shenandoah Valley, at the town of Harrisonburg, not far from Jackson's encampment. Lincoln would also soon create a new army for Gen. John C. Frémont, who was the Republican presidential candidate in 1856, and who was replaced the previous November by Gen. Henry W. Halleck as commander of the Western Department. Although Lincoln knew of Frémont's incompetence, he was politically pressured into making the appointment. The president also intended to withhold yet another division from McClellan, this one for Frémont, who was assigned to cover the approaches to Washington from western Virginia.

With the forces of McDowell, Banks and Frémont located close to Washington, Lincoln agreed to McClellan's plan. A telling sign of Lincoln's slipping confidence in his general came on March 11, when the president stripped away McClellan's authority as general-in-chief of all Union forces, leaving him only to command the Army of the Potomac.

On March 17, the Army of the Potomac sailed out of Washington for Fort Monroe. After all the recruiting, training, drilling and more drilling, the largest army ever assembled to that time was finally moving. Logistically, this endeavor was no small task. It required 400 ships to ferry over 100,000 men, 300 cannon, 25,000 animals, the mountains of supplies necessary to begin the mission and over 1000 wagons to haul them up the Peninsula. The magnitude of this effort is was so great that it took three weeks to complete.

McClellan's 100,000 man army consisted of five corps, commanded by Gens. Edwin V. Sumner of the 2d Corps; Samuel P. Heintzelman, the 3d Corps; Erasmus D. Keyes, the 4th; Fitz-John Porter, the 5th; and William B. Franklin commanding the 6th Corps.

Facing the Army of the Potomac was the South's premier military force. Commanded by Gen. Joseph E. Johnston, the Southern army consisted of two corps, under Gens. Stonewall Jackson and John B. Magruder, and five independent divisions commanded by James Longstreet, Daniel H. Hill, Ambrose P. Hill, Benjamin Huger and Theophilus Holmes.

Forecasting weather conditions as part of planning tactical troop movements was not taken seriously by military planners at the time, and probably not even considered necessary. This disregard was no more obvious than in the spring of 1862 on the Peninsula, where it rained almost continuously in driving sheets. In this setting, on April 3, the Army of the Potomac began marching out of Fort Monroe toward Yorktown, the historic battle site of Revolutionary War days. The attempt to move thousands of men and wagons through deep-rutted, sloppy miles of mud was slow, frustrating and laborious.

At Yorktown on April 5, the day before Grant was attacked at Pittsburg Landing, the Army of the Potomac experienced their first encounter with the enemy on the Peninsula. The Southern force garrisoned there was relatively small, a mere 17,000 men, facing an approaching giant of 100,000. Southern commander Gen. John B. Magruder tricked McClellan into thinking that his defenses were much

The Peninsula Campaign

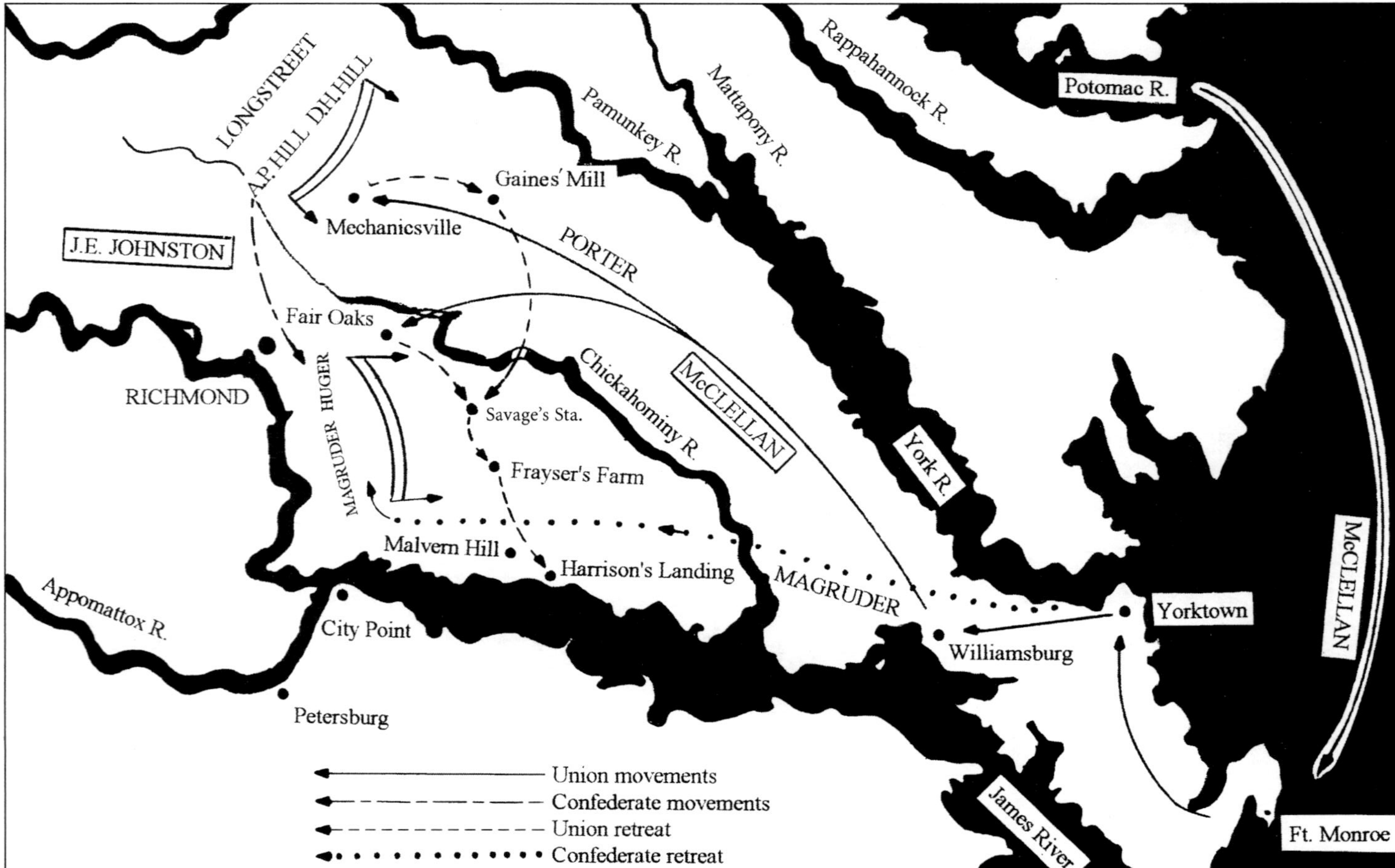

stronger by continuously shifting his troops from one area to another. The illusion thus created fooled McClellan, who was by nature overly cautious. "It seems clear that I shall have the whole force of the enemy on my hands," McClellan wired to Washington, "probably not less than 100,000 men, and possibly more." Because he thought his army outnumbered, McClellan ordered his troops to hold their positions. Despite Lincoln's angry protestations for his inaction, as well as advice from his commanders to attack, McClellan ordered his men to prepare the big guns for a siege of Yorktown. Always arrogant, McClellan even insisted that Lincoln send McDowell's 34,000 men to reinforce his presumably outnumbered army.

In Washington, as the siege of Yorktown played out, Congress abolished slavery in the District of Columbia. Lincoln also attempted to deal with the slavery issue when he tried to persuade the border states of Delaware, Maryland, Kentucky and Missouri to free their slaves. The freed slaves would then be transported to an African or South American colony, and in return the federal government would compensate the owners $400 for each slave freed. The States rejected this plan.

In Richmond, on April 16, the Confederate government approved legislation for a military draft, or conscription. It required three years of service for all able-bodied white men aged 18 to 34. Other provisions of the law exempted men owning 20 or more slaves, and also those paying other men who agreed to serve in their places. As a result of these loop holes, the conscription law was very unpopular; by many Southerners the conflict was now referred to as "A rich man's war but a poor man's fight."

While the Union army prepared their siege lines with guns so massive they required 100 horses to pull them into place, Johnston ordered Magruder and his men to withdraw from Yorktown. Knowing the defenses were much too weak to withstand the heavy shelling expected from the Union guns, the garrison evacuated on the night of May 3 and marched up the Peninsula.

In the ensuing retreat and pursuit, both armies struggled with the torrential, record-breaking rainfall and the resulting hardships. On May 5, Gen. James "Old Pete "Longstreet, commanding the Confederate rear guard was the first to exchange fire with the advancing Northern army, in the Battle of Williamsburg, named after the colonial capital of Virginia. Longstreet, a 41-year-old South Carolinian was solid and dependable and without question one of the South's best commanders. His day long engagement provided the necessary time for Johnston's army to escape, but was extremely costly. The South lost over 1,500 men in their first combat action with the Army of the Potomac. The Union lost over 2,000, a result of much confusion over the focus of command. This mix-up led regiments to intermingle, divisions to break up, and caused delays getting the back men into position.

At dusk, when Longstreet's forces pulled back, the Northern commanders requested permission to advance straight into Richmond to settle matters. Again McClellan refused, this time citing poor roads. For the rest of May, the Army of the Potomac stayed put.

While both sides hunkered down in the mud, General Jackson's Confederate Valley Army, in the Shenandoah Valley, was closely monitored.

At the south end, Massanutten Mountain divides the valley down the middle, creating smaller valleys on either side. Because of this geographical feature, the two smaller valleys were extensively used by both sides as long, north-south "super-highways." General Jackson was in the eastern valley, at Elk Run; and General Banks was on the western side of Massanutten at Harrisonburg.

At Confederate headquarters, Gen. Robert E. Lee, acting as a military advisor to President Davis, heard the artillery fire as McClellan approached Richmond. Lee knew of McClellan and his reputation as a commander overly cautious and hesitant. In addition, Lee predicted that McClellan would call for reinforcements and that these reinforcements would undoubtedly advance south through the Shenandoah Valley. Consequently, General Lee ordered Jackson's army into action.

Jackson's mission was to prevent any Union troops from leaving the valley and attacking Richmond from the north, while the Army of the Potomac attacked from the east. Both Lee and Jackson knew that such a scenario would be fatal for Richmond and the Confederacy.

From his camp at Elk Run, Jackson planned to march his small army of 4,200 men to the south, out of the valley and to the railroad depot at Charlottesville. From there, he would transport his army west to Staunton by rail, and then continue his westerly movement on foot, directly for General Frémont's division at the small hamlet of McDowell, in the western part of Virginia.

On May 8th, Jackson's men met two regiments from Frémont's

division. Following a four-hour battle fought entirely with small arms, Frémont's beaten troops retreated northward toward Franklin. Jackson then reentered the Shenandoah Valley, this time on the western side, and marched straight for General Banks at Harrisonburg. Forewarned of Jackson's intentions, Banks evacuated his camp and hastily went up the valley to his base at Winchester, where he prepared for the Confederate attack. During the ensuing chase through the valley, Jackson joined forces with a division commanded by Gen. Richard S. Ewell, and was reinforced to about 17,000 men. Continuing their pursuit of Banks, the combined Rebel armies attacked and defeated a much smaller Union outpost at Front Royal, approximately 10 miles from Winchester.

On May 25, the armies of Jackson and Ewell attacked Banks' 6,000 Union troops at Winchester. The battle was extremely one-sided, but before Jackson's superior army overwhelmed his men, Banks fled north toward the Potomac River and out of the valley.

Now that the threat of Frémont and Banks was gone, Jackson turned his attention to General McDowell's forces in Washington preparing to reinforce McClellan. To keep McDowell's forces from moving toward Richmond, Jackson unwittingly initiated a masterstroke of deception. He marched his troops 32 miles north from Winchester to Harpers Ferry, just short of the Potomac River, and then turned south again. When Lincoln learned that Jackson's army was approaching the Potomac River, the president's anxiety approached paranoia. Concerned that Washington was in danger, he rescinded his order to supply McDowell's troops to McClellan.

Lincoln's fear of Jackson also compelled him to order General Frémont's 14,000 men into the valley along with a corps from McDowell's army under Gen. James Shields. Both Frémont and Shields, on parallel paths, raced down the "highways" straddling Massanutten Mountain, one on each side, chasing Jackson who now marched his foot-weary soldiers back down to the south end of the valley. Frémont caught General Ewell's army at Cross Keys on June 8 and was handily repulsed. General Shields battled Jackson to a standoff at Port Republic on June 9.

Jackson's army covered a total of 245 miles in a month and a half of marching. They out-maneuvered three Union armies led by Fremont, Banks and Shields, and won five battles. Exhausted and battered, the Confederate Valley Army quietly slipped out of the Shenandoah Valley for Richmond, their mission accomplished.

On the outskirts of Richmond, the Chickahominy River flows east and divides the Peninsula in half lengthwise. Located less then 10 miles from the Confederate capital, the Army of the Potomac straddled the river, with most of the army on the north side. With the rain subsiding, McClellan planned to broaden his front line southward by sending four corps to the south side of the river, while keeping only Gen. Fitz-John Porter's corps in place on the north side.

On May 30th, Gen. Erasmus Keyes led the first of the four corps south across the river to Seven Pines, Virginia. The timing couldn't have been worse. That night another severe storm hit the area and turned the Chickahominy into a raging torrent. The bridges were swept away, separating Keyes from the main army. Like a tiger pursuing its isolated prey, Gen. Joe Johnston seized this opportunity to attack the divided Union force. On May 31, he sent Gen. James Longstreet and his division forward to smash the smaller, isolated corps in the Battle of Seven Pines (or Fair Oaks).

En route to Keyes, Longstreet mistakenly directed his men over the wrong road. The confusion caused hours of delay as the mixed regiments separated, which in turn delayed the battle until late in the afternoon. What should have been a unified attack failed, forcing Longstreet to retreat the next morning. To make matters worse, that evening the Confederate commander, Gen. Joseph E. Johnston, was severely wounded by a Union sharpshooter and was carried off the field.

On June 1, Gen. Robert E. Lee left his desk job in Richmond and replaced Johnston as commander of what would soon be called the Army of Northern Virginia. The 55-year-old veteran graduated second in his West Point class of 1829, and at the outbreak of the Civil War was President Lincoln's first choice to command the Union forces. Ironically, Lee's counterpart in the tiny Confederate Navy was his brother, Capt. Sidney Smith Lee.

Despite the disparity in troop strengths between the two opposing armies, Lee was committed on switching from a strictly defensive posture to taking on an offensive strategy. He was determined to press the attack and to drive McClellan off the Peninsula. For much of June, Lee assessed his predicament and formulated his strategy for defending Richmond. His first order of business was to strengthen the earthworks and fortifications separating Richmond from McClellan. On June 12, he sent his cavalry commander, Gen. "Jeb" Stuart, and 1,200 cavalrymen on a reconnaissance mission. In four days, Stuart and his men rode completely around the Army of the Potomac gaining valuable information on the location and size of McClellan's army. One vital piece of information was that McClellan now had four corps on the south side of the Chickahominy and only one, under Gen. Fitz-John Porter, on the north side. With this information, Lee drew his plan. He decided to risk splitting the comparatively smaller Army of Northern Virginia into two fronts. The smaller force of 27,000 men, commanded by General Magruder of Yorktown fame, and Gen. Benjamin Huger, would remain behind to defend Richmond against 70,000 bluecoats. With these overwhelming odds, Lee risked losing Richmond and the war, if McClellan attacked. Lee was reasonably sure that his adversary would not attack because McClellan would assume his troops outmanned and outgunned. Knowing that Porter was alone on the north side of the Chickahominy, Lee would use his larger second front to attack there.

On June 26, Lee struck with 60,000 troops, in three divisions, commanded by Gens. Ambrose P. Hill, Daniel H. Hill and Longstreet. Their target was Porter's 30,000 troops. The ensuing Battle of Mechanicsville began the so-called Seven Days' Battles. Problems hampered Lee right from the beginning. Again, the Confederate attack was sporadic and weak. Porter's men did not yield, but stubbornly resisted the Confederate assault. Lee's battle plan called for support from a fourth division, that of Stonewall Jackson, marching down from the Shenandoah Valley. Jackson's arrival proved too late, and by nightfall when the fighting stopped, Porter's corps remained in place.

During this time, McClellan learned of Jackson's imminent arrival and was convinced more than ever that his army was at a huge numerical disadvantage. True to character, McClellan fired off a telegraph message to Washington insisting on more men and absolving himself from responsibility in the event the army was defeated. "I am in no way responsible," he insisted. " I have not failed to represent repeatedly the necessity for reinforcements ... if the result ... is a disaster, the responsibility cannot be thrown on my shoulders; it must rest where it belongs." In light of his perceived dilemma, McClellan reversed his advance and pulled Porter's corps back four miles east, where he was attacked again on June 27, in the Battle of Gaines' Mill. This time, the Confederate attack was well synchronized and broke Porter's line. Reinforcements from the south side of the river held the Southern attackers back, and in so doing prevented a rout of Porter's troops. That night, Porter's corps crossed the river and reunited with the main body at Savage's Station.

On the south side of the Chickahominy, Confederate Gens. Magruder, Longstreet and Huger left their fortifications on the outskirts of Richmond and joined the fray by attacking Union troops at Savage's Station on June 29. The Confederates were again rejected. This scenario continued with Lee attacking McClellan and McClellan retreating, from Gaines' Mill to Savage's Station, to Frayser's Farm, and then to Malvern Hill. On July 2, the Army of the Potomac reached the safety of the federal gunboats at Harrison's Landing, on the James River. In the end, Lee lost 20,000 men, a quarter of his army, but from this loss he showed the profound mismatch in styles, determination and competence of the two generals.

Because these heavy losses severely diminished the fighting capacity of his army, Lee did not attack the Union at Harrison's Landing. Instead, he marched his men back to Richmond, knowing that although he was unable to accomplish the total victory he desired, he had successfully defended his capital and demoralized his enemy.

For the North, the Peninsula Campaign was a complete fiasco. The failure of McClellan's Army of the Potomac to carry out its mission was so disappointing that the Senate Committee on the Conduct of the War soundly criticized McClellan's leadership abilities. He was chastised for his failure to immediately attack Rebel forces at Yorktown, the chaotic command controls at Williamsburg, his failure to advance into Richmond after severely repelling Confederate forces at Fair Oaks, his decision to split his army on both sides of the Chickahominy River, and his decision to retreat to the James River in spite of inflicting heavy losses on the enemy during the retreating maneuvers.

McClellan responded that he did the country a service by not aggressively using his army to fight. His frequent cry was that his army was always outnumbered, and for his army to confront these superior forces and lose would have been disastrous for the country.

On July 6, President Lincoln visited McClellan's camp to assess matters personally. Again he listened to McClellan's excuses and his refusal to consider his moves a retreat, rather than a "change of base." The president rejected McClellan's arguments and ordered the Army of the Potomac to begin withdrawing from the Peninsula. Because he had no one else to lead the Army of the Potomac, Lincoln kept McClellan as commander, at least for the time being.

V
Cedar Mountain to Second Battle of Bull Run
(June–August 1862)

Disappointed by McClellan's debacle on the Peninsula, President Lincoln searched for a military leader that he believed possessed the courage to fight and the will to win. On June 26, Lincoln recalled Gen. John Pope from Pittsburg Landing, Tennessee, and appointed him as commander of a new army, the Army of Virginia. Lincoln hoped that this new army would provide the impetus for winning battles in the east. The new commander and army represented a change desperately needed by Lincoln. Pope was to consolidate and reorganize the scattered forces of General Banks and General Frémont in the Shenandoah Valley with those of General McDowell. In addition, Pope was to receive two additional corps from the Army of the Potomac, Gen. Fitz John Porter's and Gen. Samuel P. Heintzelman's.

McClellan, now commanding a much smaller army, would provide support to General Pope, a turn of events he adamantly opposed. McClellan's ego was now so badly bruised he believed Pope would be "thrashed ... & disposed of." Even Porter and Heintzelman and their troops, who were extremely loyal to McClellan, disliked Pope and were far from eager to join him. Pope, in turn, denigrated McClellan's competency and did not expect much support from his counterpart.

When Lee learned that Pope commanded a new army of some 50,000 men north of Richmond, the elation from his recent accomplishment on the Peninsula turned to profound concern. He worried that if Pope moved south and McClellan started back toward Richmond, their combined strengths would be too great to defend against. Consequently, on July 13, Lee ordered Jackson and 12,000 men to Gordonsville, 60 miles north of Richmond. Here at Gordonsville was the vital railroad junction of the Orange and Alexandria line. Jackson was to hold this junction at all costs and at the same time reconnoiter the immediate area for Pope's army. Lee planned for Jackson to circle around to Pope's rear and to cut him off from Washington. This move should have drawn McClellan away from Harrison Landing, thereby removing the threat on Richmond. The Army of Northern Virginia would then attack Pope from the front.

Two weeks later, Lee sent Gen. A.P. Hill with another 12,000 men to join Jackson at Gordonsville.

On July 22, Lincoln announced to his cabinet that he was about to issue a directive to free all slaves residing in the rebellious states. It became clear to the president that reuniting the Union would be impossible as long as slavery existed. His unsuccessful attempt in April to encourage the border states to free their slaves led to this Emancipation Proclamation. In Lincoln's opinion, Southern slaves indirectly helped the Confederate army by freeing Southern men from all other labor but to fight in the army. The freed slaves would, he thought, welcome the opportunity to join the Northern armies, thereby severely damaging the South's capability to carry on the war effort. Emancipation may even have appealed to some classes in France and England to the point that they would support the Northern side. The cabinet convinced the president that in light of the recent string of Union defeats, the timing of this proclamation now would give the appearances of a government in trouble. President Lincoln agreed to delay the proclamation until a more propitious time.

On August 3, General Halleck ordered McClellan to withdraw his remaining forces from the Peninsula to his new base at Aquia Creek, 30 miles south of Washington.

Probing about 20 miles north of Gordonsville on August 9, a portion of Jackson's army found Pope's advance units at Cedar Mountain. The federal advance force was the 8,000-man army of Gen. Nathaniel P. Banks. Seeking revenge for his defeat to Jackson in the Shenandoah Valley two months earlier, Banks did not hesitate to attack. The fact that his two divisions were outnumbered did not discourage Banks, who fully expected reinforcements at any time. The sudden attack surprised the Jackson men, and the fierce fighting set them back, but only initially. Jackson himself arrived, rallied his men, and together with Hill's division, counterattacked. Jackson regained the lost ground and more. When Union reinforcements began to arrive, Jackson returned to Gordonsville, with neither side claiming victory.

On August 13, Lee received the news that eased his fears of losing Richmond. When informed that McClellan and the Army of the Potomac were shipping out from their James River camp, Lee, along with General Longstreet and 25,000 men, moved north and reunited with the rest of the Army of Northern Virginia at Gordonsville. An additional 25,000 troops stayed behind to protect the Richmond fortifications.

The turn of events over the past two months had indeed been very significant for the Southern cause. From maintaining a defensive posture at the gates of Richmond, the Army of Northern Virginia had transformed into an offensive army that had not only repelled the largest fighting force ever assembled from the edge of their capital, but had also expelled them from the Peninsula. By consolidating his army at Gordonsville, Lee was determined to continue his offensive operations, with Gen. John Pope, and the Army of Virginia, as his targets.

Pope was at Culpeper, Virginia, in mid–August with 55,000 men. His orders from General Halleck were to sit tight and wait for the reinforcements from the Army of the Potomac, about 70,000 troops under Porter and Heintzelman. With a combined strength of over 120,000 men, he would then forge ahead with his assault on Richmond.

On August 18, with Pope somewhat on hold, Lee sent a contingent of cavalry to cut the Yankee supply line by destroying a railroad bridge spanning the Rappahannock River. The operation failed. Miscommunications and missed assignments botched the mission from the start. It backfired when a Union patrol party chanced on an unguarded river crossing and found a copy of Lee's written orders on a captured Confederate officer. These orders directed Jackson to Pope's rear. With Lee's intentions known, Pope was forced to move his army to Catlett's Station and strengthen his position, despite Halleck's order to wait at Culpeper.

Not to be out-maneuvered, on August 22 Lee ordered another cavalry raid, this time on Pope's new headquarters at Catlett's Station. In this operation, Lee evened the score when the Confederate troops found military documents noting that General Porter's 5th Corps would soon join Pope, followed by General Heintzelman's 3rd Corps. In possession of this vital information, Lee decided that his plan must be launched immediately, not after the reinforcements arrived. Again Lee ignored military logic when for the second time he split his army in the face of a numerically superior force.

On August 25, Jackson and 23,000 men set out on a march that would arch west and circle back through Thoroughfare Gap to within 25 miles of Pope's rear. At that point, Jackson's mission would be to cut Pope's communications and supply lines.

By late afternoon of the 26th, after marching 50 miles around Pope with no resistance, Jackson's men continued east and seized Bristoe Station, on the Orange & Alexandria Railroad line. At Bristoe Station they cut telegraph lines, destroyed several trains and burned down the railroad bridge, effectively severing Pope's link to Washington. Continuing his mission, the next day Jackson moved north to Manassas Junction, now the main Union supply depot. The Confederate troops were truly rewarded when they took the overflowing warehouses, full of food, ammunition, clothing and shoes. Just about everything from toothbrushes to guns was there for the taking. The hungry Rebels were overjoyed with their good fortune. The food included everything from meat and bread to lobster, candy and turkey. Not overlooked was the large supply of coffee to wash it all down. That night Jackson's men carried off whatever they could and left the rest in a fire, blazing against the night sky.

By this time, partial reinforcements had increased Pope's army to about 70,000 men, against Jackson's 23,000. When Pope learned that Jackson was in his rear and that the depot at Manassas had been destroyed, he sent a division to plug Thoroughfare Gap to prevent Longstreet and Lee from moving into the area and reinforcing Jackson. At this point, Pope still had no clue as to the location of Jackson. While Pope's search for his enemy continued, the Union force blocking Thoroughfare Gap inexplicably backed away, leaving it open for the Army of Northern Virginia.

After leaving the Union supply depot at Manassas Junction, Jackson and his men waited at Groveton, hidden in the woods on the west side of the old Manassas battlefield. On the afternoon of August 28, Jackson watched through his telescope as a division of Pope's army trudged up the Warrenton Turnpike. The Union troops, on a reconnaissance mission searching for Jackson's men, unknowingly passed before them. Jackson's army struck. With a screaming Rebel yell, the Confederate troops lashed out from the woods. Caught off guard, the Union lines formed instinctively. For two hours, the opposing lines were only 100 yards apart. Mercifully for both sides, night came quickly and the fighting stopped. In the Battle of Groveton, both armies suffered heavy losses.

Aware that Jackson was at Groveton, Pope, renowned for his braggadocio, confidently predicted that this time "we shall bag the whole crowd." The Army of Virginia was, however, scattered over miles of the surrounding territory as "search parties," out looking for the elusive Jackson. Pope immediately notified his widely-separated commanders, but it took valuable time to wait for them to arrive.

On August 29, General Pope launched the Second Battle of Bull Run. He was eager for the fight, so much so that he refused to wait for his army to organize. Of his over 70,000 soldiers, only about 30,000 were available for action. Pope ordered the federal assault, but it soon faltered. The Union Army was not properly prepared. Because they reached the battlefield at different times, their attack was sporadic, hesitant and lacked the cohesiveness needed to accomplish the impact of a unified front. As a result, Jackson's and Hill's forces, with only half the manpower, managed to hold on and wait another day for the expected Army of Northern Virginia.

General Pope's efforts may have been decidedly different with the support of his entire army. Unfortunately for Pope's purposes, the Union fighting spirit was lacking even from the troops on hand that day. General McDowell's 30,000 men, for example, provided little help. McDowell led his division so ineffectively that it was dusk before two of his regiments were in position. Worse, not one man of Porter's corps took part in the fight that entire day. Apparently Porter was under a misconception that Southern reinforcements had arrived. Accordingly, he diverted his 10,000 fresh troops away from the battle being fought only two miles away. Later that same day Porter received another order to attack. Still believing that superior Confederate forces were extended across his front lines, Porter again refused to advance his men. A few months later at his court martial, Porter admitted it was his total lack of respect for General Pope that led him to disobey the orders. In the end, Porter was discharged from the army.

On the morning of August 30, Pope was convinced that Jackson had withdrawn during the night, and that the force remaining was

The Second Battle of Bull Run (Manassas)

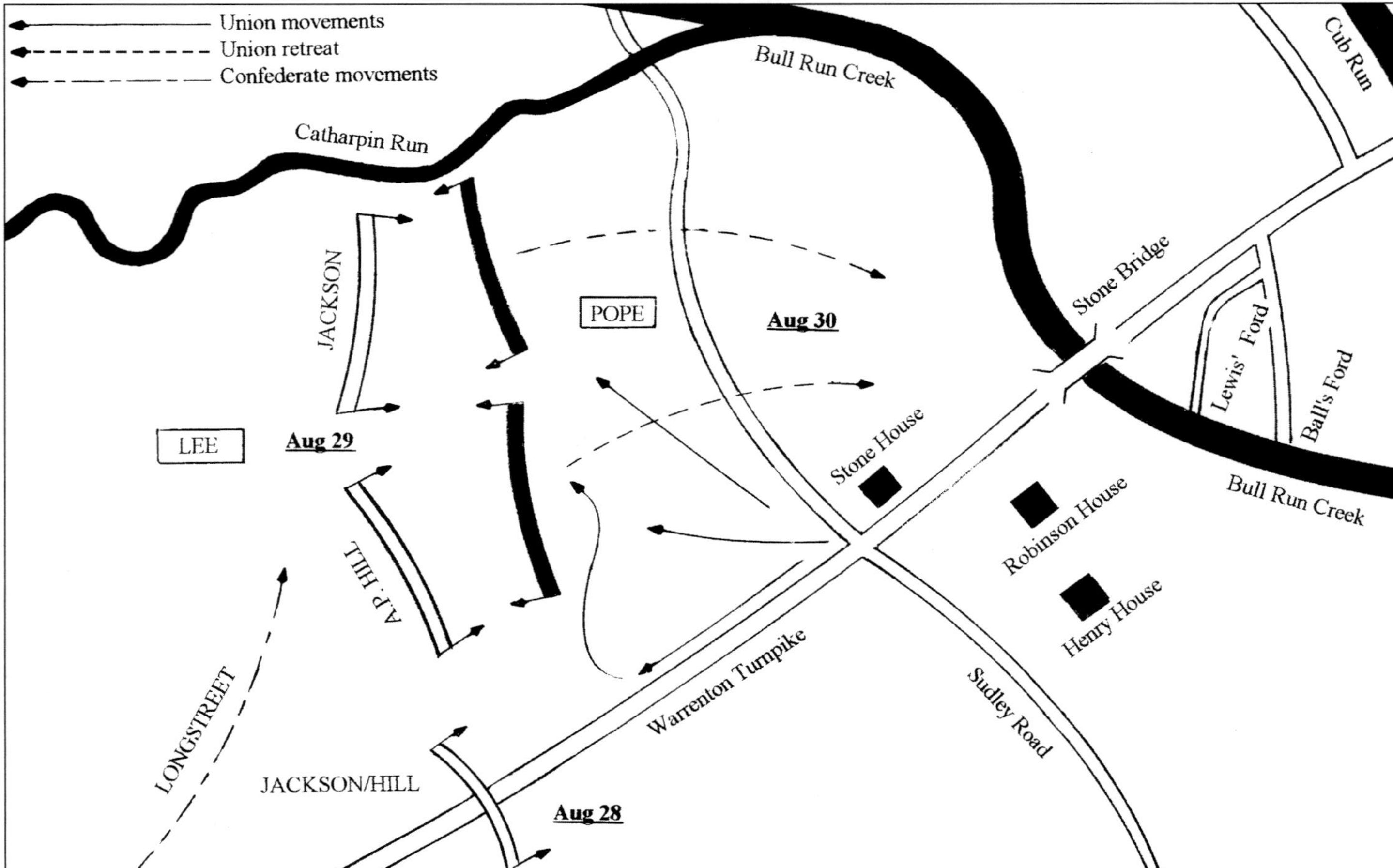

only a rear guard. Pope then narrowed his front line to advance on what he perceived as only the rear guard. Despite information to the contrary, he still believed that Lee and Longstreet were nowhere near the immediate area. In truth, Longstreet, Lee and 30,000 men had secretly arrived that morning, and with Jackson and Hill were waiting, hidden in the woods in a semi-circular trap. At noon, the Federals opened the assault and the Rebels drew them steadily into their trap. Jackson's men, firing volley after volley, fought until their ammunition ran out. When Pope finally committed his reserves, Longstreet swung his men into action. Longstreet's relentless artillery barrage and rifle fire staggered the charging Northern soldiers. The Union lines broke, confused and stunned. Sensing their advantage, Longstreet's troops came charging from the woods. The air vibrated with the shrieking, screaming Rebel yell, sending shivers through the retreating bluecoats. By four o'clock, with just enough fight left to gain the needed time, Pope ordered a full retreat across the same stone bridge used a year before by the routed troops of McDowell's army. Once Pope's men had crossed, the bridge was destroyed and the defeated Union Army trekked on to Centreville. On September 1, Jackson made one final attack on the retreating Union flank at Chantilly, only 20 miles from the nation's capital. By this time, the Confederates were too worn out to threaten seriously the fleeing Federals. After repelling them, the Union troops straggled into the fortifications of Washington. The Union losses from killed, wounded and missing came to about 16,000 and the Confederate about 9,200.

For the second time and from the same battlefield in just over one year, the South had sent the Union running back to Washington. The humiliation was not lost on the president. After all this time, all this fighting and all this bloodshed, he found himself back where he had started. Confused and disappointed, President Lincoln merged the Army of Virginia with the Army of the Potomac. Pope was sent to Minnesota, to fight the Sioux Indians, and McDowell was transferred to California. With no one else available, Lincoln reluctantly turned to McClellan. As Lincoln knew, McClellan was the only commander for whom this army could fight. The men of his command were ecstatic over "Little Mac's" return, and morale soared as the news spread through the army.

VI
Antietam to Fredericksburg
(September–December 1862)

Following his resounding defeat of Union forces at the Second Battle of Bull Run, Lee faced two strategic options. Although his army was heavily outnumbered, he could continue to exert offensive pressure on his Union rivals, or he could simply return the Army of Northern Virginia to their defensive positions around Richmond. Realistically, he knew he must seize this opportunity to sustain his momentum. His army was riding on a crest of victories, and in Lee's estimation the Northern army was stymied and their morale and motivation at this point sure to be quite low. The time was perfect to march north into Union territory. Even though Washington was too well defended to attack successfully, pulling back to Richmond now would give up all for which his men had fought and died. Besides, northern Virginia was so ravaged by war it could no longer support his army, which depended to a great extent on foraging off the land. On the other hand, Maryland and Pennsylvania would feed his men well. Furthermore, a Confederate victory on Northern soil would provide the Confederate government with an opportunity to gain support from France and England.

It was therefore a foregone conclusion that Lee would decide to muster his battle-weary army and invade Maryland, and perhaps even recruit some badly needed young Marylanders eager to fight the

Yankees. Lee's sights, though, were really on Harrisburg, Pennsylvania, where the Pennsylvania Railroad and Susquenhanna River connected the federal eastern theater to the West. Lee thought that by taking Harrisburg, he could isolate Washington from the western front.

On September 4, the Army of Northern Virginia crossed the Potomac with only 40,000 men, about two-thirds of Lee's original army. Many lacked shoes and all wore torn remnants of what were once uniforms. The officers were hardly distinguishable from their subordinates, and were far from resembling their images in the photographs they proudly sent home to their loved ones. Lee's army was lean, ragged, and dirty but also determined, loyal and aggressive.

The Confederate army reached Frederick, Maryland, on September 6. That night, while bivouacked on the fields surrounding the town, Lee issued his new orders. For the third time, he elected to divide his small army. The feasibility of this action was based, to a large extent, on Lee's ability to exploit McClellan's reputation. Combined with his perception of low morale and lack of spirit in the Union Army, Lee considered the risk worth taking, and divided his command into three smaller forces. He sent one army, under General Jackson with Gen. A.P. Hill supporting, 50 miles southwest to capture the Union garrison of about 11,000 at Harpers Ferry, the northern gateway to the Shenandoah Valley. Taking Harpers Ferry satisfied two prerequisites. Lee's communication and supply link to Richmond would be maintained, and it provided his army with an escape route, if by some unforeseen circumstances his plan went awry. With Jackson and A.P. Hill off to Harpers Ferry, Gen. D.H. Hill, a South Carolinian, took an army of about five brigades to South Mountain, a peak in the Blue Ridge chain. There, he could delay McClellan's 75,000 men from advancing toward Lee's army through the South Mountain passes, specifically at Crampton's Gap and Turner's Gap. Meanwhile, Lee and Longstreet, with the balance of the Army of Northern Virginia, moved northwest and waited at Hagerstown, not far from the Pennsylvania border. On September 10, Jackson, D.H. Hill and Lee moved their separate ways out of Frederick.

Two days later, McClellan bivouacked his men at Lee's abandoned campsites in Frederick. In an incredible stroke of luck, a Union soldier found three cigars on the ground, wrapped in a copy of Lee's written orders. McClellan now knew Lee's location, where he was going and what his intentions were. Furnished with this highly sensitive information, another commander would have broken camp almost immediately to give chase. McClellan did not move for 16 hours. Still overly cautious, he believed the lost orders may have indicated a trap, and chose not to overreact.

On South Mountain, D.H. Hill's army, poised on the ridges and secure in their concealment, watched as the long snake-like river of blue slowly advanced toward them. On September 14, the enemies met in the Battle of South Mountain. As planned, Hill had the distinct advantage of holding the high ground. The fighting was fierce, and, despite the gross disparity in sheer numbers, the battle raged the entire day. In the end, the Union advance stopped in its tracks as the stubborn Rebels poured down an incessant rain of lead from their protective shelter of trees and boulders. At dusk, the killing stopped, but neither side would claim a victory. This was especially true for Hill, who lost almost half of his troops. In spite of his huge losses, Hill accomplished his mission. With the Union advance stalled, Jackson had one more day to carry out his assignment.

That same day, Jackson began his artillery barrage from the hills overlooking Harpers Ferry. His Confederate force of six divisions was more than enough to overwhelm the Union garrison. However, incredibly, as the Union defenders watched for the Confederate attack, a lieutenant rode up to the troops and ordered a general retreat. The Commander, Gen. Dixon Miles, could not believe his ears when told his troops were evacuating their positions and spiking the battery guns. His attempt to stop the retreat was too late. Acknowledging his untenable position, Miles surrendered the next morning. Splitting the army even further, Jackson left A.P. Hill behind to secure Harpers Ferry while he rejoined Lee.

As the Union army steadily approached, Lee realized that at some point he must stop to fight. To maximize his defensive posture, he moved from Hagerstown to Sharpsburg, a small village 15 miles northeast of Harpers Ferry and only three miles from the Potomac. In selecting this site, Lee took a huge risk. His army was less than half the size of McClellan's, the Potomac River was at his rear, Antietam Creek was in his front and he had only one escape route.

Meanwhile, Jackson and D.H. Hill converged on Sharpsburg to meet Lee.

On September 15, the Army of the Potomac, about 75,000 strong, reached the edge of Antietam Creek. Commanding the six Union corps were Gens. Joseph Hooker, the 1st Corps; Edwin V. Sumner, the 2d Corps; Fitz-John Porter, the 5th; William B. Franklin, the 6th; Ambrose E. Burnside, the 9th Corps and Joseph K. Mansfield, the 12th Corps.

The next day, just three miles across the creek, Jackson and D. H. Hill's troops rejoined Lee's army and began moving into position. Lee's 52,000 troops massed along a three-mile front extending from the Potomac on the Confederate left to the Rohrbach Bridge, a little stone span over Antietam Creek on the right. (After this battle, the bridge was popularly known as Burnside's Bridge). Jackson's troops defended the left, with D.H. Hill's division in the center and Longstreet's corps protecting the right.

Jackson's 7,000 men, silently waiting near a small, white Dunkard, or Dunker, church (a pacifist sect), hid in a patch of trees, the West Woods. They looked out across the Hagerstown Turnpike that passed before them and at a cornfield on the far side. Beyond the cornfield lay the East Woods, containing the Army of the Potomac.

General McClellan's assault plan depended on the coordinated effort of a three-prong attack. The Union right wing, under Gen. "Fighting Joe" Hooker, a 48-year-old veteran of the Mexican-American War, would attack Jackson's men in the West Woods. At the same time, at the stone bridge on the right, the 9th Corps under General Burnside, a Rhode Islander and an old friend of McClellan's during their civilian days, was ordered to create a diversion to prevent Lee from shifting troops from that sector to reinforce Jackson. Hooker was to push Jackson's men into the center and at the same time close off the Hagerstown Turnpike as an avenue of escape. Burnside was then to press an all-out offensive on the right, also squeezing the Confederates toward the center. Finally, General Sumner's corps would join in and attack the concentrated Rebel force in the center. McClellan's plan was sound, and would destroy Lee's army if properly executed and coordinated. But it was not to be. Instead of all three fronts attacking in unison, delivering a massive blow along the entire Confederate line, McClellan sent them in piecemeal and lost his advantage.

The Battle of Antietam (Sharpsburg) began on the morning of September 17 when General Hooker's corps, strung out across both sides of the Hagerstown Turnpike and into the East Woods, advanced on Jackson's troops. From the East Woods, through the cornfield and down the turnpike, 12,000 Union soldiers came charging at the Confederates. The fighting was furious for two hours. Yankee troops nearly

THE BATTLE OF ANTIETAM (SHARPSBURG)

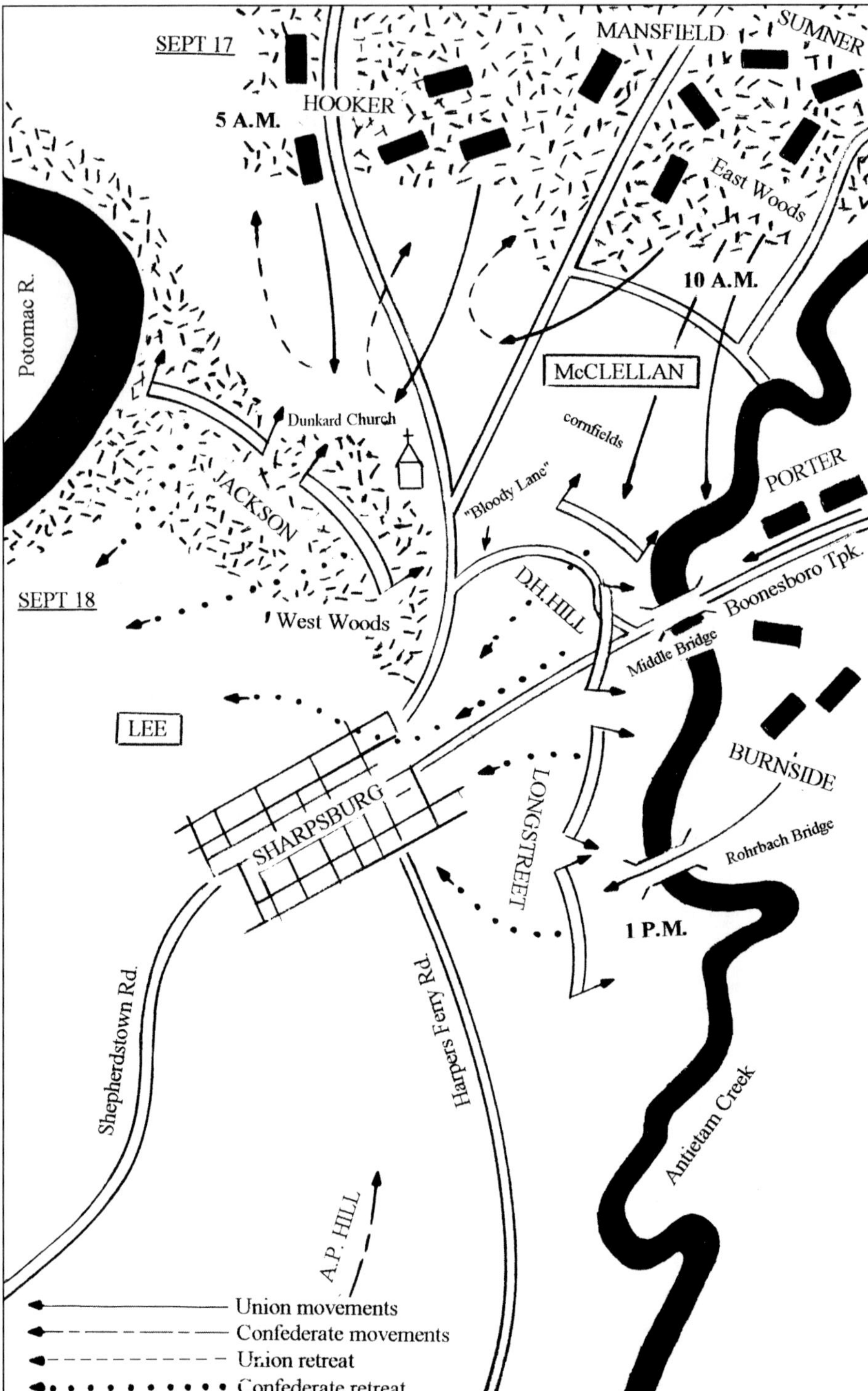

reached the Dunkard church when reinforcements from the Confederate center and left helped persuade Hooker's men that retreating was far more preferable to dying. Hooker's troops backed off to the East Woods. That Lee was able to shift troops within his lines was an indication that the battle was not progressing for General Burnside as planned at the stone bridge.

With Hooker's troops back in the fold, Gen. Nathaniel Banks, Jackson's old foe, now in General Mansfield's 12th Corps, tried his luck in a second-wave attack at Jackson's stubborn and resilient men. The bluecoats charged out of the East Woods and through the cornfield. The frenzy of the fresh Union troops momentarily caught the Rebels off guard and forced them back farther into the West Woods. By about 9 A.M., after a 90-minute battle, Banks' troops could not sustain their offensive drive and were themselves swept back.

McClellan, uncharacteristically, continued the attack on Jackson's line. He sent a third wave out from the East Woods. This time the attack was made with three divisions of General Sumner's corps. Despite the disparity in manpower and equipment, Jackson's fighting Confederates were too much for the Union forces. Sumner's front line broke and Jackson counterattacked through the cornfield. Union artillery firing from the perimeter of the cornfield ripped Jackson's men apart as they charged through the shoulder-high cornstalks. Their mangled bodies lay where they had stood, still neatly in line, cut down with the ripening corn. Jackson called an immediate retreat.

In a matter of a few hours that morning, Jackson's gritty veterans were able to successfully repulse three federal corps. Partly responsible for this fiasco was General Burnside, who ordered the men of his 9th Corps to cross over Antietam Creek via the stone bridge when they could have waded across more rapidly at a nearby ford. As they filed over the small span, column by column, the Confederate sharpshooters picked them off like tin cans on a log. This delaying tactic allowed Lee to shift reinforcement troops from that sector to Jackson's line, which ultimately saved the day for Jackson.

McClellan's attention now focused on Lee's center, defended by two brigades of General D.H. Hill's division, located in thick woods near a sunken road. This narrow road, a short-cut connecting the Hagerstown Turnpike to the Boonesboro Pike, was called the "Bloody Lane" after the carnage witnessed there. The two remaining divisions of General Sumner's corps initiated the attack around 10 A.M. The first division made three attempts to penetrate the Confederate line but was devastated by withering fire from Rebel muskets. The onrush of the second division forced Hill's men to fall back to a new position. At this point, Lee was in trouble, with his center broken. McClellan had all the trump cards to destroy the Confederate army. Instead, to the bewilderment of his commanders, McClellan called off the attack. Under the assumption that Lee was massing his reserves in that vicinity, "Little Mac" decided that "it would not be prudent" to continue the assault on Lee's center.

By this time, General Burnside's 9th Corps had finally crossed Antietam Creek, but still faced a relentless barrage of Rebel firepower. The Confederates held the high ground and stubbornly resisted the federal assault. Leading the Southerners was Brig. Gen. Robert Toombs, the former CSA secretary of state, who became bored with politics and resigned for a career of fame and excitement. After intense fighting, Burnside's men drove the Rebels back from the crest of the hills and into Sharpsburg. For the second time that day, the Army of Northern Virginia found themselves in dire straits. The Union was about to close Lee's only escape route, a ford over the Potomac, which meant certain doom for the scrappy Southern fighters. Suddenly, as if in a scene from an epic novel, General A.P. Hill and his 3,000 Confederate troops arrived unexpectedly from Harpers Ferry. Hill's forces slammed into the surprised Union flank and sent them back to the banks of Antietam Creek.

That night, Lee assessed his broken army. Despite the heroic bravery of his men and the fact that they had consistently held their own against staggering odds, he knew his exhausted troops would not endure another day of fighting without rest and food. That test would surely come the next morning.

But the next day, McClellan did not attack. He was too busy meeting with his commanders, discussing tactics and calling for reinforcements. Lee abandoned his plan to continue marching north, and on the night of the 18th, the Army of Northern Virginia, now just 38,000 hungry, sick and weary men, crossed the Potomac and limped back into Virginia.

Even though McClellan commanded an army that outnumbered Lee's forces by three to one, he remained at his headquarters while the Rebels crossed the Potomac. In spite of Lincoln's orders to pursue Lee and finish the war here and now, McClellan let the Army of Northern

Virginia escape. Merely stopping Lee from further incursion into Northern territory was interpreted by McClellan as a victory. President Lincoln was livid over his commander's failure to advance his army at this most opportune time.

The Battle of Antietam was one of the bloodiest of the Civil War. Battlefield casualties of 26,000 men were four times the amount suffered by American soldiers at the Normandy beaches in 1944, and the number of Americans who lost their lives in one day at Antietam was more than double the number that fell in the War of 1812, the Mexican War and the Spanish-American War, combined.

Five days after Antietam, Lincoln met with his cabinet and reminded them that in April he had posed the subject of emancipation, but had delayed a final decision until the Union had won a major victory. Lincoln admitted that although Antietam was not as decisive as he would have liked, the fact that the Confederate army was expelled from Northern soil was sufficient to announce formally his proclamation.

Lincoln's Emancipation Proclamation went into effect on January 1, 1863. Under this edict, slavery would be abolished in only those states engaged in a rebellion against the Union. To most people this meant that Lincoln was freeing the slaves in the Confederate states, where he had no authority, while preserving slavery in the North. In reality, Lincoln had no power to abolish slavery in the free states, but could use his authority under the War Powers Act to seize enemy resources. The slaves were considered enemy resources, and made Union forces armies of liberation.

On October 3, the president visited McClellan at his Antietam camp. Lincoln tried to convince his commander that the time to attack Lee's ragged army would never be better then the present. McClellan would not hear of it. He refused to move until his wagons were restocked with rations and his men properly fed and given new shoes. He even complained that his horses were tired. In Washington, General Halleck, also communicating orders to commence operations against the enemy, was totally disgusted and vented his angry frustration to McClellan, but with little effect.

The Army of the Potomac finally headed for the Virginia border on October 26. Because they moved so slowly, Lee was able to establish a defensive perimeter at Culpeper while Jackson marched his corps into the Shenandoah Valley.

President Lincoln finally decided to replace McClellan. On November 5, Gen. Ambrose E. Burnside, commander of the 9th Corps, reluctantly agreed to assume command of the Army of the Potomac. Twice before Burnside had been offered this command and both times he had refused it, because in his heart he knew his limitations better than his admirers did. He eventually accepted only to prevent the appointment of another general, presumably Hooker, whom Burnside considered even less capable than himself.

When Burnside assumed command, the Army of the Potomac was encamped across the fields of Warrenton, Virginia, on the south side of the Rappahannock River. Across the river, less than 30 miles away, was the Confederate army. Now replenished to about 65,000 men, Lee's army was divided between his two corps, Longstreet's and Jackson's, with the latter still in the Shenandoah Valley.

General Burnside's first act was to reorganize his army into three Grand Divisions, commanded by Sumner, Franklin, and Hooker. Each Grand Division comprised two corps. Sumner's right Grand Division contained the 2d and 9th corps, Franklin's left, the 1st and the 6th corps, and Hooker's center, the 3d and the 5th.

Once Burnside's staffing arrangements were complete, the Army of the Potomac broke camp and marched for Richmond, by way of Fredericksburg, a riverside city 35 miles to the southeast. The new commander plan was to follow the Rappahannock to the small town of Falmouth, cross the river over pontoon bridges, and seize Fredericksburg. Burnside would then entrench his men in defensive positions along the hills behind the town. With the Union army positioned between Lee's divided forces and the Southern capital, Burnside would advance straight into Richmond. First, however he would have to get the jump on Lee.

The Army of the Potomac began to march south on November 15. Two days later, two divisions of General Sumner's Grand Division reached Falmouth, directly across the river from Fredericksburg.

In the best of plans the unexpected will usually happen, and in this case, Burnside learned his pontoons would not arrive on time, forcing a delay in his crossing the river. The pontoons did not arrive until November 25. Perhaps understanding more fully the significance of this delay, General Sumner proposed to Burnside that instead of waiting for the pontoons, his men should cross the river and establish a position in the hills before Lee could respond. Burnside refused.

Since timing was the critical element in this mission, the delay proved disastrous.

General Lee heard of Sumner's arrival at Falmouth the following day, the 18th, and dispatched Longstreet's corps to head off the Union army at Fredericksburg. Longstreet marched his troops along the north side of the Rappahannock; they reached Fredericksburg on the 21st. Confederate pickets were quickly scattered along the rooftops and in the windows of the abandoned houses along the river's edge to harass the men in blue and delay their crossing.

While the Union army waited for their pontoons, General Jackson's corps arrived from the valley and the Confederates dug in on the hills behind Fredericksburg. For Burnside, this was the worst-case scenario for his offensive. Lee now commanded the advantage with forces controlling the heights on a three-mile crescent line. In approximately three weeks, the Confederates solidly entrenched themselves along the four hills overlooking the town. On the left side, the men of Longstreet's corps were poised and waiting on Marye's Heights, Taylor's Hill, and Telegraph Hill, grimly anticipating the Union attack. The divisions of Jackson's corps made up the Confederate right side extending from Prospect Hill to Deep Run Creek, a small inlet to the Rappahannock. Burnside's men would be sitting ducks on the open fields below.

Across the river, 147 artillery pieces were strung out along the heights overlooking the river, primed and ready to support over 100,000 men who were preparing to attack. It was a formidable army indeed.

On November 26–27, the president and General Halleck travelled to the Union camp to discuss the options available to Burnside now that his plan was unraveling. This visit underscored Lincoln's desire to press the attack despite risks that were now fairly obvious. Unlike the president's efforts to persuade McClellan, this not-so-subtle pressure greatly influenced the Union commander. Burnside decided to attack the enemy defenses head-on. Although his commanders complained and criticized this seemingly futile attack, their loyalty to Burnside won them over.

Before dawn on the morning of December 10, Union engineers began the arduous task of constructing six pontoon bridges across the 150 yards of the Rappahannock River. Of the six bridges, the two under construction for General Franklin's troops a few miles downriver were

THE BATTLE OF FREDERICKSBURG

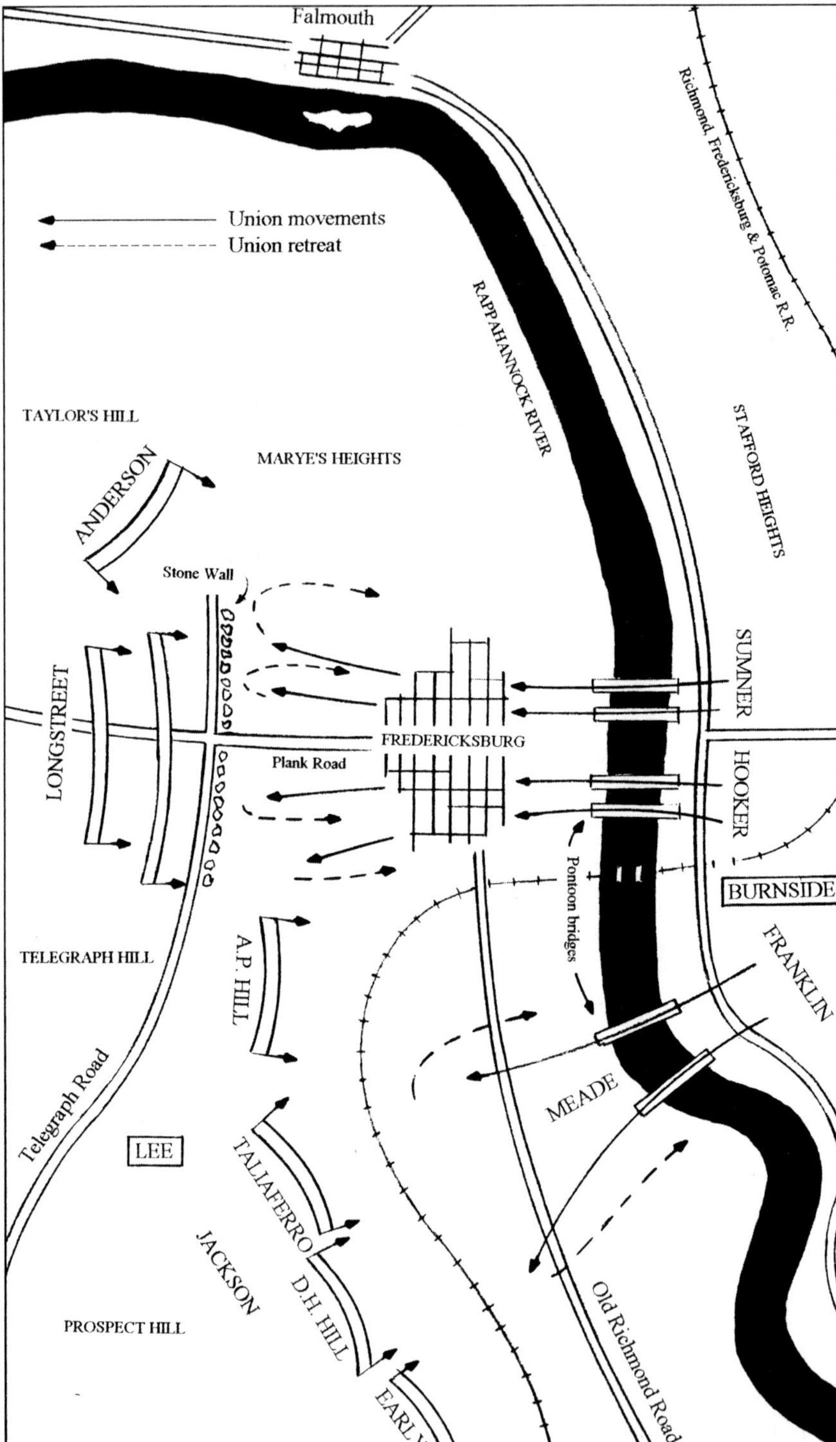

built with hardly any resistance from the Confederate defenders. Franklin's 40,000 men, along with part of Hooker's Grand Division, easily crossed the river on December 11. Directly in front of Fredericksburg, the same project was a great deal more hazardous. Across the river from the Union army, the Confederate pickets were now alerted to the Union activity. From their windows and rooftops the Confederate sharpshooters had a field day using the Union troops for target practice, particularly those who were working on the bridges. Each new effort made by Burnside's men to work at the river's edge attracted sniper fire, forcing the Union men to run for cover. Apparently disgusted with the Confederate harassment, Burnside ordered a barrage of shot and shell. Burnside's artillery practically destroyed the now-deserted city of 3,500, but failed to dislodge the enemy snipers. Finally, rowing across the river in pontoon boats, a contingent of federal troops chased the irritating Rebels out. With the pickets removed, the bridges were completed and Sumner's Grand Division allowed to cross unmolested on December 12.

As the morning fog rolled away on Saturday, December 13, the Battle of Fredericksburg began to play out. The first Union assault from Franklin's Grand Division was under Gen. George G. Meade. Born in Spain, the 47-year-old Mexican War veteran gave the order that sent his division straight into Jackson's line on the Confederate right. Initially held up by Confederate artillery fire, the Union troops penetrated a gap in Jackson's line and threatened disaster for Lee's men. Confederate reinforcements swung over from both flanks and squeezed the Union Army out and back in retreat. Another attempt by Franklin, this time at Deep River Creek, also failed. Having lost 5,000 men, a discouraged Franklin, despite orders to the contrary, chose not to renew the attack.

At the base of Marye's Heights on the Confederate left, 2,500 of Longstreet's men patiently waited along a sunken road behind a stone wall. With muskets loaded and ready, they peered over the shoulder-high wall toward the town, looking for signs that the Union attack was about to begin. At a given signal, the federal troops poured from the streets of the bombed-out town and quickly formed into their ranks. In true Napoleonic style, they made two groups of three brigade lines. As the first line moved steadily forward over the open field toward the stone wall, Confederate batteries, firing from the hills, decimated the Union ranks. When the Union advance came within range of the stone wall, hundreds of Confederate musket barrels, resting across the top of the wall, fired in one ear-splitting blast, followed by a second volley, and another, all in quick succession. The rapid fire devastated the onrushing Yankees. The remnants of the Union line, overwhelmed by the Confederate fury, hastily retreated as shell and canister (a special type of encased shot designed for firing at close range) continued to rake the field. Union Gen. Darius N. Couch, surveying the carnage from a church steeple with disbelieving eyes, lamented, "Oh, great God! See how our men, our poor fellows, are falling."

Incredibly, the same scenario was repeated in five more Union attacks. Dead Union bodies strewn over the field, sometimes three deep, were themselves impediments to the orderly advance of the Union lines. This horrific carnage went on until nightfall. As Confederate General Longstreet remarked to Lee that bloody afternoon, "General, if you put every man now on the other side of the Potomac on that field to approach me over the same line, and give me plenty of ammunition, I will kill them all before they reach my line." Not one Union soldier came within 100 feet of the wall; worse, the Union wounded were left on the field to die in the bitter cold night.

The next morning the Confederates were anxious to renew the battle. From their artillery positions on Marye's Heights to the firing line at the stone wall, the Rebels gazed in disbelief at the horrible sight in front of them. Thousands of Union dead lay strewn across the open fields. The tangle of bodies would pose an obstacle to the new federal assault. Indeed, a new assault on Marye's Heights was not to be. The Union recorded 13,000 casualties that day, most of them on the field before the stone wall at Marye's Heights. Even though he was planning to lead the next attack himself, Burnside was persuaded by his commanders to withdraw. On the night of December 15, the Army of the Potomac retreated across the Rappahannock River.

VII *Confederate Counteroffensive: Iuka to Stones River* (June – December 1862)

After their evacuation of Corinth in June, General Bragg and his two corps, led by Polk and Hardee, remained bivouacked at Tupelo, Mississippi. In the comfort of their camp, the worn-out soldiers recuperated from their bloody and heartbreaking defeat at Shiloh. While his men recovered, reorganized and retrained, Bragg worked out his ideas for an aggressive counterattack aimed at recovering his losses in Tennessee and Kentucky. He pinpointed Louisville as his ultimate target. That the huge Union army he faced at Shiloh was now split apart made this move all the more appealing and feasible.

Bragg's plan was simple. Gen. Sterling Price, the victor at Wilson's Creek in Missouri, would stay behind to defend central Mississippi and to prevent the enemy from advancing on Vicksburg. After defeating the Union forces in this area, Price would rejoin Bragg in Kentucky. At the same time, Gen. Edmund Kirby Smith, presently at Knoxville, would advance into Kentucky and make a demonstration close to the Ohio border near Cincinnati. Finally, Bragg would take his men north through Tennessee, join Smith in Kentucky and advance on Louisville.

In July, General Price and his 15,000 soldiers headed out to engage the Union forces defending Corinth, and Bragg began boarding his 35,000 troops on the railroad to Chattanooga. It happened that Union Gen. Don Carlos Buell and his Army of the Ohio were also heading for Chattanooga. Transporting his men by rail was a brilliant maneuver for Bragg, and enabled his army to reach Chattanooga first. In several ways Buell was at a tremendous disadvantage. Not only was his army following the Memphis & Charleston Railroad line on foot, but to complicate matters, they were under orders from Halleck to stop and repair the line along the way. Between the repairs and the constant raids from the Rebel cavalry, Buell's men made very little progress. Unable to reach Chattanooga before Bragg, General Buell marched north to Nashville, and waited there for Bragg to attack.

Bragg had other ideas. On August 28 he put the second phase of his campaign into operation by marching his men out of Chattanooga toward the Kentucky border and Louisville.

Earlier, on August 14, General Smith had begun his northward march into Kentucky with about 20,000 troops. At Richmond, Smith had encountered 6,500 Union soldiers which he had handily driven off, had moved on to occupy Lexington, and was now continuing his march north toward Frankfort, the Kentucky capital, and Cincinnati.

In Cincinnati, the residents were panicked over the news of General Smith's approaching army. With rumors of an imminent attack, martial law was imposed, businesses closed and all able-bodied men, armed with weapons from shotguns to squirrel rifles, gathered in the city square.

While General Smith carried out his part of the plan, Bragg's Confederate troops pressed their relentless advance north through Kentucky. Closing in on Louisville, the Rebel soldiers paused long enough to capture a small Union garrison on September 17 at Munfordville. At this point, the Army of Tennessee marched east to join General Smith, who was approximately 30 miles from Louisville.

On September 13, General Price and his 15,000 men reached the town of Iuka, Mississippi, just short of the Tennessee line, and about 20 miles east of Corinth. Concerned that the Confederates were on their way to reinforce Bragg, Grant moved to block Price from crossing the Tennessee border. He immediately dispatched two divisions under Gen. Edward Ord to Burnsville, a small town about seven miles west of Iuka. Arriving on September 18, General Ord's orders were to attack Price the following morning. While Ord marched to Burnsville,

Gen. William S. Rosecrans and two infantry divisions left Corinth with orders to attack Iuka from two different directions. All three Union attacks would be launched simultaneously on the 19th. That morning, however, Rosecrans wired Grant that his army was behind schedule and would arrive later in the afternoon. Disappointed, General Grant informed Ord about this new turn of events, telling him that he should attack only after hearing the gunfire from Rosecrans' engagement with the enemy.

General Ord never heard a single shot.

Apparently, when Rosecrans finally arrived in the late afternoon of the 19th, the enemy confronted his advance force and beat the Union army back before nightfall halted the fighting. The wind direction that day was such that no sound from the battlefield reached Ord's camp, and resulted in no response from Ord.

Later that night, when a courier delivered Rosecrans' report of the fight, an astonished Grant ordered General Ord to attack early the next morning. When Ord arrived at Iuka, he found General Price and his Confederates gone, having retreated to Ripley, Mississippi, during the night. General Rosecrans' army now occupied the town.

Still waiting for Bragg in Nashville, Buell finally realized his mistake. Feeling somewhat disconcerted, Buell left an occupation force in Nashville and on September 7, marched his army toward Louisville.

In Louisville, as in Cincinnati, citizens were terror stricken over the approach of the Confederate army. Women and children abandoned the city, and earthworks were constructed to prepare for the imminent invasion. To the immense relief of the Louisville citizenry, on September 25 Buell reached the city ahead of Bragg and Smith, who were in Frankfort, preparing to attend the new governor's inauguration.

Back at Ripley, Mississippi, Gen. Earl Van Dorn arrived from Vicksburg with his small army and joined forces with General Price. Continuing to press Bragg's counteroffensive, Van Dorn's goal was to drive the Union forces from northern Mississippi before Grant could move on Vicksburg. Van Dorn took charge of the two armies, now numbering about 25,000 men, for an attack on Rosecrans' 21,000 troops still defending Corinth. When Confederate troop movements convinced Grant of Van Dorn's intentions, reinforcements were ordered to Corinth under the command of Gens. Stephen A. Hurlbut and James B. McPherson. Not one to be outmaneuvered, on October 4

Bragg's Counteroffensive Into Kentucky

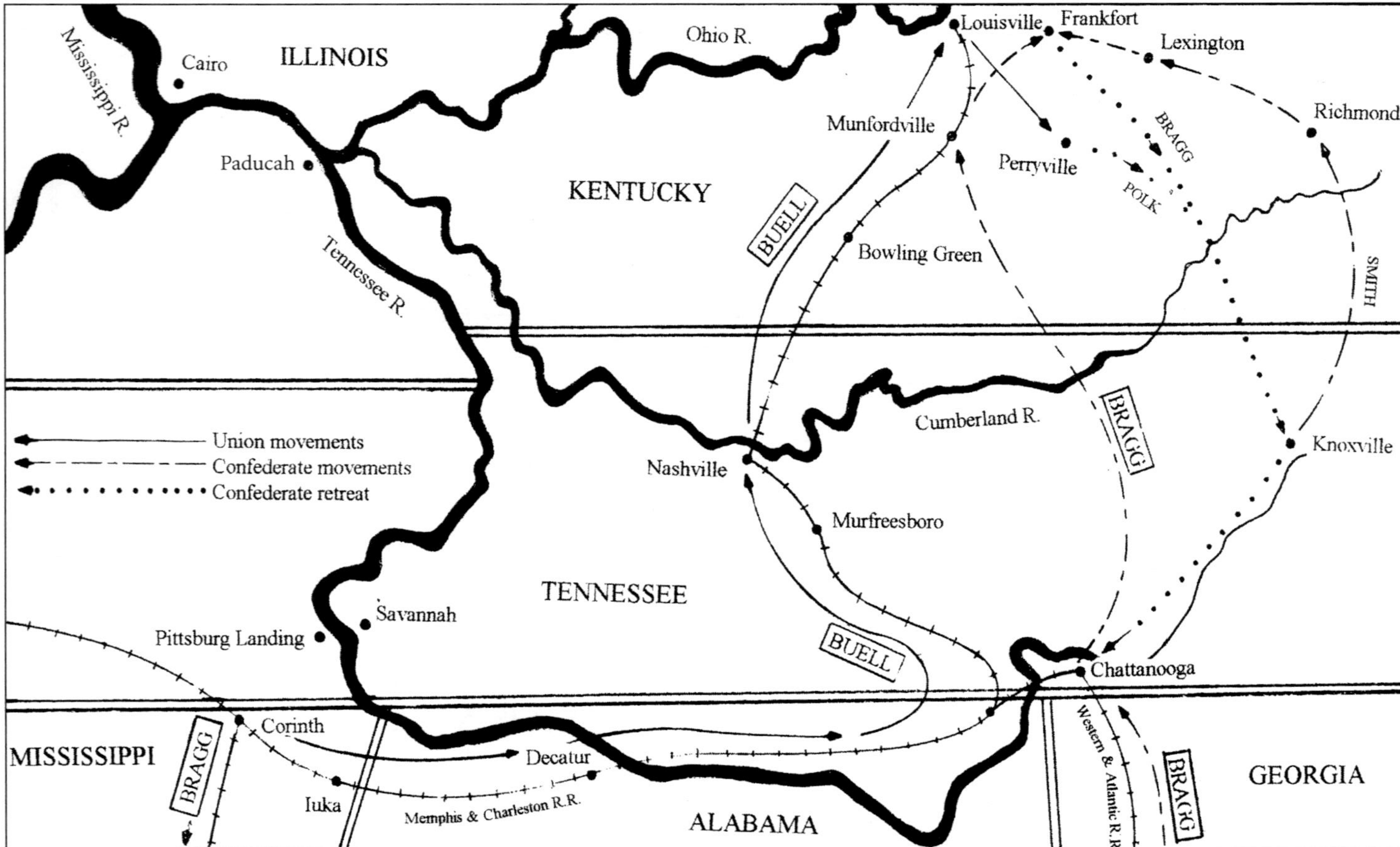

Van Dorn ordered an all-out attack on Rosecrans' army before the reinforcements arrived to assist the Union forces. The Union defenders held their position long enough for Van Dorn to realize that he was about to be crushed between Rosecrans and the two rapidly approaching Union armies. Van Dorn escaped, but not before losing an estimated 1,500 killed.

Buell finally mobilized his army on October 1, after receiving several threatening messages from Washington on his do-nothing attitude. The Army of the Ohio numbered close to 60,000 men and was a magnificent sight. The immense wagon train snaking out of town covered over 22 miles. The ammunition alone required 75 wagons for each corps.

On October 4, General Bragg and General Smith were still in Frankfort attending the inauguration ceremonies of the new Confederate governor of Kentucky. As Buell marched his Army of the Ohio toward Bragg's main body of troops on the outskirts of Frankfort, he ordered a division out of formation to harass the proceedings at the capitol building. A sudden and unexpected burst of Union gunfire disrupted the festive occasion and created much confusion in the Confederate leadership. This small demonstration of Union force convinced the Southern generals that the entire Army of the Ohio was somewhere in the Frankfort area. Worse yet, not expecting Buell to attack so soon, Bragg's 40,000 men were widely scattered around the surrounding countryside, except for some 15,000 men under General Polk who "escaped" Buell's threat and went to Perryville.

When Buell's advance corps reached Perryville in the evening of October 7, parched from the unusually dry and hot weather, they immediately headed for the nearest water at Doctor's Creek, only to find Polk's troops already there. A battle for the drinking rights ensued between a Union brigade under Gen. Philip Sheridan and Polk's Rebels. Polk's army won the fight and controlled the river, at least for the time being.

Early the next morning, Sheridan renewed the attack. This time the tables were reversed when the Union drove Polk back from the river and even from the hills beyond. Buell's Army of the Ohio straggled into Perryville throughout the rest of the day.

In Frankfort, General Bragg learned of the Confederate loss at Perryville, but because of the October 4th incident, he assumed that Buell's main army was still near Frankfort. Consequently he disregarded

Polk's urgent pleas for reinforcements, and ordered a counterattack on what he saw as only a portion of the Union army.

In the afternoon of October 8, Polk carried out Bragg's orders by sending two divisions against what was in reality the entire Union left wing, the corps commanded by Gen. Alexander McCook. The Confederate attack was intense. Luckily for Polk, most of McCook's men were young recruits in battle for the first time. They were easily broken and swept from the field.

So far, the Confederate invasion of Tennessee and Kentucky had met little resistance, but the loss at Corinth did not bode well for Bragg's campaign. That evening the Confederate commanders met to discuss plans for continuing their counteroffensive. During the meeting, Bragg learned that Polk was confronting Buell's entire Army of the Ohio and not just a portion of it. But more important, with Van Dorn's defeat at Ripley, Bragg knew that reinforcements would not be coming any time soon. Fearing that Grant was now free to aid Buell, the Confederate commander ordered Polk out of Perryville that very night. Polk rejoined the rest of the Confederate army in the retreat to Tennessee.

General Bragg's ambitious attempt to regain Kentucky and Tennessee failed. By the end of October, the Confederate army had retraced its steps and was back in Knoxville, where General Smith had begun his campaign in August. From Knoxville, Bragg's army marched full circle back to Chattanooga.

General Buell, who had the advantage of troop strength and battlefield control, chose not to chase Bragg any farther than Bowling Green. Instead, he returned his army to Nashville to reestablish his base of operations. When word of Bragg's unmolested retreat reached Lincoln, it so enraged the president that he lost little time replacing Buell with General Rosecrans as commander of a new Army of the Cumberland.

General Rosecrans refused to leave Nashville until satisfied that his army was ready. Despite several appeals from Washington for action, his first priority was to stock up on enough supplies and rations to carry him through some 20 days in the field. In addition, he organized his new army into three wings. Gen. A.M. McCook, the 20th Corps, would command the right wing; Gen. George H. Thomas, commanding the 14th Corps, would control the center; and the 21st Corps went on the left wing under Gen. T.L. Crittenden. On December 26,

Rosecrans and 42,000 men marched from Nashville along with their huge wagon train of rations. Bragg by this time had moved out of Chattanooga with 38,000 men and was now about 30 miles southeast of Knoxville in the town of Murfreesboro.

The Northern army struck first, on Wednesday, December 31, in the Battle of Stones River (Murfreesboro). Rosecrans' plan was to severely smash the Confederate right using Crittenden's left wing. To insure a sledge-hammer assault on this sector, Rosecrans transferred over a portion of McCook's right wing to strengthen the left. With the Union right wing now weakened, Rosecrans gambled that McCook could successfully perform his part of the attack. To alleviate any misconception, McCook assured Rosecrans that he could contain the enemy for the time necessary for Crittenden's troops to accomplish their objective and for the plan to work. Meanwhile, Thomas would drive his army forward into the center and push the Confederates to the left.

On the morning of the attack, the plan quickly unraveled. McCook could not hold his position after all, and within one hour the Union right flank was swept back. Running from the woods screaming at the sudden reversal, the Union soldiers cried out, "We are beaten, the right wing is broken! The enemy is sweeping everything before them." With the Union right broken and in full retreat, Rosecrans swung all available manpower and artillery from Crittenden's wing to make a stand on the Union right. Quickly lined up on Rosecrans' only escape route, the Nashville Pike, Union batteries waited for the Confederate avalanche to sweep out of the woods. Suddenly the screaming Rebel yell reverberated through the winter air as the Confederate troops burst into the clearing between the opposing armies. In a huge roar and blinding flash, the Union guns fired in one gigantic explosion. Instantly the field was lost in a cloud of smoke. Again the Union line fired and again the ground trembled with the thunder of battle. When all was over, the dead Rebel troops, many hundreds of them, gave witness that the Confederate left was finally stopped. Reporting his observations after the battle, one Union officer remarked, "When our batteries advanced, they found no Rebels between the woods and the turnpike except the dead, dying and disabled. There were hundreds of these, and their blood soaked and reddened the ground."

That night, at a meeting in Rosecrans' quarters, the Union

commander decided to renew the battle. As if by some unspoken agreement, on January 1 both sides remained in camp, leisurely preparing for the upcoming showdown.

The battle resumed on January 2. This time General Bragg switched his offensive punch from his left, which had failed two days earlier, to General Breckinridge's corps on his right flank. Rosecrans' army was now on the far edge of the easily fordable Stones River. When the Confederates reconnoitered the prospective battlefield, they spotted a huge mass of Union artillery assembled on a low rise in the distance. From this observation, a Confederate disaster was predicted, and General Breckinridge tried unsuccessfully to dissuade Bragg from carrying out the attack.

Late in the afternoon of January 2, Breckinridge's unsuspecting troops trod off to an almost certain death. Watching his corps begin their advance, the commander declared no responsibility for the results of this battle about to be waged against his will. To Gen. William Preston he exclaimed, "General Preston, this attack is made against my judgment and by the special orders of General Bragg. If it should result in disaster, and I be among the slain, I want you to do justice to my memory and tell the people that I believed this attack to be very unwise, and tried to prevent it."

As the Confederate lines advanced, the Union defenders suddenly appeared. A fierce fight ensued which forced the Union soldiers to retreat across the river. As the advancing Rebels were drawn closer and closer to their fate, the men in blue ran for cover. Suddenly the 58 pieces of Union artillery opened a barrage of shell and canister, erasing huge sections of Confederate fighters. Nevertheless, the survivors were determined, and stubbornly maintained their steady course as the terrible carnage continued around them. Try as they might to cross Stones River, the Confederates were unable to withstand this merciless barrage. Only 90 minutes after leaving, the Rebels fled for the safety of their camp.

Having suffered about 11,700 casualties, on January 3 Bragg again gave up the field to the Union. Demoralized and weakened, Bragg's Army of Tennessee retreated further south to Shelbyville and Tullahoma. When news of Bragg's retreat reached the Southern newspapers, he was severely criticized for not continuing his December 31st assault on Rosecrans' broken right wing, and also for ordering Breckinridge's corps into what was clearly perceived as a Union trap.

Exhausted and spent, both sides went into their winter quarters to remain until the following summer.

In the West, the Union side had an incredible year. With the exception of Vicksburg and Port Hudson, every Confederate outpost on the Mississippi River lay in Northern hands. In addition, most of Tennessee, Mississippi and Kentucky were now under federal control. For the most part, the Western generals, in one year's time, had practically won their war. From Fort Henry and Fort Donelson in February to the victory at Stones River, Tennessee, the following January, the Union commanders and their troops in the West had every reason to be proud of their accomplishments.

VIII
The Vicksburg Campaign
(December 1862–July 1863)

Union military action on the Mississippi River was both swift and decisive in 1862. From Cairo, Illinois south to Vicksburg, federal victories included Island Number 10 in April, as well as Fort Pillow and Memphis in June. Responsible for much of this effort was Flag Officer Andrew H. Foote, one of the Union's foremost naval commanders at the north end of the Mississippi.

At the south end of the Mississippi, sailing north to Vicksburg from the Gulf of Mexico, Adm. David G. Farragut captured New Orleans in April, and Baton Rouge and Natchez in May. The following month at Vicksburg, however, Farragut found the Confederate batteries along the sides and summit of the two-hundred-foot bluffs too much to handle. Consequently, as 1862 ended, 250 miles of the Mississippi River between Port Hudson, Louisiana, and Vicksburg, Mississippi, remained in Confederate hands.

Defiantly encapsulated within its fortifications, seemingly impregnable, Vicksburg challenged Union military power. If this last bastion of Confederate resistance fell, the Union would have free navigation of the entire Mississippi River.

After turning away Confederate Gen. Van Dorn at Corinth on October 4, 1862, Grant, now serving as commander of the Western Department, began his campaign to capture the prize, Vicksburg.

Grant organized a joint army and naval operation enlisting the services of Adm. David D. Porter, naval commander of the Mississippi

Squadron. A 49-year-old Pennsylvanian, Porter had been brought up in a family rich in navy heritage. As a young naval officer, he had served under his father in the War of 1812; his adopted brother was Flag Officer David G. Farragut, whose flotilla had captured New Orleans in April.

Grant planned to march his 40,000 troops south along the Mississippi Central Railroad line from Jackson, Tennessee, to the Union supply depot at Holly Springs, Mississippi. Following his layover at Holly Springs, Grant's army would then march 90 miles farther to Grenada. Only if his advance went unchallenged would he proceed deeper into hostile country, to Vicksburg. Meanwhile, from Cairo, Illinois, Porter would sail his fleet of gunboats to Memphis to rendezvous with Gen. William T. Sherman and his troops. On December 20, Porter's boats, loaded with Union soldiers, supplies and artillery, would sail down the Mississippi toward the outskirts of Vicksburg.

The scheduling of Sherman's departure date, December 20, was evidently not a random occurrence, but the result of an internal power struggle between Grant and his second-in-command, Gen. John A. McClernand, a prominent Democrat and politically-appointed general. General McClernand wanted the glory and fame that he expected would reward the commander capturing Vicksburg. Without Grant's knowledge, he persuaded the president and Secretary of War Edwin M. Stanton to grant him a separate and independent command. In addition, McClernand would have the full authority to advance on Vicksburg at the same time that Sherman and Porter left on their own missions. McClernand, currently in Springfield, Illinois, raising additional troops, planned to join his own army at Memphis and embark there for his advance down the Mississippi on December 28.

In General Grant's opinion, "Two commanders on the same field are always one too many." When informed of McClernand's independent command, Grant asked Washington for further clarification. General Halleck, in a rare display of support, told Grant that he alone was in charge of this mission. Halleck ordered McClernand's army divided into two corps, reserving one for General Sherman.

Grant was concerned that McClernand, Sherman's senior, would assume command of the entire force at Memphis once he arrived. As a result, Grant told Sherman to leave Memphis before McClernand arrived, with not only his own corps but with McClernand's troops as well. Sherman did so on December 20. When McClernand reached Memphis to find his army "kidnapped," he was enraged. On appealing to Washington, McClernand was told to stop complaining for the good of the service, and was sent to join Sherman and Porter on the outskirts of Vicksburg.

Defending Vicksburg was Confederate Gen. John C. Pemberton, a Pennsylvanian in command of the Army of Mississippi. Grant fully expected Pemberton to challenge the Union's overland advance with the bulk of his main army drawn away from Vicksburg. While Grant occupied Pemberton, Porter and Sherman would continue down the Mississippi and disembark at Chickasaw Bluffs, on the Yazoo River just north of Vicksburg. There, Sherman would attack the northernmost Confederate defense line along the bluffs of the Yazoo River with 30,000 troops. With the main Confederate army still miles away fighting Grant, Sherman would then march directly into Vicksburg.

The plan failed.

Grant's army depended on the availability of food and other supplies to drive its forward movements. To satisfy this requirement, a base was established at Columbia, Kentucky, to supply materials to Grant's forward base at Holly Springs, Mississippi, a stretch of 150 miles through enemy territory.

While Grant and Pemberton were fully engaged at Grenada, Mississippi, General Van Dorn's cavalry skillfully slipped around to the rear of Grant's army on December 20, the same day Sherman and Porter set off from Memphis, and destroyed the Union supply depot at Holly Springs. Besides destroying all the munitions, food and forage, Van Dorn also captured 1,500 Union defenders. Gen. Nathan B. Forrest and his cavalry also destroyed miles of Grant's railroad and telegraph lines to Columbia, effectively cutting off the Union's supply line to the front as well as severing Grant's communications link to his base. Having to rely on such a long supply and communications link through enemy territory proved impracticable and a costly mistake, but it taught the Union generals a memorable lesson.

Deprived of his supplies and communications, Grant aborted the mission and retreated to Grand Junction, Tennessee. Sherman and Porter were unaware of this development and continued to carry out their roles in the campaign. Their operation, the Battle of Chickasaw Bluffs, appeared fairly simple for Sherman to execute, at least on paper. Bringing his troops up the Yazoo River on December 26 and 27, Sherman found the terrain much worse than anticipated. Confronted with impassable swamps, quicksand and strategically-placed Confederate sharpshooters and artillery, he was unable to advance any closer then 150 to 200 yards from the Rebel fortifications. Sherman and Porter were finally persuaded to evacuate after 2,000 Union troops were killed and after learning that Grant had retreated from Grenada. Sherman's army withdrew to the mouth of the Arkansas River on January 2, the same day General McClernand arrived from Memphis.

In Grand Junction without food for his army and so far from his base, Grant was forced to order foraging expeditions, a novel experience for the western army. Traveling under armed escort, wagon trains scoured a 30-mile area. To Grant's amazement, enough food and forage was brought back to live on for two months. This was another lesson Grant would not forget during future operations far from home.

Meanwhile, Pemberton took his army back into the fortifications surrounding Vicksburg while Sherman, Porter and McClernand travelled about 50 miles up the Arkansas River. There on January 11, they attacked and captured 5,000 Confederates garrisoned at Arkansas Post.

As Grant anticipated, with McClernand's arrival at Chickasaw Bluffs the command-structure problem resurfaced. Because McClernand was now the senior general officer on site, he assumed command of the entire Union force for this most critical mission. To say Sherman and Porter were disturbed by this development would be an understatement. They telegraphed an urgent request to Grant questioning McClernand's capability and fitness for such a task, and asked for McClernand's replacement. Grant, also quite concerned, knew that McClernand was by vocation a politician, not a soldier. To gain Democratic support for the war, Lincoln had commissioned McClernand a brigadier general, despite his having no military experience, along with several other Democratic congressman. To leave him in command would have seriously compromised the entire effort to capture Vicksburg. As a result, Grant ordered the entire Union force to move to Young's Point, Louisiana. Arriving there personally on January 30, Grant assumed the field command himself.

This section of the country was having an unprecedented period of continuous rain. Living conditions were extremely difficult for both Union and Confederate soldiers. The torrential downpours and high water levels everywhere convinced Grant that any substantial or serious troop movements could not be attempted until spring, or March at the earliest. Not wanting to keep his troops idle the entire winter, Grant filled their time by carrying out "experiments." The goal of these make-work projects was to find a way to bypass the heavy concentration of Confederate batteries stretched out along 10 miles of riverbank in front of Vicksburg. Even though Grant thought this a futile effort, his troops would be busy and the folks back home satisfied that the army was doing something.

The Union army's first attempt to find a water route around the Confederate batteries entailed completing a canal started the year before. Beginning at Young's Point, it cut across a mile-wide finger of land and would allow Porter's boats to bypass Vicksburg. Under General McClernand, 4,000 men worked through the month of March dredging the canal to a depth of 12 feet when the high water suddenly broke through a dam built on one end, shutting down the project. Even if the effort had been successful, new Confederate batteries positioned nearby would have made navigation through the canal extremely difficult.

A concurrent endeavor found Gen. James B. McPherson's corps breaking the levee at Lake Providence. By removing old timbers that clogged the waterway, McPherson's men exposed an existing water route from the lake, down the Red River to the vicinity of Port Hudson, a run of over 500 miles below Vicksburg. This distance was determined to be excessive and as a result, the Red River route was considered impractical and was also abandoned. From February to April, three other laborious and futile attempts were made to penetrate other swamps, bayous and rivers around Vicksburg. If nothing else, these projects whiled away the winter.

As April approached, the high water was noticeably receding. A flurry of activity took place as preparations ensued to begin the highly dangerous mission required to overcome Vicksburg.

From their widely scattered camps, the Union forces were ordered to concentrate at Milliken's Bend, the staging site for the combined army and naval forces. Soon afterwards, at a strategy meeting with his commanders, Grant disclosed the full details of his plan to run the Confederate batteries and disembark on the eastern bank below Vicksburg. Grant's three corps, led by McClernand, McPherson and Sherman, would march south overland from Young's Point. Meanwhile, Porter would attempt to force his fleet past the Vicksburg batteries and rendezvous with the infantry below Vicksburg at the small river town of Hard Times. Once the rendezvous was made, Porter would ferry Grant's troops across the Mississippi to the east side of the river.

First, Porter would have to run his fleet by the Confederate batteries, primed and waiting to demonstrate their massive firepower, that lined the river.

Despite his generals' concerns, and their recommendations that he withdraw the army to Memphis and begin anew, using the lessons so far learned, Grant was determined more than ever to continue his campaign. He told his commanders that to go back now would be perceived by the North and the South as a retreat and a sign of weakness. In spite of the risks, they were committed to push on. The risks were fairly obvious. If the fleet was destroyed, the army would be marooned deep in enemy territory with no supplies, no reinforcements and no communications. So confident was Grant in his plan that he dismissed his commanders' concerns and ordered Porter to proceed.

Even General Halleck recognized the necessity of this mission. To Lincoln, Halleck wrote, "In my opinion, this is the most important operation of the war. To open the Mississippi River would be better than the capture of forty Richmonds." Lincoln agreed, saying that "Vicksburg is the key, the war can never be brought to a close until the key is in our pocket."

Before Porter committed his boats to the risks of running the batteries, he conducted a test of the Rebel firepower. For the test, a dummy gunboat was constructed from a coal barge. Covered with coal tar and assembled with smokestacks holding smoking combustibles, the "gunboat" looked fairly realistic, especially in the moonlight. Launched downriver one moonlit night, the dummy rode the current before the Rebel guns. Spotting the boat silently approaching, the Confederates opened fire from the on shore batteries. In spite of all the gunfire, the dummy gunboat continued on its course, sailing past Vicksburg.

Several days later, Admiral Farragut's fleet was moored below Vicksburg very much in need of coal. Learning of his brother's dilemma, Porter sent several barges loaded with coal down the river. This time the boats sailed by Vicksburg without a single shot fired. It was discovered later that the Rebels, humiliated over being tricked by a dummy gunboat, were not about to be fooled again in wasting ammunition by falling for the same trick a second time.

Grant's Army of the Tennessee was organized with Gen. John A. McClernand commanding the 13th Corps, Gen. James B. McPherson the 17th Corps and Gen. William T. Sherman the 15th Corps.

THE ROAD TO VICKSBURG

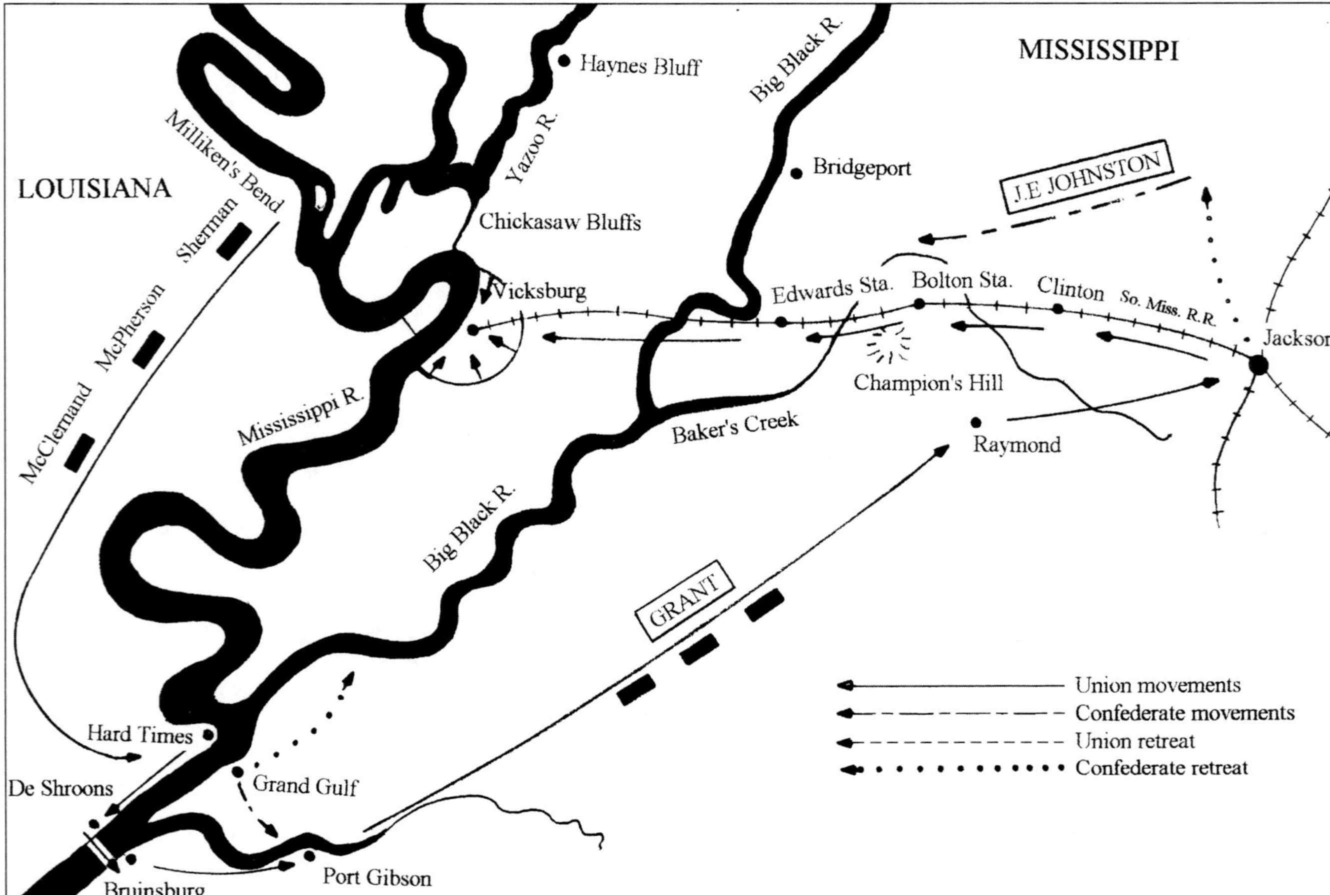

McClernand's four divisions were ordered out first, on March 29, with the 17th and 15th Corps to follow in that order.

On the pitch-black, moonless night of April 16, while General Pemberton and his commanders attended a grand ball in Vicksburg, Porter began his run on the Confederate batteries. The fleet consisted of Porter's flagship, six gunboats, three transports towing barges of coal, and one steamer. The boats were manned almost entirely by 150 army volunteers. Perhaps to drive home a point to his commanders, Grant's confidence in the success of this operation was evident in the fact that joining him on board his headquarters boat was his 12-year-old son, Frederick, who stayed with Grant's army for the duration of the campaign.

To occur concurrently with Porter's run, Grant ordered a cavalry brigade of over 1,500 men to conduct a series of strategic raids beginning on April 17. Commanded by Col. Benjamin Grierson, the cavalry went on a two-week campaign of destroying Confederate rail lines, supplies and depots. Grant meant to force Pemberton's attention away from the Union maneuvers taking place on the Mississippi.

As Porter's fleet approached the waiting batteries like a parade of ducks in a shooting gallery, the river was transformed into a blazing panorama of light. Houses and barns were torched along the riverfront, eerily illuminating the passing ships. Citizens poured out of their homes, filling the streets to witness the loud and fiery spectacle. Instantaneously, the shoreline exploded as Confederate artillery, from the base to the crest of Vicksburg's hills, opened their barrage. The constant chatter of muskets added to the deafening scene. On each transport, groups of Union soldiers were stationed below deck. Working feverishly by candlelight, they tried to stop up shell and bullet holes with cotton and gunny sacks. After three hours of continuous gunfire, the fleet got through without a single casualty. Every vessel, however, suffered considerable and varying degrees of damage.

Possessing more confidence after their first successful attempt, the Union men repeated the run on April 22 with another volunteer crew on board six more ships. Towing a dozen barges loaded with additional provisions and supplies, the ships made it through, but half the barges were lost.

On April 27, exhausted from a difficult march of 65 miles through deep mud, partially submerged roads and swamps, the last of McClernand's corps finally arrived at Hard Times, on the western bank of the

Mississippi River and only 30 miles below Vicksburg. The name of the town was fitting, considering what the men in blue were experiencing. Nearby, just below and across the great river, was Grand Gulf. Fortified since February, the Rebel garrison watched intently as the Union troops and Porter's fleet gathered on the river's edge, well out of Southern artillery range.

Planning for every contingency, on April 27 Grant set General Sherman into action on a scam to confuse the Confederate commanders at both Haynes' Bluff and Vicksburg. Grant's goal was not only to confuse but to divert attention from the Union's amphibious landing, and to draw Pemberton's troops away from Vicksburg. In this operation, Sherman, still at Millikens Bend, orchestrated a noisy demonstration using eight gunboats and one infantry division. After sailing up the Yazoo River to Haynes Bluff, Sherman's troops landed nearby and marched in sight of the Confederate garrison to announce their presence. Under cover of dense woods, they were taken back downriver to board another gunboat for a second trip to the garrison. Employing all eight boats, this ploy was repeated for most of the day, and as Grant found out later proved quite successful. Apparently fooling the commander at Haynes' Bluff into believing a major attack was imminent, Pemberton diverted 3,000 reinforcements to Haynes' Bluff that had been on their way to the vicinity of Grand Gulf to challenge Grant's river crossing.

Grant did not have to deal with the Confederate Navy. There was none to speak of in the area, except for a number of iron-plated wooden steamships. The Southern government authorized building only two ironclad gunboats for the Mississippi, the CSS *Arkansas*, which was scuttled near Baton Rouge in August 1862 to prevent it from falling into Union hands, and a sister ship that was never completed.

With McClernand's corps at Hard Times and McPherson's troops arriving any day, the Union planned to ferry 10,000 of McClernand's men on transports across the Mississippi to the east side on April 29. From that point the Union would storm the Confederate garrison at Grand Gulf while Porter's gunboats provided the necessary cover. Porter's eight gunboats failed to accomplish their part of the plan. After five hours of trading cannon fire with little effect, Porter backed off and the transports delivered McClernand's men back to the west side. Recognizing the futility of attacking the well-fortified entrenchment at Grand Gulf, Grant and Porter decided to run the ships by the Grand Gulf batteries instead. Porter would then rendezvous with McClernand's troops, who were directed to march farther downriver. That night, Porter's run went without a hitch and the rendezvous was accomplished at the small town of De Shroon's.

The next morning, after many months of struggle, Union forces finally reached the east bank of the Mississippi. Porter's transports delivered McClernand's entire corps and one division of McPherson's, a total of about 23,000 men, to the town of Bruinsburg without incident.

Meanwhile, Gen. Joseph E. Johnston, fully recovered from his injuries received at Seven Pines the previous May, was quite aware that as the Union army crossed the Mississippi they were very much divided between the sides of the river. Recognizing this opportunity as an excellent time to attack his enemy, Johnston sent a message to Pemberton ordering him to assault Grant with his entire force. Twice the order was sent and twice disregarded.

Even though Pemberton did not attack, the Union commanders were well aware that the Confederate forces were eager and ready to fight. To reach their grand prize the Union commanders knew they must first deal with the bloodshed and carnage expected as the Confederate troops at Grand Gulf, Raymond, Jackson and Haynes' Bluff would challenge every step of their advance.

Grant's first objective was to establish a base at Grand Gulf, a mere 12-mile march from Bruinsburg. The evening of April 30, on the day they arrived, General McClernand's corps was the first on the road and the first to encounter Rebel defenders. Five miles from Port Gibson, the road split into two smaller roads. General McClernand split his corps as well, three divisions taking one road, one division, under Gen. Peter J. Osterhaus, the other. Osterhaus' division was now isolated from the rest of the corps. Taking advantage of McClernand's blunder, on the morning of May 1, most of the 8,000-strong Confederate garrison from Grand Gulf, under Gen. John S. Bowen, attacked Osterhaus' isolated division. Osterhaus' troops were beaten back with heavy losses, and reinforcements from McPherson's army quickly came up to assist the embattled division. By nightfall, after a day of bloody and persuasive fighting, the Rebels were driven back to Grand Gulf.

On May 2, Union soldiers entered Port Gibson completely

unmolested. In addition, the day Union troops occupied Port Gibson, the Confederate garrison at Grand Gulf abandoned their fortifications. To avoid being trapped between Porter's fleet and Grant's army, the Rebel soldiers were in full retreat north.

With the Army of the Tennessee now firmly in place at Port Gibson and Grand Gulf, Grant's immediate concern involved supplying rations to his thousands of troops. Abandoning his plans to use Grand Gulf as a base and mindful of the fact that roads from Milliken's Bend could not support the number of wagon trains required, Grant put to use the lessons learned from the previous December. Although his men would receive partial rations, such as hard bread, coffee, sugar and salt, which were being delivered on boats running the Vicksburg batteries, they would depend on the country for the rest.

Considering the number of rich plantations in the area, Grant's men needed very little in the way of rations. They gathered hogs, cattle, sheep, and poultry as well as a wide variety of vegetables from the surrounding farms and plantations. Once growing cotton, the farmers now planted only the crops necessary to feed the Confederate army.

By May 6, the Army of the Tennessee was again at full strength, McPherson and Sherman having now arrived.

Almost from the beginning, Grant resolved to capture Vicksburg by siege. To accomplish that objective, the supplies and reinforcements that steadily streamed into Vicksburg by rail from Jackson, the state capital, had to be stopped. On May 6, General McPherson's corps led the way north to capture Jackson and destroy the railroad to Vicksburg. While the Union army swept its way north, Gen. Joseph E. Johnston arrived in Jackson to assume command of the Confederate army in Mississippi. Confederate strength was estimated at about 12,000 men arriving with Johnston and 50,000 under Pemberton, located on the rail line at Edward's Station, just east of Vicksburg.

Encountering Confederate soldiers on the outskirts of Jackson, on May 14 the Union army drove the Confederate pickets back into the Rebel main line of defense. Two corps, those of Sherman and McPherson, were assigned to carry out the attack from two different directions at three points. Recognizing that his forces would be attacked from three sides, Johnston ordered the vastly outnumbered Confederates to withdraw north from the city. In the statehouse that night, Grant slept in the same room which Johnston was said to have occupied the night before.

At this point, Grant planned to advance methodically from town to town west from Jackson, along the Southern Mississippi Railroad line leading straight into Vicksburg. General Sherman and his corps would stay behind in Jackson temporarily to destroy the railroad line, the rail depot, and any facilities, such as the arsenal and factories, used to support the Rebel war effort.

Receiving information that Grant's army was moving west toward Vicksburg, General Johnston, not one to be outwitted, set out to attack Grant's army at Clinton, the first town on the line west of Jackson. From his camp about six miles north of Jackson, the Confederate commander began a 20-mile march to Bolton Station, down the line and just west of Clinton. General Johnston was committed to the principle that a concentrated and highly mobile fighting force had the best chance to defeat Grant. With this philosophy in mind, he directed General Pemberton to follow the rail line east to meet him at Bolton Station, where both forces would combine to attack the Union army. Grant received a copy of Johnston's order to Pemberton from a Union loyalist in the Confederate service and immediately sent Sherman and half of McPherson's corps to Bolton Station. He then ordered McClernand's corps with McPherson's remaining troops west along the rail line to intercept Pemberton.

For the second time, Pemberton ignored Johnston's orders. Instead, he left a portion of his command within the Vicksburg fortifications, and with the remainder of his army, 17,000 men, marched south from Edward's Station. Pemberton hoped to cut the Union communication link with their supply base and in turn provoke an attack. Pemberton was not aware that Grant had abandoned his base some time ago and on this foray ran into General McPherson's army instead.

In the Battle of Champion's Hill, the two adversaries met just east of Baker's Creek on May 16 and waged a brutal fight for over four hours. Two divisions from McPherson's command were the first engaged and almost immediately became fully involved. The remainder of McPherson's army was brought up for reinforcement. Three times the Rebel and Yankee lines swept the field. First one side enjoyed the advantage, then the other. Soon, McClernand's advance division also joined in the battle, suffering heavy casualties. In response, Grant ordered McClernand to bring up his last two divisions to assist. McClernand ignored the order. The 15,000 Union troops, fighting without further reinforcements, tried to cover all the roads and appeared to have Pemberton trapped when he escaped over the one route inadvertently left unguarded. The Confederate army retreated to within 10 miles of their main fortifications in Vicksburg. There Pemberton set up camp near the east bank of the Big Black River. The Battle of Champion's Hill accounted for the heaviest casualties of the Vicksburg campaign. For the South, over 3,000 were killed or wounded. The North suffered 2,300 casualties. "The most obstinate and murderous conflicts of the war," is the way one Union commander described the battle.

As a result of Pemberton's escape to the Big Black, Grant ordered Sherman, then at Bolton Station, to divert from his march west. He sent Sherman to Bridgeport, a town located on the banks of the Big Black River and about 10 miles north of the Confederate army's presumed location. Meanwhile, McClernand's corps, following the rail lines, continued their advance west toward Vicksburg, with McPherson close behind.

In the early morning hours of May 17, McClernand's two advance divisions found Pemberton's camp at the Big Black River and prepared to attack, with General McPherson's troops, bringing up the rear, held in reserve. With the two Union divisions deployed, Grant's line covered Pemberton's entire front. Precipitously, Gen. Michael K. Lawler, advancing in his shirtsleeves, led his brigade in a charge toward the Confederate center. Inexplicably, the Rebel center broke, panic stricken, and fled across the river back into Vicksburg, burning the bridge behind them. Assuming the advantage, the Federals quickly charged into the open Confederate center and captured over 1,700 of Pemberton's men who were trapped, unable to get across the burning bridge just set on fire by their companions.

In the streets of Vicksburg, the citizens were dismayed and could not believe their eyes at the sight of Pemberton's men, their "protectors," returning gaunt and emaciated, and acting like a wild and unruly mob. In the meantime, Haynes' Bluff was also evacuated.

Advancing 180 miles with five victories and no defeats to their credit, the Union army relentlessly marched forward. Crossing the Big Black, the men in blue found themselves looking straight into the Vicksburg fortifications. Sherman, looking down on the Yazoo River, could not contain his joy when he stood on the very spot the Confederates had held on his abortive mission the previous December. McClernand and McPherson also arrived and took their positions surrounding Vicksburg. Sherman was on the right, McPherson in the center and McClernand on the left. Together they formed a 15-mile arc choking off all land escape. On the river, Porter's fleet completed the encirclement so that by May 18, the investment was complete. Grant could now breathe a sigh of relief. His critics had said it could not be done.

Gambling that the Confederates were worn out and demoralized, Grant ordered his troops to storm the Rebel works on May 19 and again on May 22. Both attacks were severely repulsed, with the Union forces suffering extremely heavy losses. At this point Grant saw the futility of attacking the strong Confederate fortifications and put his siege into effect. With nothing going into Vicksburg, Pemberton had to use only the supplies on hand. Grant was determined to wait him out. To "outcamp" Pemberton, Grant set to work building roads to establish supply links to the river below, clearing woods for campsites, constructing batteries, bringing in reinforcements and making sure that the cavalry kept an eye on General Johnston. The Confederate general was only 50 miles from the Union army, collecting reinforcements and heading toward Grant's rear.

To prepare for Johnston's approaching army, Grant had to conduct offensive action against the enemy in his front, and construct defensive entrenchments for fighting the enemy to his rear. For the Union's offensive capabilities, Grant's 15-mile front line was dotted with 220 field pieces, along with several heavy naval guns donated by Admiral Porter. Defensively, reinforcements were brought in to man the newly built entrenchments. Grant's army during this period grew to about 71,000 men.

Since December of the previous year, when McClernand had attempted to gain control of the Vicksburg campaign from Grant, a smoldering animosity had existed between the two generals. It exploded to the surface when McClernand wrote a message to his men that the other corps commanders interpreted as doing "a great injustice to the other troops engaged in the campaign." This message found its way north and was printed in the Northern newspapers, which were read by the Union troops at Vicksburg. When Grant was informed of this by Sherman and McPherson and read the article, he was so incensed that he relieved McClernand of his command on the spot and ordered him back to Springfield, Illinois. McClernand received a command in Texas but resigned in November 1864.

Elsewhere during the siege, on June 7, Confederate forces tried to destroy the Union supply line at Milliken's Bend. A Rebel brigade commanded by Gen. Richard Taylor attacked two new Union regiments, but after intense fighting was turned back. The chief significance of this battle was the Union regiments' composition entirely of black contrabands, fighting in uniform for the first time. Although not unique to the Union army (General Banks was employing black troops at Port Hudson), when word of their achievement reached Washington, even skeptics were convinced that the use of black soldiers would hereafter change the "sentiment of the army." Attitudes were quite different on the Confederate side. The Rebel command responded angrily when told that a number of black ex-slaves had been captured and brought back as Union soldiers. While most were thrown into prison, some were sold back into slavery.

While Grant's siege played out, the 3,000 citizens of Vicksburg were bombed around the clock from Porter's gunboats on the Mississippi. Somehow, throughout this ordeal, the people of Vicksburg endured their many hardships. Their spirits were kept up to some extent by the local newspaper, now printed on wallpaper, that told them to hold on because Johnston was coming to their rescue. Although the city's business community was practically shut down, most of the people went about their own affairs and ignored the daily shelling. Many citizens fled, however, to the protective shelter of some 500 caves dug in the hillsides to survive the incessant barrage from Porter's gunboats. The caves served especially those who were now homeless or those who had abandoned their homes in fear of their lives. These caves were usually furnished with some of the comforts of home and were a welcome respite from the terror raining down. The primary hardship was the lack of food. The people could not afford the exorbitant prices for the few food items still found in some shops. Around this time, the cat and dog population noticeably dwindled. As for the army, Pemberton had only 60 days of rations on hand for his troops. Having consumed their horses and mules, the soldiers now ate only ground peas and meal, and found ingenious ways to catch the rats, their only source of meat.

Finally, on July 1, Pemberton learned of a Union full-scale attack planned for the 6th. Without food and without much hope for support from Johnston, Pemberton's resolve weakened to the point that he considered evacuating the city. During a meeting with his four commanders, they convinced him that an evacuation would fail. As a result, on July 3, white flags of truce began to appear on the Rebel works. Following several written exchanges concerning terms of surrender, Pemberton capitulated on Independence Day, July 4. Vicksburg was won! (The citizens of Vicksburg refused to celebrate the Fourth of July from that day on. It was not until World War II that the national holiday was again recognized by the city's inhabitants and given its proper tribute.)

The terms of the surrender were not unconditional. Grant decided to parole all the captured Rebels. In this way, Grant saved the government the expense, the time, manpower and resources needed to ship 30,000 prisoners to the North, only to be paroled from there. Besides, he needed the transports for his own use.

When Gen. Franklin Gardner, the Confederate commander at Port Hudson, learned that Vicksburg had surrendered, he recognized the vulnerability of his position and the futility of continuing his struggle. Consequently, Port Hudson, the last Rebel holdout on the Mississippi and also besieged at the hands of Gen. Nathaniel P. Banks and his Army of the Gulf, surrendered unconditionally on July 9.

Also learning of Pemberton's surrender, General Johnston, for much the same reasons, retreated back to his works at Jackson, but was closely pursued by General Sherman and his 15th Corps. On July 17, following several days of shelling by Sherman's artillery, Johnston made a hasty night retreat. Too far ahead for Sherman to pursue, Johnston marched east, taking his army halfway to Alabama.

The news of Vicksburg's surrender caused much celebration in Washington and in the Northern states. The Mississippi River, from Cairo, Illinois to the Gulf of Mexico was back in the hands of the Union. Militarily, the Vicksburg defeat cut the Confederacy in half. President Lincoln was delighted, announcing, "Grant is my man and I am his for the rest of the war." For some people in the North, the end of the war was now in sight. To others more perceptive about the realities of war and its politics, there was still much more to accomplish.

Rather than resting on his laurels, Grant lost little time in seeking approval from General Halleck for his next campaign, a move on Mobile, Alabama. Not only would this movement place the Army of the Tennessee deeper into enemy territory; strategically it would also enable Grant to threaten Bragg's rear at Chattanooga. In addition, his army would be able to destroy the supply lines feeding not only Bragg but Lee as well. Grant was so optimistic over the benefits of his plan that he tried to persuade the general-in-chief on two different occasions, only to be refused both times.

As he had after Corinth the previous June, Halleck reduced the strength of Grant's army. He ordered the 13th Corps, McClernand's unit now commanded by Gen. Edward O.C. Ord, to join General Banks' Army of the Gulf, and ordered portions of the two remaining corps transferred to other parts of the country where most needed.

General Grant was promoted to major general and given command of the newly created Military Division of the Mississippi, including the Army of the Tennessee, the Army of the Cumberland and the Army of the Ohio.

IX
The "Mud March" to Chancellorsville
(January–May 1863)

Demoralized from his bloody defeat at Fredericksburg, General Burnside ordered the Army of the Potomac back across the Rappahannock River to their Falmouth camp. There, suffering even further from a bitter cold Fredericksburg winter, the Union soldiers huddled together in their quarters on the south bank of the river. Overcome by anger and distrust, they struggled to understand the frailties of their leaders. Since their devastating defeat at the base of Marye's Heights, morale had declined to its lowest point in the war. This disaffection was not limited to the rank and file. Several generals went so far as to complain directly to Lincoln about their dissatisfaction with Burnside's leadership. General Hooker, Burnside's second-in-command, was the most flagrant of them all. Hooker believed he had been wrongfully denied the commander's position in November. Secretly scheming against Burnside, Hooker plotted to win the command for himself.

As for Burnside, he sensed the loss of esteem and felt compelled to explain the circumstances of his defeat. Maintaining that the manner of attack had not been his responsibility, he insisted that he, too, was only following orders and even offered to resign. In the days following his humiliating retreat, Burnside's frustration smoldered and his guilt deepened. Determined to vindicate himself, Burnside reconnoitered the Rappahannock, searching for an ideal crossing point to launch a new attack. He desperately wanted another try at the enemy, not only for the sake of his troops but also to relieve his own feeling of incompetence.

Perhaps sensing the mood of his defeated army, President Lincoln wired a message to the troops, attempting to assure them that their loss was not the result of a mistake. Lincoln's words rang hollow and were not accepted very kindly by the Union soldiers. They brought snickers and jeers, because in their hearts the men knew the battle at Fredericksburg had indeed been a terrible mistake. They also knew that it was pure folly to attack an enemy head-on while the enemy controlled the surrounding heights. Meant to lift their spirits, Lincoln's message insulted their intelligence.

Finally settling on a plan to redeem himself, on January 20, in the dead of winter, Burnside ordered his army to break camp. Equipped with his pontoons, he marched his men upriver to recross the Rappahannock. Rain began falling, and before long turned to torrential downpours. For three days and three nights the rain was relentless. Caught in this deluge, the Army of the Potomac was able to travel about three miles a day. Artillery and caissons mired axle-deep in the soft runny mud, the wagons could not roll and the men were exhausted.

In contrast, across the river the Confederate troops were quite delighted, and watched the Union spectacle in amusement. They erected large wooden signs by the river, taunting the Northern soldiers with gibes, such as, "Yanks, if you can't place your pontoons yourself, we will send you help." On January 23, the luckless Burnside ordered his men to return to camp at Falmouth, ending what became known as "Burnside's Mud March."

With equipment firmly anchored in the soft mud, the move back to camp also presented a very difficult challenge. With the entire army pitching in, a corduroy road was quickly built adequate to move the wheeled vehicles back on the night of January 23, with the men following the next day. Once back in Falmouth, the exasperated and weary troops went into their winter quarters, not to be disturbed until spring.

Two days later, Lincoln relieved Burnside of his command, sending him to lead the Army of the Ohio. As his replacement the president selected, to no one's surprise, Gen. Joseph "Fighting Joe" Hooker.

The Union troops took this news with a sense of joy and relief. The veteran officers, who knew Hooker and had served with him in combat, considered the president's selection a "grave error." Aware of his scheming against Burnside, the officers questioned the quality of his character, not to mention his reputation for unsavory morals.

Hooker rapidly reorganized his army, abandoning Burnside's Grand Divisions in the process. He also instituted a system of insignia badges. Worn by each soldier, the color-coded patches identified the troops' combat units. More important, they gave the men a unique form of identity, which they could show off proudly. Food was also substantially improved and more furloughs were handed out. Soon, morale noticeably improved to the point that even the most skeptical senior officers were forced to reassess their initial opinions of General Hooker.

Entering West Point at the age of 14, Hooker graduated in 1837 and served with distinction in the Mexican War, where he reached the rank of lieutenant colonel. Known as "Fighting Joe," a nickname earned from his aggressive style on the Peninsula, Hooker also had a reputation as a ladies' man. (It is believed the term "hooker" was used at times in reference to the many women visiting the general's tent. These women were often referred to as "Hooker's women" or simply "Hooker's"). As commander, the 49-year-old Massachusetts native relished his new authority.

During the long, dull months of winter, the men occupied themselves the best they could. Troops on opposite sides of the river were caught in the same grip of nature. To relieve the boredom they often met to trade rations such as coffee, molasses, tobacco and reading material, to name a few of the items that were always in demand by one side or the other. During these periods of truce, friends and even relatives, fighting for opposing armies, would greet each other and laugh and talk as if the war never existed. On both sides, the troops found many diversions to break the monotony of winter camp life. Glee clubs were formed for singing, and theatrical performances such as minstrelry and plays were staged. Even snowball battles were held in which entire regiments would attack and counterattack, taking prisoners until a winner was declared. Playing cards, as well as dominos and checkers, was always a favorite, as were reading and writing letters home.

In early April, the president and Mrs. Lincoln visited the Union camp at Falmouth. Thoroughly supportive of his troops, Lincoln always looked forward to meeting with the soldiers and officers and to encouraging them in their service to their country. Joining Hooker at his headquarters, Lincoln listened to the commander's plan and strategy for the upcoming spring offensive, occasionally offering his advice and counsel. Before departing for Washington, the White House visitors were treated to a grand review of the Union army and a splendid dinner party.

Back in camp, rested and yet restless, the troops prepared for battle. After the long winter layoff, an endless list of chores, details and tasks had to completed before moving an army of over 100,000 men with hundreds of wagons, teams of artillery and thousands of horses. The Union's marching army at this time consisted of seven corps, about 134,000 men.

On April 27, Hooker could wait no longer and ordered his army to begin their spring offensive. "Fighting Joe" marched four corps and two divisions of a fifth 25 miles up the Rappahannock River to Kelly's Ford. The remaining two divisions of his right wing were ordered to stay behind in their bivouac. Because their camp lay directly in sight of the Confederate lookouts across the river, Hooker wanted to fool the Rebels into believing the Union army was still in camp.

By this time of course, Lee was well entrenched in and around Fredericksburg, with fortifications close to impregnable. Because of this, Hooker had no intentions of committing the same mistake his predecessor had made, and refused to challenge Lee in his own back yard. Instead, Hooker intended to cross the river with nearly five corps at Kelly's Ford without Lee's knowledge, and assemble at Chancellorsville.

Chancellorsville consisted merely of the fields and woods surrounding one house, the Chancellor House. A brick two-story mansion with pillared porches, this dwelling was occupied by the women of the Chancellor family, their children and several slaves. It would also serve as Hooker's headquarters.

The following day, the 28th, the two remaining corps of about 22,000 men, now forming the left wing under the command of General John Sedgwick, marched three miles downriver below Fredericksburg to make a demonstration. They hoped to occupy Lee's forces in that sector while Hooker's right wing crossed the Rappahannock. At about the same time, the Union cavalry set out on a mission to destroy the railroad lines supplying Confederate materials and troops. By denying him this vital communications link, Hooker believed he could force Lee's withdrawal to Richmond.

Arriving at Chancellorsville on April 30, the entire Union right wing regrouped without incident. Completely fooling Lee, the Union army crossed the river without fighting or loss of life. Hooker's campaign, to this point, had been a smashing success; his popularity soared. With his right wing now in the Confederate rear, and Sedgwick's wing occupying the Confederate front outside Fredericksburg, Hooker's strategy was to march down on Lee's rear, directly along the Plank Road, and trap the Confederate army in the center. Expecting to draw Lee from his fortifications, Hooker would then fight Lee on the field he chose. As Hooker would boast, "The enemy must either ingloriously fly, or come out from behind his defenses and give us battle upon our own ground, where certain destruction awaits him."

At this time, the Army of Northern Virginia, about 60,000 men, consisted of two divisions of Longstreet's corps (Longstreet and two divisions being away at Petersburg, Virginia); the four divisions of Jackson's corps, including A.P. Hill, D.H. Hill, Isaac Trimble and Jubal Early; as well as Gen. J.E.B. Stuart's cavalry, and about 170 guns.

Receiving information on April 28 that Sedgwick was crossing the river on pontoons, the Confederate troops did nothing. For two days they were content to watch the men in blue file across their floating bridge and parade around the riverbank in a show of force. On the 30th, after learning from Stuart of Hooker's presence at Kelly's Ford, Lee quickly ordered his Rebel troops to the rear. General Longstreet's two divisions were sent up the Plank Road to challenge the advancing Union army. Jackson's corps would follow that same night, leaving behind Early's division and Gen. William Barksdale's brigade, about 9,000 men, in Fredericksburg to keep an eye on Sedgwick.

On May 1, the Battle of Chancellorsville began when the two opposing armies, marching toward each other on the Plank Road, clashed head-on. Two Union corps, after advancing only three miles from Chancellorsville, engaged in a fierce battle with the two Longstreet divisions. After receiving word of the encounter, then raging along a front of several miles, Hooker inexplicably ordered all Union troops back to Chancellorsville over the objections of his corps commanders. Ordered to retreat from high ground ideal for battery emplacements to a defensive position in wholly unsatisfactory terrain,

THE BATTLE OF CHANCELLORSVILLE

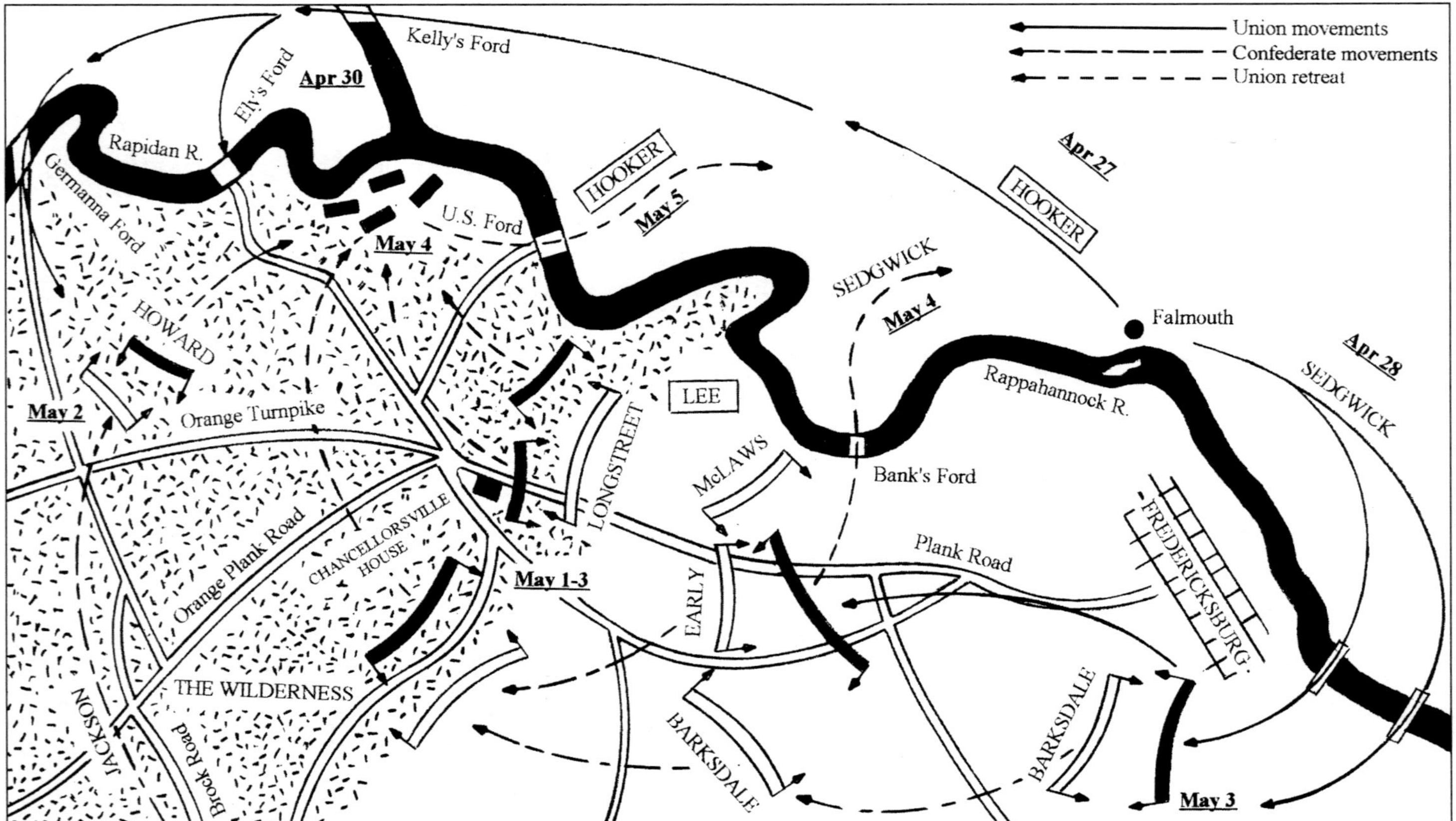

Hooker's corps commanders were incensed and confused over this quick turnaround of events. They could not understand why Hooker's first command in the face of the enemy was to retreat.

That night in the Confederate camp, only a mile and a half from Union lines, Lee was briefed on the location of the Union troops. Silhouetted against the glow of their campfire, Lee and Jackson huddled together planning the next day's history.

The following morning, May 2, Union soldiers were greeted with heavy bombardment from Confederate artillery batteries. The heavy Rebel guns were moved during the night to the same high ground that Hooker abandoned the day before. The shelling lasted well into the afternoon, but to the confusion of the Union army, the Rebel troops did not attack. A few Union commanders and several scouts reported sightings of Confederate troop columns moving quietly through the woods toward the extreme right flank of the Union army, the camp of the 11th Corps under Gen. O.O. Howard. Regimental commanders from the endangered Union corps reported to division headquarters, expressing their concern and seeking advice. They were laughed at and told to advance their pickets. At his headquarters, Hooker was sure the artillery shelling was just a cover. In fact, "Fighting Joe" was convinced that the Rebels were no threat at all because, as he saw it, Lee was in full retreat to Gordonsville, and the troops seen marching through the woods were actually Lee's withdrawing forces on the Gordonsville Road. Hooker treated any report contrary to these pre-conceived opinions with indifference.

In reality, the troops belonged to Gen. Stonewall Jackson, who was cleverly circling to his left along back roads and obscure rail beds to bring his corps to the rear of Hooker's right flank. In the late afternoon of May 2, Jackson forces broke from the woods and completely surprised the Union's 11th Corps. Hooker's announcement that Lee was withdrawing his forces to Gordonsville had caused the Union army to relax its guard. As one Confederate lieutenant colonel remarked later, "The soldiers were in groups, laughing, chatting, smoking, probably engaged here and there in games of cards and other amusements, feeling safe and comfortable." Caught unaware, the men of the 11th Corps were severely routed as masses of charging and screaming Confederate soldiers burst from the woods along a two-mile front. The panic scattered men, horses and wagons in every direction as the wounded and dead lay everywhere. Keeping his wits, Hooker quickly rode out to his battered right flank and commandeered enough men and artillery from three or four corps in the immediate vicinity to hold off the enemy until dark. When the dust had settled, Jackson's attack on Hooker's right flank had proved a tremendous success.

During the night, Hooker assumed that Lee must have evacuated his entire army from Fredericksburg and was now concentrated in the vicinity of Chancellorsville. Considering that scenario, Hooker sent a dispatch to his left wing ordering Sedgwick and his two corps to Chancellorsville, expecting them to arrive by morning on Lee's rear. Sedgwick would find the order impossible to follow. During the night, Union engineers also reestablished their front lines so that by the morning of May 3, Jackson's force of about 28,000 troops was significantly outnumbered on two sides by about 40,000 Union men with approximately 35,000 more close by. At this point, a concentrated attack by Union forces would have undoubtedly proved fatal for Jackson's corps. No attack was ordered. Completely demoralized, Hooker fell into a depressive state. He became despondent over Lee's assertiveness, which had frustrated all of his efforts.

Meanwhile General Sedgwick received Hooker's message at 11 P.M. on May 2. His forces at that time were only three miles below Fredericksburg. To march the 15 miles to Chancellorsville during the night in any military context was considered nearly impossible. To compound the difficulty, Lee had not withdrawn his entire army from the city as Hooker had assumed, but was still entrenched on his old battlefield, with Barksdale and Early waiting and watching for Sedgwick to make his move.

Attempting to follow his commander's orders, Sedgwick marched his 22,000 men toward Fredericksburg. Fighting Barksdale's brigade at every step of the way, the Union's left wing did not reach Fredericksburg until daylight. At Fredericksburg Sedgwick's men found themselves back at Marye's Heights, the site of the previous December's disaster. Two attempts were made to storm the Confederate works before the Union troops penetrated the thin defenses with a bayonet charge, again suffering heavy losses. Continuing his march, by mid-afternoon Sedgwick's men were only about six miles from Chancellorsville when they were attacked by reinforcements commanded by Gen. Lafayette McLaws, sent down from Chancellorsville to support General Early. The next day, McLaws and Early combined forces and this time the Union troops could not sustain their drive.

The attacking Confederates were instructed before the charge to "advance at double-quick ... you will not stop until you get the order to halt. You will never get that order." Overpowered and exhausted, on May 4 Sedgwick was forced to withdraw across the Rappahannock over Bank's Ford.

Back at Chancellorsville, the elation of their huge victory of May 2 was quickly replaced as sadness and shock befell the Confederate army. Their commander, Gen. Stonewall Jackson, was accidentally shot by his own troops that very night. Inspecting his lines around 8 P.M., Jackson and an entourage of staff and couriers rode too close to the federal lines. Coming under fire from the Union side, Jackson and his men wheeled their horses and quickly rode back toward their own side. Confederate troops from a North Carolina brigade mistook the shots for an attack and fired back in the darkness as Jackson rode by, hitting him three times. He was wounded in the left wrist and hand by one ball, the right hand by a second and in the left arm, shattering the bone completely. Shortly after midnight his left arm was amputated, but after eight days, on May 10, he died from pneumonia. For Lee, the loss was tremendous, too much even for words of regret. For the South, the loss was overwhelming.

At the break of dawn on May 3, the Rebels opened their attack on the Union army, now in the role of defending Chancellorsville. The entire Union line was fully engaged against the 28,000 men of Jackson's corps, temporarily under cavalry commander Gen. J.E.B. Stuart. From the high ground, the Confederate batteries still poured shell and shot into the Yankee lines. Around 8 A.M., disbelieving eyes peering from the second floor windows of the Chancellor House saw a distant Union corps returning from the front, and then another. With banners held high, their streamers were unmistakably spotted through field glasses as trailing off in the wrong direction. Before long, an angry scene unfolded as Union officers raced up the steps of the Chancellor House protesting their lack of ammunition and the irresponsible breakdown in the command structure that took the ordnance men away from the action.

Hooker did little but act as an observer. Still very much despondent over Lee's brilliant maneuvering, Hooker spent the morning on the front porch of Chancellor House. Leaning against a post, he strained his ears and scanned the horizon listening and looking for sounds and sight of Sedgwick's forces, as if expecting Sedgwick to ride up and save the Union army. As the commanding general watched the proceedings he gave no orders, no instructions, and asked for no reports. The corps commanders knew they were on their own.

At one point, the Southern soldiers took possession of a small clearing within artillery range of Hooker's headquarters and began firing. Suddenly, the pillar Hooker was attached to exploded into a cloud of splinters. A Confederate artillery shell had made a direct hit on the post, just missing Hooker but sending him sprawling on the floor. Quickly gathering himself up, still shaken, Hooker joined his staff on horseback and rode off to the rear, abandoning the field without notifying anyone.

Shortly thereafter, around noon, Gen. Danius N. Couch, second in command, was summoned to Hooker's new "headquarters" where he found the general lying down. Told by Hooker to take command, General Couch was ordered to draw back all the Union forces and establish another new defensive line about a mile to the rear. By this time, Lee was within 200 yards of the Chancellor House, which was now in flames, and the occupants, military and civilian, were fleeing into the woods on the road to United States Ford. Lee did not press the attack but stayed within striking distance, knowing full well the day was his.

On May 4, fighting at Chancellorsville had for the most part ceased. Lee turned his attention to Sedgwick, who had broken by Fredericksburg and was approaching Salem Church, only about six miles away. In response to this threat, Lee ordered Gen. L.C. McLaws and five brigades away from Chancellorsville to join forces with Early.

The Union army welcomed this lull, using it to entrench and to analyze their predicament. That night, while a terrible storm swept the area, Hooker convened a council of his generals, and asked each of them to state his case for advancing or withdrawing the army. The vote favored advancing to fight the enemy. After listening to their arguments, Hooker decided to withdraw across the Rappahannock River.

Less than two hours later, General Couch received a message from Gen. George G. Meade, the commander of the 5th Corps. The message informed Couch that Hooker, astonishingly enough, was already on the other side of the Rappahannock and that the river conditions were so bad from the storm that communications were severed and the bridges possibly lost as well. Now finding himself in full command,

Couch decided to suspend the crossing and to proceed with the campaign. A few hours later, Hooker restored communications and Couch was sternly instructed to resume the evacuation.

In the end, Chancellorsville casualties totaled 17,280 for the Union and approximately 13,000 for the Confederacy. The newspapers castigated the leadership of the Army of the Potomac. How, they asked, could an army of over 100,000 men cross a river to challenge another army of merely 50–60,000, and retreat defeated not once, but twice after losing nearly 20,000 brave men? Asked years later why he failed, Hooker replied, "For once I lost confidence in Hooker, and that is all there is to it."

X
Turning Point: The Road to Gettysburg (May–July 1863)

In the spring of 1863, the Union armies were fighting on three different fronts. General Grant's Army of the Tennessee was methodically fighting its way through Mississippi toward Vicksburg. General Rosecrans' Army of the Cumberland was in Nashville, Tennessee, preparing to launch its spring offensive against Bragg. General Hooker's Army of the Potomac was still struggling with Lee in Virginia.

The Confederate successes at Fredericksburg and Chancellorsville were hailed by a jubilant South as further proof that the Confederate soldier was far superior to any Yank on the battlefield. Confederate supporters had been preaching this view from the very beginning, when the Union boys had been sent running from the Manassas battlefield two years earlier. In reality, the troops on both sides of the front line struggled immensely to overcome adversity. While the Army of the Potomac lacked capable leadership, the Army of Northern Virginia lacked human and material resources. Despite their limitations to wage effectively a war against the North, the Confederate army, at least in the East, enjoyed tremendous advantages over their enemy in several respects. Foremost was the immense skill and outstanding quality of their military leaders, such as Generals Lee, Jackson and Longstreet. Second, the commanders enjoyed a higher degree of support, cooperation and responsiveness from the Southern war department in formulating and carrying out their battle plans. In addition, the Army of Northern Virginia did not suffer from constraints of political influence and considerations.

Flushed with victory, the Army of Northern Virginia celebrated in this, their finest hour. Morale soared and confidence in their superiority reached an all-time high.

At a high-level meeting in Richmond on May 15, Lee convinced President Davis, Secretary of War James A. Seddon and all but one cabinet member that with the Army of Northern Virginia sufficiently strengthened, he could succeed in a second invasion into Union territory. With Washington threatened, Lee argued, the likelihood that Lincoln would consider discussing peace terms favorable to the Southern cause was a distinct possibility. Additionally, it was generally accepted that a battlefield win on Union soil could still create favorable sentiment in Europe for diplomatic recognition of the Confederacy. Supporting Lee's proposal was the undeniable fact that war-ravaged Virginia could no longer provide the food and materials desperately needed by the Southern soldiers. On the other hand, the North, bloated with food reserves, livestock, clothing and armaments, could furnish the Confederate army with everything they needed.

Agreeing to Lee's plan, the Confederate government consented to his request for additional troops. By June the Army of Northern Virginia was ready to strike with three infantry corps totaling nine divisions, a cavalry division and 69 artillery batteries, a total force of some 75,000 men. Commanding the 1st Corps of McLaws, Hood and Pickett was Lee's dedicated warhorse, Gen. James Longstreet. Gen. Richard S. Ewell, one of Jackson's division commanders, who had left a leg on the second Manassas battlefield, was now leading Jackson's old outfit, the 2d Corps, comprised of the troops under Early, Rodes and Johnson. Gen. Ambrose P. Hill, veteran of the Seven Days' Campaign, Cedar Mountain, Antietam, Fredericksburg and Chancellorsville, was promoted to command the new 3d Corps of Heth, Pender and Anderson. Gen. J.E.B. Stuart would lead the cavalry.

On June 3, Southern troops commanded by Gens. Longstreet, Stuart and Ewell marched to Culpeper, Virginia, the birthplace of General Ewell, about 10 miles northwest of the Rappahannock River, while General Hill's corps stayed in place watching Fredericksburg.

Hooker, still smarting over his loss at Chancellorsville, continued to miscalculate the true scope of Lee's movements. He mistakenly believed that the only Rebel force shifted to Culpeper was Stuart's cavalry and that the entire Rebel infantry was still bivouacked somewhere around Fredericksburg. He was not certain of that. Even the information obtained from occasional spying forays from tethered hot air balloons proved inconclusive. To be positive, Hooker ordered a cavalry force of about 10,000 troops, led by Gen. Alfred Pleasonton, to conduct a raid on Stuart's camp at Culpeper. Their primary mission was to confiscate every document from Stuart's headquarters that might disclose Confederate troop positions and General Lee's intentions.

On June 8, the first phase of Lee's northward campaign was set in motion. Sending his 2d Corps from Culpeper, Lee's orders to General Ewell were to clear the Shenandoah Valley of all Yankee resistance. Soon after Ewell's departure, the remainder of Lee's army would follow.

On that same day, Pleasonton and his cavalry crossed the Rappahannock River and on June 9 attacked Stuart's 10,000 cavalrymen in and around Brandy Station, about halfway between the river and Culpeper. Caught by surprise, the embarrassed Stuart battled with the Union cavalry on three different fronts for over 12 hours. During the height of the battle, Stuart's headquarters were ransacked and anything remotely suggesting Confederate plans was taken. Finally persuaded to withdraw by the approaching Confederate infantry from Culpeper, the Union troops retreated across the river, satisfied that with the documents taken, the mission had been a huge success.

This encounter was the only true cavalry battle of the war. Over 20,000 expert horsemen fought against each other that day and most significantly, the Union cavalry demonstrated for the first time that they were second to none.

In the Shenandoah Valley, the federal army currently occupied four towns: Berryville, Winchester, Martinsburg and Harpers Ferry, where the bulk of the troops, about 10,000 men, were bivouacked. General Ewell, with his 2d Corps, snaked into the valley through Chester Gap on June 12 and pushed directly for Berryville. Within hours, the commander at Berryville, in advance of the approaching Confederates, evacuated his brigade to Winchester. Two days later, the federal unit at Martinsburg retreated across the Potomac to the Union camp at Maryland Heights. Pressing steadily forward, Ewell's troops then attacked the combined Union forces at Winchester, driving the Northerners from the town with heavy losses. Following their eviction from Winchester, the Union soldiers continued their retreat, this time to Harpers Ferry on June 15.

General Ewell's objective, to drive the Union forces from the Shenandoah Valley, was accomplished on June 17 when the federal garrison abandoned Harpers Ferry. They also retreated across the Potomac to Maryland Heights. In his sweep of the Shenandoah Valley, Ewell's army captured 4,000 Union soldiers, 28 pieces of artillery, hundreds of small arms, horses, and fully provisioned wagons, all in just five days, with a loss of only 269 men. As a result, the Confederate Stars and Bars crossed the Potomac into Maryland for the second time. Unchallenged, Lee's men set up camp near Hagerstown and Sharpsburg.

General Lee's invasion strategy was going so well that on June 21 he told Ewell to continue his advance straight on to the occupation of Harrisburg, the Pennsylvania capital. This objective had eluded Lee the previous September, but was now within his reach. As a result of this order, General Ewell divided his corps, sending divisions under Gens. Robert E. Rodes and Edward Johnson to Carlisle, Pennsylvania, and the remaining division under Gen. Jubal A. Early to York, Pennsylvania. Reaching their destinations on June 27 and 28 respectively, the two armies were to converge on Harrisburg from two different directions. Harrisburg was a bedlam of activity. Railroad stations were crowded with shouting and screaming mobs. Merchants were packing up their goods, and everyone was rushing around in near panic.

General Hill and General Longstreet, having departed Fredericksburg and Culpeper on the 14th and 15th of June respectively, followed the route left by Ewell through the Shenandoah. They reached Chambersburg and Fayetteville, Maryland, on June 27.

At this time, General Stuart's orders were to guard the same South Mountain passes that D.H. Hill had defended the year before against McClellan. When the Union army was spotted crossing the Potomac River, Stuart was to notify Lee immediately. From that point on, the cavalry was to watch the enemy's movements and report them directly to Confederate headquarters.

Lee committed a grave error at this point. He let Stuart leave his post with three brigades of his cavalry to conduct a raid. Unfortunately for the Confederate army, Stuart failed to leave instructions with his replacement, Gen. Beverly H. Robertson, to notify headquarters when Hooker crossed the Potomac, and on the location of the Union army.

On June 13, soon after reviewing the stolen documents from General Stuart's headquarters at Culpeper, Hooker moved the Army of the Potomac north. The Union army crossed the Potomac at Edwards Ferry on the 25th and 26th undetected, and by the 27th three Union corps were in the South Mountain passes and two more in Frederick, all within striking distance of the Confederate rear.

Since the beginning of Lee's northward march, Hooker had suffered a series of frustrating rejections to his ego at the hands of his immediate superior, General Halleck, and on occasion from the president himself. First proposing to attack the Confederate troops at Fredericksburg in early June, Hooker was tactfully told to get his priorities straight, that with Lee about to invade Union soil and place Washington under threat of attack, instead of challenging Fredericksburg, Hooker should have been more concerned with protecting the nation's capital. Soon after the battle at Brandy Station, Hooker recommended to the president that since Lee's army was heading north, the time was right to invade the lightly defended Richmond. Again, sensing that he still did not have a commander motivated to fight, Lincoln had to remind Hooker that his goal was to defeat Lee's army, not Richmond. Confronted with the bulk of Lee's army near South Mountain in Maryland, Hooker ordered the Union's 12th Corps to join the troops from Maryland Heights on a coordinated drive on Harpers Ferry. The purpose of Hooker's plan was to cut Lee's communications to Virginia. General Halleck's position on the use of the troops at Maryland Heights was completely contrary to that of Hooker's. Halleck adamantly opposed abandoning the Heights, and rejected Hooker's plan immediately. Hooker was highly critical of his predecessor, but now he understood from firsthand experience the limitations under which General Burnside had suffered. He also understood now what Burnside had meant after the loss at Fredericksburg when he had remarked that he, too, had been only following orders.

Begrudged that he was consistently unable to exercise his full authority as a commander to the degree he felt necessary, and because he was convinced that the government did not support his efforts, Hooker resigned his command of the Union army on June 28. (He would be reactivated in September, however, when Lincoln transferred the 11th and 12th Corps to the Army of the Cumberland and placed Hooker in command.)

The new Union army leader, the fifth in less than a year, was a relatively unknown quantity, Maj. Gen. George G. Meade. The 48-year-old Meade, born in Cadiz, Spain, was educated at the U.S. Military Academy. Following his exemplary service as division commander at Antietam and Fredericksburg, Meade was promoted to command the 5th Corps at Chancellorsville.

The army Meade inherited on June 28 was about 82,000 strong, composed of seven corps of infantry and three divisions of cavalry. The Union corps commanders were John F. Reynolds, 1st Corps; Winfield S. Hancock, 2d Corps; Daniel E. Sickles, 3d Corps; George Sykes, 5th Corps; John Sedgwick, 6th Corps; O.O. Howard, 11th Corps; and Henry W. Slocum, 12th Corps. The Union cavalry was under the command of Gen. Alfred Pleasonton, with divisions commanded by Generals John Buford, William Gregg and Hugh Judson Kilpatrick.

Up until the 28th of June, the Confederate army's march north had met very little in the way of a serious challenge. With no report from the cavalry, Lee believed the Union army had yet to cross the Potomac. Elated with his success, that morning Lee told Longstreet and Hill to proceed with their march and to join General Ewell, whom he expected to be in Harrisburg by the time they arrived. That night, however, Lee received the shocking news that the federal Army had not only crossed the Potomac several days earlier, but also was close enough to threaten his rear.

Thus, the first breakdown in Lee's invasion strategy occurred. Suddenly, Lee found himself seriously compromised without the reconnaissance information the cavalry should have been providing all along. Without knowing that Hooker had crossed the Potomac, Lee had unwittingly permitted the Union to close the gap between the two armies to the extent that pressure was now being exerted on his forces. Lee was forced to modify his plans in the middle of his northward march to accommodate the emergency. Both commanding generals would soon find that swiftly developing events, not they, would control the action.

That same night, Lee cancelled the travel orders to Longstreet and Hill and sent a message to General Ewell bringing his march on Harrisburg to a halt. Referring to Hooker, General Lee's report stated, "In the absence of the cavalry it was impossible to ascertain his intentions; but to deter him from advancing farther west and interrupting our communications with Virginia, it was determined to concentrate the army east of the mountains." Doing that, Lee ordered all Confederate forces to converge on Cashtown, nine miles northwest of Gettysburg.

On June 30, one of Hill's division commanders, Gen. Henry Heth, sent a brigade out of Cashtown on a unique assignment. Information received in the Confederate camp mentioned a supply of shoes available in Gettysburg, currently a rare commodity in Lee's army. Considering the number of troops having to march barefoot, the Rebel command would have been remiss if an attempt were not made to "procure" them. Coincidentally, a federal cavalry column under the command of Gen. John Buford was on patrol and heading for Gettysburg at the same time. When both sides made visual contact on the western outskirts of the town, the Confederates went no farther, but returned to Cashtown.

On receiving the news of the Union presence from Heth, General Hill informed Lee and Ewell and then prepared his division commanders (Heth, Pender and Anderson) for an advance toward Gettysburg the next day. General Lee had no intentions of fighting at Gettysburg, but now the second breakdown of his invasion plan occurred when Hill precipitated the unwanted battle by taking his command on an unauthorized march and engaging the enemy without orders.

At Gettysburg meanwhile, after calling for help, Union General Buford decided to remain in place, and strategically positioned his dismounted troopers in the woods, crevices and rocks along Seminary Ridge. About a mile directly east, a second ridge, Cemetery Ridge, ran roughly parallel to the first and resembled an inverted hook. The point of the hook was Culp's Hill, curving west to Cemetery Hill. The shaft was Cemetery Ridge, ending at two wooded and boulder-covered hills, Little Round Top and Big Round Top. Between these two ridges and opposite Cemetery Hill lay the town of Gettysburg.

Responding to Buford's appeal for help from his headquarters in Taneytown, General Meade sent in the Union's 1st Corps as reinforcements. Commanded by Gen. John F. Reynolds, the corps was famous for its lead division, which contained five regiments known as the "Iron Brigade." Distinguished by their black hats, these troops gained the reputation as the hardest-fighting unit in the Army of the Potomac. On the following day, the Iron Brigade would be decimated.

On the morning of July 1, the unauthorized advance of two Confederate columns, specifically the 3d Corps divisions of Generals Henry Heth and William D. Pender, were observed approaching along the Cashtown Road. Soon the bloody and infamous Battle of Gettysburg, fought from July 1 to July 3, would be underway. The battle raged on all morning between the Union cavalry forces of General Buford with reinforcements arriving from General Reynolds' 1st Infantry Corps, and Hill's two divisions, who were supported by a battalion of artillery. Both sides suffered heavy casualties, but for the North a particularly tragic loss was General Reynolds himself, who was shot and killed by a Confederate sharpshooter while directing troop movements from the woods. Soon after, in the early afternoon, the Union's 11th Corps arrived, General Howard now assuming command of the field. By this time the Union force fought desperately to maintain its position on Seminary Ridge, but was slowly forced back into the western outskirts of Gettysburg.

Receiving General Hill's message while marching from Carlisle to Cashtown, General Ewell turned his two divisions toward the sound of the battle and joined the engagement shortly after General Howard's arrival on the field. Ewell's presence on the battlefield was a welcome relief for the battered 2d Corps, which could now withdraw to Seminary Ridge.

Suddenly feeling the devastating effects of the fresh Confederate reinforcements, Howard called for assistance from the 3d Corps commander, Sickles, and from General Slocum and his 13th Corps. Before the Union reinforcements reached the field, General Early and his division arrived from York. Now completely overwhelmed by the sheer disparity in numbers, the Union army withdrew through the streets of Gettysburg in a near-rout to the higher ground of Cemetery Hill, site of the town's Evergreen Cemetery. Meeting them as they streamed up the hill was General Hancock of the 2d Corps, sent by Meade to take command.

From the crest of Seminary Ridge, Lee watched intently as the battle raged below him. General Ewell's two divisions had Gettysburg well secured from one end to the other and his third division, Early's, was threatening Culp's Hill. At that point Lee delegated to General Ewell the authority for continuing the fight by attacking the enemy

The Battle of Gettysburg (second and third day)

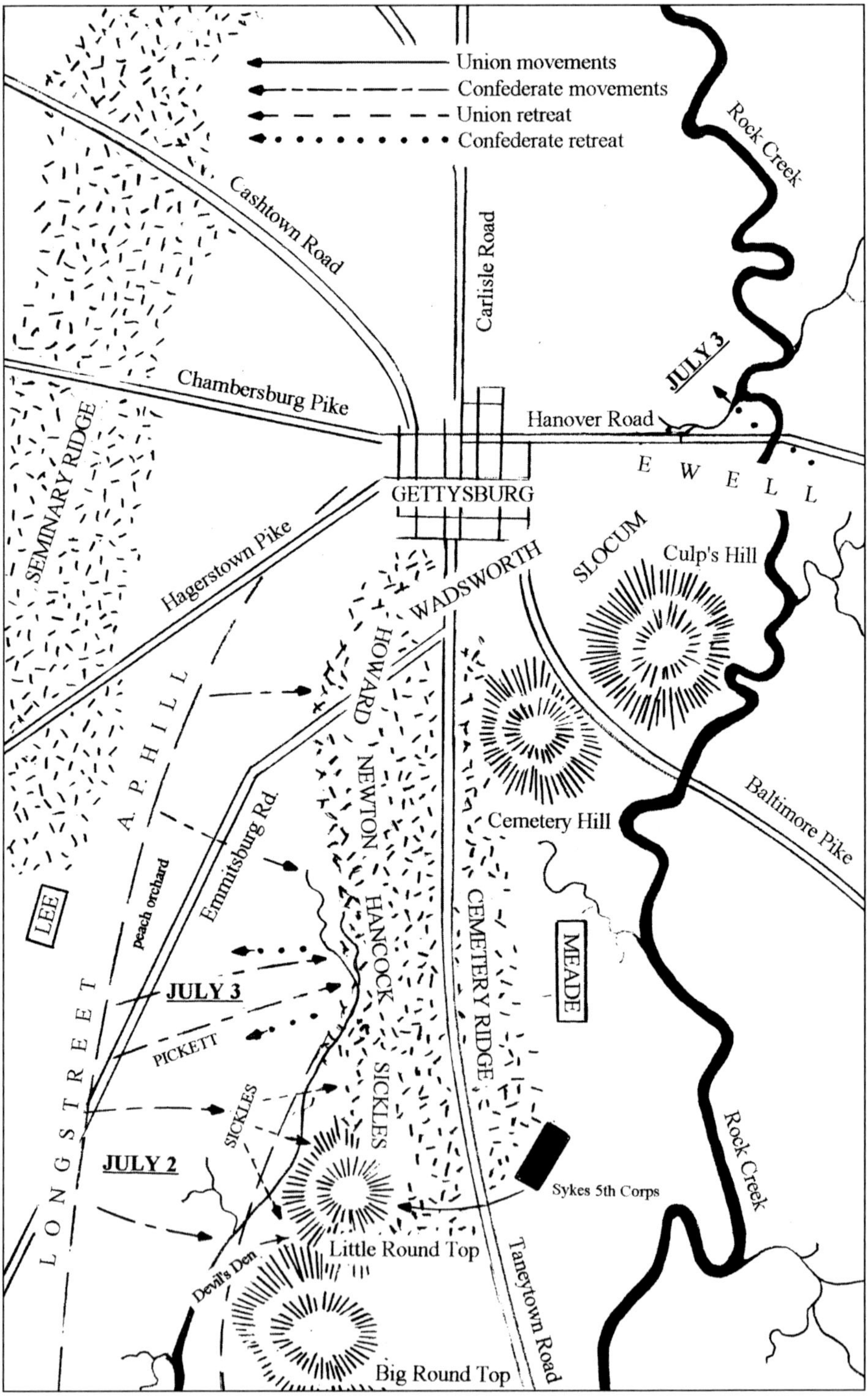

on Culp's and Cemetery Hills, "if practicable." Ewell decided against an attack. His judgment was based on the fact that he had only 8,000 men left, and that his corps was in no condition to continue fighting an enemy he knew occupied a formidable position. Nevertheless, Ewell's decision was a highly controversial one that would be debated for years to come. The decision was criticized as overly cautious in a sure-win situation by some and supported by others as prudent, considering the condition of Ewell's corps. With Ewell's decision made, Lee called off the Confederate pursuit for that day.

As nightfall approached on July 1, Ewell's corps remained in place near Culp's Hill and Cemetery Hill, poised to attack the Union's right in the morning. General Hill's two divisions were back on Seminary Ridge where his third, Anderson, was marching to join them. Two divisions of Longstreet's corps, led by McLaws and Hood, were trudging in from Cashtown, while Pickett's division was temporarily held back at Chambersburg as rear-guard. For the Union forces, the four corps of Newton (Reynolds' replacement), Sickles, Slocum and Howard dug in among the trees and boulders of Culp's and Cemetery Hills. Shortly after midnight, General Meade himself arrived.

On the morning of July 2, General Ewell's front line stretched from the outskirts of Culp's Hill and through the town of Gettysburg. Located to the right of Ewell's Corps, General Hill's lines arched onto and beyond the length of Seminary Ridge and then extended into the adjacent peach orchard. To Hill's right, when they arrived, Lee would form the two divisions of Longstreet's corps, continuing on through the peach orchard and perpendicularly across the Emmitsburg Road.

As did his counterpart, General Meade wanted to fight on a field of his own choosing; in this case Meade preferred the area behind Pipe Creek. Finding himself on Cemetery Hill, he spent the morning inspecting his lines and directing new arrivals to their positions. Convinced that most of the Confederate troops were in place and ready to attack, Meade believed himself outnumbered, and assumed a defensive posture. The balance of Meade's army, the 5th, 6th, and 2d Corps, did arrive, however, straggling in sporadically between 7 A.M. and 4 P.M.

Incredibly, the Confederate attack did not open until after 4 P.M. because of unexpected delays getting Longstreet's two divisions in place. Apparently, one of Hood's brigades was late to arrive and, strangely enough, instead of using available reserves to fill in the line, the Confederate army waited for the brigade. Later, Longstreet blamed the delay more on the reconnaissance officer who had been ordered to lead the 1st Corps to their position in line. Longstreet claimed that the officer's circuitous route was overly cautious in preventing their detection from a Union signal station on Little Round Top, and was thus much too slow. After the war many Southerners were severely critical, and blamed Longstreet for this delay. In their opinion, the delay gave the Union reinforcements the time to arrive, which ultimately caused the Confederate army to lose the battle, and in essence the war itself. At any rate, the delay worked to Meade's advantage.

By the time Longstreet's 13,000 men had settled in, most of the Army of the Potomac was on the field and its supporting artillery in position. The Union line began at Culp's Hill and Cemetery Hill at its northern extreme, then extended for two miles along Cemetery Ridge to the two Round Tops. Defending Culp's Hill was Slocum's 12th Corps and Wadsworth's division from the 1st Corps led by Wadsworth. On Cemetery Hill, Howard's 11th Corps reached Newton's 1st Corps. To Newton's left covering the Union center was Hancock's 2d Corps, and finally in front of the Round Tops on the Union's extreme left was Sickles' 3d Corps. In reserve was the 5th Corps under Sykes. Sedgwick's 6th Corps had yet to arrive from Manchester, a 22-mile march.

General Sickles did not fancy his assigned place in line. He complained to Meade that the low ground made him particularly vulnerable to attack, and that the rugged terrain in this area would not accommodate his artillery. Fully aware that Longstreet's corps was forming their lines to his front 1,400 yards across the peach orchard, Sickles unilaterally changed his position. At 2 P.M., he moved his men about a half-mile forward to an area on the edge of the peach orchard better suited to his needs. In making this move, Sickles created a break in the continuity of the Union line, and was now isolated from the main body. In addition, he not only exposed the flanks of his entire corps (two divisions), but the left flank of Hancock's 2d Corps as well.

While Meade prepared to receive an attack at any moment, in the Confederate camp that morning Lee had yet to decide on a plan of action. Not hearing a word from General Stuart's cavalry put him at a disadvantage. Nevertheless, around 11 A.M., Lee devised a battle plan following a meeting with his corps and division generals. The Confederate general decided to concentrate his assault primarily on the Union left, General Sickles' position. Ironically, General Longstreet, outspoken in his opposition to this operation, would have the honors of carrying out this mission, with the support of Anderson's division. Hill and Ewell's corps would provide diversionary artillery fire, but would attack in earnest only if and when an opportunity made it necessary.

Shortly after 4 P.M., following an opening Confederate artillery barrage, Hood's division began its advance. With bayonets flashing in the hot, July sunshine, the two gray lines swept through the peach orchard and across the Emmitsburg Road. Met by withering fire from the Union 3rd Corps, Hood's men momentarily withdrew as McLaw's division continued the attack. Spurred on by the tenacity of McLaw's charge, Hood's troops renewed their fight, and before long Longstreet's corps penetrated the break in the Union line.

Fighting now raged from Cemetery Hill to the Round Tops. Longstreet's corps and Anderson's division swept to the front, fighting the Union forces of Hancock's 2d and Sickles' 3rd Corps. As Lt. F.A. Haskell of the 2d Corps related from his vantage point on Cemetery Ridge, "Now came the dreadful battle picture, of which we for a time could be but spectators. Upon the front and right flank of Sickles came sweeping the infantry of Longstreet and Hill. Hitherto there had been skirmishing and artillery practice — now the battle started; for amid the heavier smokes and longer tongues of flame of the batteries began to appear the countless flashes and the long, fiery sheets of musket fire. We saw the long gray lines come sweeping down upon Sickles' front and mix with the battle smoke. Now the same colors emerged from the bushes and orchards on his right and enveloped his flank in the confusion."

With momentum clearly on the Rebel side, around 6 P.M. General Sickles had an easy decision to make. Overwhelmed on all sides and taking heavy casualties, the Union 3d Corps had little choice but to retreat to their original position. As Sickles' fleeing troops climbed the slopes of Cemetery Ridge, they were met by divisions of the 12th Corps shifted by Meade from Culp's Hill to fill the hole previously left by Sickles' move. Confused and mingled with men of the 12th, many of General Sickles' troops found shelter in the so-called Devil's Den, an 80-foot elevation of massive boulders located in front of Little Round Top. Concealed in the rocks of the Devil's Den, the Union soldiers made a valiant effort to hold off the charging Rebels, but again were overpowered and forced to withdraw. In the process, General Sickles was severely wounded, losing a leg, and was carried off the field. Meanwhile, on McLaw's left, General Anderson's division, in unison with Longstreet's men, charged into the lines of Hancock's 2d Corps stretched out along Cemetery Ridge. Now reinforced with the divisions from the 12th Corps, the Union force did not waiver, and in the ensuing battle, Anderson suffered a heavy loss of life.

When Confederate action had begun earlier that morning, diversionary cannonading into the Union right mistakenly convinced Meade that the battle would concentrate in that sector. In that regard, Meade paid very little attention to the defenses on his left. When Longstreet's troops began their forward movement at 4 P.M., however, Meade sent his chief engineer, Gen. Gouverneur K. Warren, to inspect the lines on the extreme Union left. Standing on the summit of the 200-foot Little Round Top, Warren realized that here was the key position of the entire Union line, and was shocked to find the hill unoccupied by Union soldiers. Spotting the Rebel troops among the boulders below, Warren rode off searching for available troops. Finding the reserve force of the 5th Corps nearby, Warren directed a brigade of infantry and one artillery battery to the vacant position in the Union line just as three Confederate regiments began their assent of Little Round Top.

The Union brigade assigned to the summit of Little Round Top lost about a third of its men that afternoon, but their tenacious fighting spirit carried the day and was credited for saving the entire Union's line. Special credit went to Col. Joshua L. Chamberlain and his 300 men of the 20th Maine regiment, who bore the brunt of the battle for Little Round Top. When their ammunition ran out, it was their bold and determined bayonet charge down the rugged sides of Little Round Top that turned the tide and assured the North of its victory. After the war, Chamberlain was awarded the Congressional Medal of Honor for this action.

With the exception of General Sickles' 3d Corps, the Army of the Potomac was steadfast in its resolve and as a consequence remained firmly in possession of its front line. The Confederate troops occupied Devil's Den, the ground at the base of the Round Tops and the Emmitsburg Road. Other than their cannonading, Hill's two divisions were relatively idle on Seminary Ridge, and Ewell's only action was an 8 P.M. attack on the 12th Corps entrenchments, found mostly vacated when the troops had shifted to Cemetery Ridge earlier. Most of Ewell's troops were driven off when the returning divisions found their works occupied, and vowed to get the rest in the morning.

On July 3, shortly after sunrise, General Lee arrived unexpectedly at Longstreet's headquarters to discuss his new orders. During this early morning session, Lee revealed the details of his latest plan to defeat Meade's army. Staunchly opposed by Longstreet, nearly to the point of insubordination, Lee's plan called for a direct, head-long infantry charge across 1,500 yards of open pasture and wheat fields to the Union center at Cemetery Ridge. Reminiscent of Marye's Heights at Fredericksburg, but with the roles reversed, Hancock's 2d Corps would await the Confederate charge safely protected behind a stone wall. To reach the wall, the Confederate line would not only have to survive the Union artillery barrage, but then fight their way through the line of musket fire from Hancock's troops. To assist in this effort, General Ewell, on the Confederate left, had already been advised to initiate an attack on Culp's Hill in concert with the infantry charge on the center.

Almost immediately, Lee's plan began to break down. During the course of the commanders' meeting, two Union divisions carried out their vow of the previous night and struck Ewell's men first. Opening an artillery attack at dawn, the Union troops overpowered Johnson's division and around 11 A.M. drove the Confederates across Rock Creek. The 12th Corps succeeded in recovering their abandoned works and thus forced Lee to eliminate Ewell's role in the attack.

To carry out the Confederate charge, Longstreet's only inactive division, Gen. George E. Pickett's, was selected as "division of direction." Having recently arrived from Chambersburg, Pickett's fresh division of three brigades would be supported by two divisions of Hill's corps, Pender's and Heth's. Because of recent battlefield injuries, Generals Isaac Trimble and James J. Pettigrew now commanded the divisions. Altogether, the Confederate attacking force would number approximately 15,000 men.

Listening impatiently, General Longstreet was not impressed. Trying to argue against the plan, Longstreet said to Lee, "General, I have been a soldier all my life. It is my opinion that no 15,000 men ever arrayed for battle can take that position." As Longstreet continued his argument, Lee refused to hear or talk about it any longer and abruptly ended the meeting.

Meanwhile, director of artillery, Col. Edward P. Alexander, was tasked with establishing the firing line for the offensive batteries that would precede Pickett's charge. The Confederate guns formed one continuous line along Seminary Ridge from the town to the peach orchard. The 150 pieces stretched almost two miles. When finally in place, the sight of this massive assemblage of firepower was awe-inspiring and a sight not easily forgotten. With keen interest, the Union commanders watched through their field glasses as each Confederate gun rolled into position. From this information, it was a foregone conclusion that Hancock's center would be attacked, preceded by an artillery barrage of monumental proportions.

Ironically, General Longstreet would give the order to commence fire. It was a demoralizing duty for someone who disapproved not only of the attack but also the manner in which it would be conducted. He could not, however, find the courage to give his own division commander, Pickett, the order to charge. To perform this painful duty, Longstreet ordered Colonel Alexander to select the most favorable viewing point to watch the artillery exchange. Then, from monitoring the activity of the 80 Union guns, Alexander would determine when conditions were right for the charge to begin, and would relay this information by courier to General Pickett. Around noon, Alexander received the first of two messages from Longstreet. The tone of Longstreet's notes gave Alexander an uneasy moment because in them, Longstreet appeared to be shifting the responsibility for initiating or calling off the charge entirely onto Alexander's assessment of the battlefield below. Anxious over this new interpretation of his role, Alexander wrote back to Longstreet that his judgment would be based solely on the intensity of the Union's return fire, and would not include the enemy's presence on the battlefield, which would be obscured by the smoke. Later, Alexander wrote, "If that assault was to be made on General Lee's judgment it was all right, but I did not want it made on mine."

At one o'clock sharp, Longstreet reluctantly issued his order to the Washington Artillery of New Orleans. Two rounds were then discharged signaling the entire Confederate line to commence fire. In an instant the ground trembled as over 100 pieces of artillery fired at the same moment, and within minutes the largest artillery dual of the war was under way. What was at first a tremendous spectacle was unbelievably amplified into a catastrophic explosion of firepower. Stunning the senses, nearly 200 guns were employed simultaneously, raining death and destruction everywhere. Intended to soften up the Union line prior to Pickett's charge, the Confederate gunners overshot their targets. Although there were many Union casualties, the barrage mostly damaged the town's Evergreen Cemetery, destroyed about 250 battery horses and a dozen caissons.

Critically assessing the Union onslaught with much trepidation, Alexander decided to wait 15 minutes for the Union fire to diminish before cueing Pickett to advance. Finally, after 25 minutes, or about 1:25 P.M., Alexander could wait no longer. Pickett was told that even though the enemy's fire had not abated, to receive adequate support he must come at once.

General Pickett was eager to lead this charge. The 38-year-old soldier had been relatively untried and longed to prove himself. Nevertheless, Pickett searched out his commander, Longstreet, for last-minute advice and guidance. When Pickett asked his commander if he should advance, Longstreet could not find the words to answer, but knowing it must be done, he managed an "affirmative bow."

The Confederate gunners had already ceased their firing in deference to their brave comrades preparing to charge across the open expanse. Within minutes of Alexander's message to Pickett, the Union artillery barrage also stopped. Now the wheat fields, taking on an almost unnatural pall, were relatively quiet. At around 1:40, Longstreet visited Alexander at his post overlooking the battlefield. As they looked out at Pickett's courageous men about to embark on what for most would be their final mission, Longstreet said, "I don't want to make this attack. I would stop it now but that General Lee ordered it and expects it to go on. I don't see how it can succeed." His reservations were correct.

At 3 P.M., Pickett's line began its march through the shimmering heat of the wheat fields. As soon as the Rebel line drew within range, the Union guns were again in force. The devastating killing power of close-range canister, grapeshot and shell and thousands of chattering muskets littered the field with many hundreds of dead and dying Confederate troops. Within a few minutes, Pickett's three brigades were reduced to a handful of stragglers limping back to the Rebel side. Losing two-thirds of his division, Pickett was devastated. Pettigrew's supporting brigades, advancing 200 yards behind Pickett, did not fare much better. Many, however, successfully breached the Union defenses and drove back the panic-stricken defenders. After only 20 minutes, the Union troops rallied and with fanatical fervor drove the fleeing Rebels back across the body-strewn fields.

General Lee met the few Confederate soldiers fortunate enough to make it back to their lines. Riding along the edge of the woods, cool and collected, Lee tried to return his men to the fight, assuring them that "All this will come right in the end. We'll talk it over afterwards, but in the meantime good men must rally." Too loyal for their own good, most of them returned to the battle. Lee knew in his heart that the fight was lost, and in less than an hour the battle was over. After three days of fighting, Lee's grand Northern invasion had been defeated, and he abandoned his efforts to dislodge the Army of the Potomac.

On the night of July 4, the same day Vicksburg surrendered to Grant, the Army of Northern Virginia retreated toward the Potomac River. The pursuit by the Union army was feeble and halfhearted, a probable result of the stormy night, with its heavy rain and driving winds. Reaching the Potomac on the 11th, Lee found his pontoon bridge at Falling Waters destroyed. Tearing down wooden buildings in the immediate area, the Confederate army set to work building a new span, and crossed on July 13. The Army of Northern Virginia arrived on the south side of the Rapidan River, near Gordonsville. Here at Gordonsville, Lee's army licked their wounds and reflected on their losses for almost a full year, until their next engagement the following May.

Regarding total casualties (killed, wounded, captured and missing), the battle at Gettysburg was the costliest of the war, with a total slightly over 51,000. The Confederate losses were about 28,000 killed, wounded and missing, roughly a third of Lee's army. The biggest loss was to the Southern cause. To many citizens of the Confederacy, the double disasters of Vicksburg and Gettysburg were grave omens. Chances of gaining European recognition were now considered hopeless. Without adequate resources, another invasion into Northern territory was out of the question. A month later, General Lee, deeply depressed, offered to resign his commission, but was refused.

Washington greeted the Gettysburg victory with mixed emotions. Despite the 23,000 casualties, some celebrated the victory as the greatest accomplishment of modern warfare, while others, especially President Lincoln, were quite unhappy. Lincoln was angry that Meade had allowed the Confederate army to escape across the Potomac. With

Lee's army severely weakened, exhausted, hungry, and practically out of ammunition, Lincoln had not only expected Meade to counterattack, but had waited impatiently for the results. In the president's opinion, this was indeed an opportune time to press a final and decisive blow. An attack at this moment would have compelled Lee to surrender, ending the war. Lincoln was stunned at the last opportunity, saying, "Our Army held the war in the hollow of their hands and they would not close it." Learning of Lincoln's dissatisfaction, even Meade offered to resign, but was also refused.

On November 19, Lincoln visited the battlefields of Gettysburg, battlefields that would be long remembered. On the crest of Cemetery Hill, the president dedicated the Soldiers' National Cemetery to the Union men who had died on that field. His eulogy immortalized their sacrifice, and guaranteed that they did not die in vain.

XI
Chickamauga to Chattanooga (June–November 1863)

Following the Battle of Stone's River, the Confederate and Union armies were camped a mere 30 miles apart in central Tennessee. The Northern soldiers were near Murfreesboro and the Southerners in the Duck River Valley area. The long and monotonous months of winter passed uneventfully for both Rosecrans' Army of the Cumberland and for Bragg's Army of Tennessee, thanks in large part to General Rosecrans' inflexibility.

Considering the fact that Johnston and Lee were being pressured concurrently, Johnston in Mississippi and Lee in Virginia, the Lincoln administration wanted desperately to harass Bragg in Tennessee at the same time. The consensus was that with all three Confederate fronts fighting simultaneously, the Rebel armies would find it very difficult, if not impossible, to reinforce each other. Stubbornness prevailed as General Rosecrans insisted he must wait until receiving his supplies, and his men were, in his opinion, ready to fight. As Washington feared, Bragg's army served as a convenient source of Confederate reinforcements. While Rosecrans procrastinated, most of Bragg's troops were sent to assist General Johnston's efforts to lift Grant's siege of Vicksburg. Although severely weakened by this action, Bragg's depleted force remained bivouacked across the area between Shelbyville and Chattanooga, Tennessee, unmolested.

As a result of this manpower drain on Bragg's army, Rosecrans was repeatedly ordered to attack. Lincoln, Stanton, Halleck and even Grant at Vicksburg all agreed that with Bragg's troop strength reduced, the advantages lay with the North if an advance on Bragg was carried out immediately. Remaining steadfast in his own philosophy, Rosecrans casually disregarded the orders.

On June 23, Rosecrans, or "Old Rosy" as his men called him, considered his supplies adequate and his troops ready for battle. He marched out of the Murfreesboro area with about 58,200 troops for Bridgeport, Alabama, a small town on the Tennessee River 30 miles west of Chattanooga. Taking full advantage of its proximity to the Tennessee River as well as its strategic connection to the Memphis & Charleston Railroad, Bridgeport was considered an ideal site for Rosecrans' supply depot.

Receiving word of the Union movement in his direction, General Bragg had little choice considering his weakened position but to abandon middle Tennessee. As Rosecrans advanced, Bragg's army retreated via railroad through the Cumberland Mountains and south across the Tennessee River to Chattanooga.

At this time, the Army of the Cumberland comprised three corps: the 14th Corps under Gen. George H. Thomas; the 20th Corps, commanded by Gen. Alexander M. McCook; and the 21st Corps under Gen. Thomas L. Crittenden.

Following their arrival at Bridgeport, Rosecrans met with his commanders and outlined his next objective: to dislodge Bragg from Chattanooga. Rosecrans also informed his corps commanders that threatening Bragg's all-important supply line would force the Confederate troops to come out in the open to fight, or to surrender Chattanooga.

To accomplish this goal, on August 16, Thomas and McCook were ordered to march their corps below Chattanooga to take out Bragg's supply line from Atlanta. Bragg played into their hands by evacuating Chattanooga on September 7, and concentrating his troops at Lafayette, Georgia, 25 miles farther south. Within days, General Crittenden's corps marched out of Bridgeport and soon occupied Chattanooga, now used as Rosecrans' base of operations.

This maneuver by Bragg was only a sham to lull the Union army into a trap.

Since the fall of Vicksburg in July, nearly two complete divisions of Bragg's army had returned from Mississippi to replenish the ranks. In addition, when Union General Burnside, commander of the Army of the Ohio, drove a Confederate division out of Knoxville in early September, the displaced Rebels moved south and fell in with Bragg, as did 8,000 troops under the command of Gen. Simon B. Buckner. The Army of Tennessee was now approximately equal in strength to the Army of the Cumberland.

When reports of Bragg's withdrawal from Tennessee reached Richmond, Confederate President Jefferson Davis reacted quite angrily. Already frustrated over the fall of Vicksburg as well as Lee's defeat at Gettysburg on the same day, the news of the Confederate army now abandoning Tennessee to the Union without a fight caused Davis much distress. He responded to this latest crisis by ordering in his veteran big guns, the divisions of John B. Hood and Lafayette McLaws from General Longstreet's 1st Corps. The Confederate president hoped they would show the Army of Tennessee how fighting was supposed to be done. With Longstreet's 12,000 reinforcements on board, Bragg's army of about 66,000 would be numerically superior, but Longstreet and his men would not arrive until mid–September.

From his new camp, Bragg strategically deployed his forces to cover the mountain roads from the outskirts of Lafayette north to Lee and Gordon's Mill, only 12 miles south of Chattanooga. Bragg planned to draw each Union corps to his position and destroy them as they emerged from the mountain passes; he would then return to Chattanooga.

While the Confederate general set his trap, the three corps of the Army of the Cumberland were fairly spread out. Each corps was isolated from the others and unable to provide reinforcements if any one of them was in need, a situation on which Bragg's plan hoped to capitalize. Crittenden was still near Chattanooga, McCook was marching up from Alpine, Georgia, a town 50 miles south of Chattanooga, and Thomas was in the mountains, halfway between the other two.

The first to approach Bragg's trap was Crittenden's 21st Corps. Advancing south from Chattanooga toward the Confederate army on September 10, Crittenden detected the presence of a large Rebel force near the town of Ringgold, and immediately retreated. In the mountains, when General Thomas' 14th Corps approached Dug Gap, Thomas discovered a large concentration of enemy troops in his front, and he also wisely pulled back. As a result, Bragg's grand plan became all too obvious and quickly fell apart. Had Bragg's commanders on the front lines exercised more patience he might have succeeded, but by showing their hand so early, instead of being drawn into the trap, the Union troops were warned of its presence and drew back. Frustrated, Bragg moved his men to the south bank of Chickamauga Creek to do battle there.

When Bragg's ruse was discovered, General Rosecrans called for his corps to close in and assemble in the valley of Chickamauga Creek, on the opposite bank from the Confederate army. Responding to the moment's urgency, the three Union corps endured forced night marches, arriving in the early hours of September 19; General Thomas on the left at Kelly's farm, General Crittenden to Thomas' right, and finally General McCook's corps defending the right side of the Union line.

The bloody Battle of Chickamauga was inadvertently set in motion on September 19 when Thomas, not knowing where Bragg's army was, or even if they had crossed the river, took two brigades on a reconnaissance mission to find them. What they found instead was the Confederate cavalry under Gen. Nathan B. Forrest on a routine patrol, with a strong contingent of Rebel infantry support. Thomas' men withstood heavy fighting which seesawed throughout the day, and were able to hold their position when nightfall halted the battle.

After a nine-day train journey, the first brigades of Longstreet's corps reached Ringgold on September 18. During the night, General Longstreet and his staff arrived at the Confederate camp and convened a council of war to discuss Bragg's plans for the upcoming action. With a much larger army at his disposal, Bragg deployed his troops into two wings. General Polk would command the right, and Longstreet the left. Bragg meant to attack severely the Union left flank, Thomas' corps, and push it into the center, while additional units from Polk's corps, reinforced by General Breckinridge's division, attacked in quick succession from the right to the left, until the entire Confederate front mercilessly rolled back the Union line. By the time the meeting ended, the Confederate commanders were extremely confident that with their superior numbers and their excellent field advantage, they would defeat the Army of the Cumberland in the morning.

Thanks to accurate predictions of Bragg's intentions, General Thomas' forces were heavily reinforced and extended farther to the Union left, past Lee and Gordon's Mill. At 8:30 A.M. on September 20, the now familiar Confederate yell was heard as Polk's troops charged into the waiting Union lines. Thomas' men were severely tested as the relentless Southerners swept forward.

Recognizing the need to shore up his left side even more, at 11 A.M. Rosecrans ordered two divisions on the right-center of his line to move on the double-quick from their positions to reinforce Thomas on the extreme left. After that movement, a second order by Rosecrans directed two adjacent divisions (Gens. Jefferson C. Davis and Thomas J. Wood) to shift laterally to the right to close up the line down to Gen. Joseph J. Reynold's division. But two huge mistakes were made that would cost the Union dearly. When Rosecrans gave his order to close up on the right to Reynolds division, he failed to know that General Reynold's was in fact farther down the line, with another division between his and Wood's. Consequently, General Wood, although confused by the strange order, failed to request a clarification. Instead, following his orders literally, he withdrew his division to the rear and marched to the right flank to provide support to Reynold's division, as directed.

General Wood's move created a huge hole in the Union line, which was at once spotted by the trained eye of General Longstreet, who immediately sent in the veteran Texans of Hood's division. The screaming Rebels wasted little time charging into the gaping hole, splitting away the entire Union right wing, killing and capturing thousands of panic-stricken men in blue and capturing fifty pieces of artillery.

To save what he could of his army, the exasperated Rosecrans hurriedly ordered the fleeing remnants of Crittenden's and McCook's forces back to Chattanooga. General Thomas, on the Union left, was cut off from the rest of the Union army and left to fight it out alone from his formidable position on Horseshoe Ridge.

Following the rout of the Union right wing, General Longstreet set his sights on taking Horseshoe Ridge, and was determined to take it before the day was over. Refused additional men from the Confederate right, Longstreet then ordered his 5,000-man reserve unit to advance up the steep sides of Thomas' position and attack the Union right flank and rear.

At around 4 P.M., General Thomas' position on Horseshoe Ridge was far from secure, with Confederates swarming in his front and on both flanks. With Thomas' men the only Union fighting force in the immediate area and grossly outnumbered, Horseshoe Ridge, or

Snodgrass Hill as it was also called, became the center of attention. It attracted practically the entire Army of Tennessee, all pressing to surround gradually Thomas' weary troops. Fighting furiously to prevent such an occurrence, every man on Horseshoe Ridge was consumed by the overwhelming pressure being exerted on all sides by the Rebel fighters. No matter how determined Thomas' troops were to resist, it was only a matter of time before Longstreet's men would gain a foothold on an adjacent ridge and threaten an attack on Thomas' rear, his only means of retreat. With his soldiers completely occupied elsewhere, Thomas had no one to spare to fight this new danger that promised to envelop his forces. Low on ammunition since the supply wagons had fled to Chattanooga with the fleeing right wing, Thomas' men were forced to ration their dwindling supply.

Acting on his own instincts, without orders, Gen. Gordon Granger, commanding the federal reserve units, arrived at Horseshoe Ridge at the right moment. Responding to Thomas' most urgent threat, the approaching reserves from Longstreet's corps, Granger's brigades repelled the Confederates from the ridge and saved Thomas from almost certain defeat. In the light of the setting sun, the Union troops quickly withdrew from Horseshoe Ridge and marched for Chattanooga to rejoin their comrades-in-arms. For his gallant defensive action, General Thomas won a nickname, the "Rock of Chickamauga."

The Battle of Chickamauga's historical significance did not capture the public's imagination, as Gettysburg or Vicksburg did. Chickamauga did, however, lay claim to one glaring historical footnote. It was the bloodiest two days of the Civil War. With 16,170 men lost for the North and 18,450 for the South, this battle ranked second behind Gettysburg in total casualties.

When news of General Thomas' withdrawal from Horseshoe Ridge reached Confederate headquarters, Bragg did not pursue the broken lines of the Union army, a choice that set off an explosion of anger and frustration in his own command. Incensed over Bragg's leadership or its apparent absence, a bitter Gen. Nathan B. Forrest refused to serve any longer under Bragg. After directly confronting Bragg over the conduct of the battle, Forrest returned to Mississippi to assume another command. Even the relatively low-keyed Longstreet was motivated to write to the secretary of war, "I am convinced that nothing but the hand of God can help as long as we have our present commander." Bragg's popularity had always suffered, but now it had reached a new low. One soldier remarked, "He was looked upon as a merciless tyrant. He loved to crush the spirit of his men. Not a single soldier in the whole army ever loved or respected him."

On the other hand, the commanders in Rosecrans' army were surprised that they were not pursued and somewhat thankful for Bragg's apparent shortcomings. Because of Bragg's failure to pursue, the Union commanders had time to regroup and reorganize their fragmented divisions and to fortify their positions. Bragg missed his chance for a certain victory by delaying his move toward Chattanooga until 4 P.M., September 21. By the time the Rebel army arrived on the 22nd, the Army of the Cumberland was entrenched and ready to fight.

Chattanooga, Tennessee, a railroad town of about 2,500 people, was vital to Southern interests. Only a few miles from the Georgia state line, Chattanooga enjoyed the advantages of having several major railroads passing through its railway depot. The Memphis & Charleston Railroad, the Nashville & Chattanooga Railroad, the East Tennessee and Georgia Railroad, and the Western Atlantic Railroad all converged there and branched off into the heart of the Confederacy. They went northeast to Knoxville and Richmond, southeast to Atlanta, and northwest to Nashville and Louisville. Because of the city's status as a rail center, Union occupation of Chattanooga was essential.

Surrounded on three sides by the convoluting Tennessee River, the town's extreme southern limit stretched out across the Lookout and Chattanooga Valleys in the shadow of Lookout Mountain and Missionary Ridge. Although now occupying this Southern prize, the Army of the Cumberland had little reason to rejoice. They were trapped in the jaws of a siege.

Following Rosecrans from Chickamauga, General Bragg's army entrenched in a line of fortifications across the commanding heights of Lookout Mountain, then curved through the valleys below and finally along the crest of Seminary Ridge. The Army of the Cumberland, trapped between the river and Bragg's army, could not escape and was unable to overcome Bragg's formidable position.

By holding Lookout Mountain, Bragg also controlled the railroad, the river, and the 22-mile road to Bridgeport, the Union supply depot. By choking off the river road, Bragg forced the Union army to depend on a 60-mile circuitous route to transport their supplies from Bridgeport through the mountains, until long periods of torrential rains inundated the area and transformed the mountain roads into rivers of mud. To make matters worse, without food, hundreds of weak and dying pack mules were unable to maintain this difficult effort. Eventually, Rosecrans was forced to abandon his supply line altogether. Then his problems really began to escalate. Before long, thousands of mules and horses died from starvation, and his men, on partial rations of hard bread, awaited the same fate. There was insufficient clothing for the approaching season, ammunition was running out and medical provisions were in short supply. For heat, the troops burned wood from razed homes, having already consumed all of the rail fences and trees in the area. The situation was indeed a desperate one.

The urgency of Rosecrans' dilemma was profoundly felt in Washington. President Lincoln decided he needed someone in charge at Chattanooga who would take direct control, someone who had proven himself capable of handling responsibility in a winning fashion. Therefore, on October 16, Lincoln not only chose General Grant for this assignment, but also appointed him to command the new Military Division of the Mississippi, making Grant supreme commander of all western forces.

Included in this new command was the Army of the Ohio, under General Burnside; the Army of the Tennessee, soon to be under the command of General Sherman; and the Army of the Cumberland under General Rosecrans. Upon accepting his new command, Grant relieved Rosecrans of his duties, assigned him to St. Louis, and appointed the "Rock of Chickamauga," General Thomas, as the new commander of the Army of the Cumberland.

On October 23, General Grant and his staff reached Thomas' headquarters from Louisville, traveling the last 40 miles from Jasper on horseback through the mountains to the Union camp. Grant's initial assessment of conditions at Chattanooga portended either starvation or surrender. General Grant believed that the fundamental solution to this issue lay in finding a way to open a more direct road to Bridgeport for the much needed food and supplies.

At this point, both the Army of the Tennessee, following the fall of Vicksburg, and the Army of the Potomac, now bivouacked on the Rapidan River after the battle at Gettysburg, were relatively inactive. With all the attention now focusing on Chattanooga, both armies were called upon to support General Grant's plan to lift the siege. General Halleck borrowed two corps from the Army of the Potomac, the 11th under Gen. Oliver O. Howard, and the 12th, commanded by Gen. Henry W. Slocum, to form a 20,000-man right wing. Reactivated since his post–Chancellorsville resignation, Gen. Joseph "Fighting Joe" Hooker, now at Bridgeport, would take command of this wing for an assault on Lookout Mountain and the valley below. General Sherman, now commanding a smaller Army of the Tennessee (17,000 men), would concentrate on the Union left from the Chickamauga Creek to the north end of Missionary Ridge, and in the process threaten Bragg's supply lines. With both of the Confederate flanks fully engaged, Thomas' 35,000 man Army of the Cumberland would advance from the center to the Rebel works on Missionary Ridge. Strange as it may seem, although Grant and the thousands of reinforcements were sent to help them, the commanders and the troops of General Thomas' army resented the implication of all this support and vowed to make amends to demonstrate the tenacity of their fighting spirit.

Meanwhile, informed that a plan for opening a new and shorter route to their supply depot in Bridgeport was already being worked on by Gen. William F. Smith, Thomas' chief engineer, both Grant and Thomas approved the plan and put Smith in charge of its implementation. To carry out this clandestine operation, 4,000 men were selected and divided into two groups. One group of 1,800 men under Gen. William B. Hazen would ferry 60 pontoon boats down the Tennessee River to Lookout Mountain. The second group, under General Smith, would move through the woods with the planking and other materials for laying the bridge. Their objective was to confront the Confederate pickets patrolling the area and to seize the entrance to Lookout Valley. That accomplished, a pontoon bridge would be laid out across the river at Brown's Ferry. Once across the bridge, the men would connect with General Hooker's troops arriving from Bridgeport, thereby reestablishing a link with their supply depot. The "cracker line," as the men called it, would also provide Hooker with a secured route to his target, Lookout Mountain.

Under cover of darkness, on October 27, the daring mission got underway. Blessed by heavy surface fog, the seven-mile boat ride was uneventful. Quietly approaching Lookout Mountain at dawn, Thomas' men met only cursory fire from the lightly defended landing site as the Confederate pickets quickly withdrew. By ten o'clock, the bridge was constructed and a rendezvous made with Hooker's troops.

Under General Grant's leadership, in only four days Bragg's siege of the Army of the Cumberland was broken, thanks to this well-planned and perfectly executed operation. Within a week, the men were back on full rations, and in the following weeks ammunition was again plentiful, new clothes were received and morale was restored.

Along with the responsibility of rescuing the Army of the Cumberland, Grant, as commander of all western armies, also had to confront other problems of equal urgency. At Knoxville, General Burnside and his Army of the Ohio were being severely pressed by Longstreet, who was bent on recapturing the city. To reduce the internal friction and bickering between Bragg and his commanders, Longstreet and his 20,000 men as well as 5,000 cavalrymen belonging to General Wheeler were removed from Chattanooga and sent to challenge Burnside on November 4, following a meeting between Bragg and Confederate President Davis. Burnside's dilemma was compounded by his army's location miles from the nearest supply depot. Burnside found himself in a situation similar to that facing Thomas at Chattanooga. Under siege, the Army of the Ohio was low on food and ammunition, most of the animals had died from starvation, and Burnside needed help desperately. Concerned that eastern Tennessee might be lost, dispatches from Washington repeatedly asked that Grant find some way to assist Burnside. All Grant could do for now was to wire Burnside that he must hold on until reinforcement troops could attack Longstreet from the rear.

The Battle of Chattanooga was triggered on November 23, when Grant suspected Bragg of preparing to withdraw his army. Informed by a Confederate deserter the day before that Bragg was leaving the front, Grant ordered two divisions of General Granger's corps forward under Gen. Thomas J. Wood and Gen. Philip H. Sheridan to make a demonstration on Bragg's front to test the validity of his suspicions. More important, Grant was still under extreme pressure from Washington to assist General Burnside at Knoxville. Unable to do anything for Burnside until Bragg was dealt with, Grant decided to act. In carrying out their little "demonstration," however, the Union troops drove the Rebel pickets back to their main line at the base of Missionary Ridge. This in turn allowed the Union to take easy possession of Orchard Knob, a small hill halfway between Chattanooga and Missionary Ridge.

On the morning of the 24th, General Hooker's army was poised to strike. His men were concealed in the woods at the base of Lookout Mountain, patiently waiting for the orders to advance. In the center, General Thomas' troops were positioned on Orchard Knob opposite Missionary Ridge, and on the Union left, the men of General Sherman's two divisions located the pontoon boats previously hidden in the woods and silently crossed the Tennessee River in the early-morning darkness. Crouching in their newly dug trenches, they waited for the signal to assault Bragg's right flank at the north end of Missionary Ridge.

At 1 P.M. Sherman's men were the first to go in, charging a half-mile across the open valley to the edge of the ridge. After successfully fighting their way through heavy fire from musketry and artillery for two-and-a-half hours, Sherman's men were shocked to find their captured hill separated from the main ridge by a boulder-strewn ravine. All their fighting had been for an obscure hill, and their attack on the main ridge would have to be repeated the next day.

Although Sherman's forces were not entirely successful, the presence of the railroad line to the Confederate supply depot in Sherman's vicinity caused Bragg to shift heavy reinforcements from his extreme left, Lookout Mountain, to his right to protect his all important supply line.

With the Confederate defenses on Lookout Mountain severely weakened, General Hooker attacked. Ascending 2,200 feet of steep mountainsides in a heavy fog, Hooker's men, now consisting of three divisions, were completely shrouded and lost from view. In the "Battle Above the Clouds," Hooker's men bravely withstood the sporadic fire from above and decidedly drove the enemy from the crest of the mountain and across the valley to Missionary Ridge.

By November 25, Bragg's entire army had consolidated almost entirely along the crest of Missionary Ridge. The exceptions were Longstreet's and Buckner's divisions, which Bragg had sent away on November 4 and 22 to attack Burnside at Knoxville. Still heavily occupied on both flanks by Sherman and Hooker, the Confederate army massed for a showdown.

At 2 P.M., Grant gave the order to attack the center at the base of Missionary Ridge. The assault would be along a two-mile front where the first of three tiers of rifle pits were located. The second tier was midway up the sides and the third on the crest with a line of Confederate artillery. Grant's order for the attack specifically instructed the men to carry only the line at the base of the ridge to prevent reinforcements from going to Bragg's right flank. As four of Thomas' divisions swarmed over the Confederate rifle pits under a devastating barrage of canister, musketry and artillery from above, the Rebels were overwhelmed by the swiftness of the Union attack and quickly surrendered. Although Grant's orders were to carry only the first level of rifle pits, the Army of the Cumberland, encouraged by their success, seized this opportunity to make good on their vow to avenge their defeat at Chickamauga. Unable to resist the urge to continue up the ridge, the men of the Army of the Cumberland, many yelling "Chickamauga! Chickamauga!" rushed up the steep 800-foot slopes of Missionary Ridge. Thomas' men soon overtook the second level of Bragg's works, now mostly abandoned, as scores of Rebels retreated in a wild rout to the crest. From his vantage on Orchard Knob, Grant watched through field glasses as the Union banners were planted on the summit. "Thomas, who ordered those men up the ridge?" Grant asked angrily. "I don't know, I did not," replied Thomas. As the Union troops reached the summit, the Army of Tennessee fled in a panic-stricken retreat down the south face of Missionary Ridge toward their supply depot at Chickamauga Station. General Sheridan and his division took up the chase.

As Thomas' men assembled on the summit of Missionary Ridge, they celebrated with unbridled excitement over their enormous achievement. Cheering wildly, several Union soldiers, spotting General Granger approaching on horseback shouted out, "What do you think of this, General?" To which the General replied, "I think you disobeyed orders, you damned rascals."

After the battle, General Bragg, stunned and disappointed, blamed his defeat on the men defending his left flank. Allowing Hooker's men to penetrate their lines, the Confederates broke and ran for their lives. Unable to stop them and with darkness near, Bragg claimed he had no choice but to order a withdrawal. As Bragg wrote, "No satisfactory excuse can possibly be given for the shameful conduct of our troops on the left in allowing their line to be penetrated. Had all parts of the line been maintained with equal gallantry and persistence, no enemy could ever have dislodged us."

Now able to respond to Burnside's plight, Grant ordered General Sherman to Knoxville. On the night of December 4, as Sherman approached with his Army of the Tennessee and a corps from the Army of the Cumberland, Longstreet retreated to Rogersville, ending the 16-day siege. As the attacking army, the Union lost twice as many troops at Chattanooga as the Confederates, 752 men, compared to 361 Confederate dead. In numbers captured, the disparity was telling. Over 6,000 Rebels were captured and sent away to Northern prison camps, as opposed to the Confederate capture of only 350 from the Northern side.

To General Bragg, the Confederate defeat at Chattanooga was caused by the penetration and breakdown of their left side. Many more blamed the decision to detail General Longstreet and his 20,000 men to Knoxville at a most critical moment, when his presence and his expertise as well as the capabilities of his men were most needed.

For the Confederate government, the omen must have been clear. Within the latter half of 1863, the South's three principal military forces, the Army of Mississippi, the Army of Tennessee, and the Army of Northern Virginia, all waging war against the Union in three separate theaters of operations, had suffered humiliating and critical defeats. Nevertheless, the war went on.

XII
From the Rapidan to the James
(March – June 1864)

With the Civil War well into its third year, the momentum was clearly on the Union side. The mood in Washington was one of guarded anticipation, not only of ultimate victory, but also of peace and reconstruction of a war-torn country.

A grateful Congress, now recognizing the military genius in Grant, reactivated the rank of lieutenant general, and with all the pomp and ceremony suitable for such an occasion, bestowed this highest of honors on Grant at a White House ceremony on March 3. The rank of lieutenant general, last held by George Washington in 1779, represented the supreme command of all Union forces, or general-in-chief. For the first time, all military operations for the 17 district commands would be coordinated and directed by a single commander. With this move, General Halleck was relieved of all direct military responsibility and shifted down to serve as Lincoln's chief-of-staff.

Lincoln was elated that at last he had a commander who would take over the military responsibilities and act accordingly, something Grant's predecessors failed to do and which, Lincoln admitted, only forced him to intervene in military matters. That was a function he very much disliked.

From his office in Washington, Grant's first order of business was to fill the vacancies resulting from his promotion and to reorganize his new command. Not surprisingly, on March 18, Grant promoted General Sherman to lead his previous command, the Military Division of the Mississippi; Gen. James B. McPherson would now command Sherman's old unit, the Army of the Tennessee. The new general-in-chief was particularly concerned about what he considered the ineffectiveness of the cavalry. Although he had nothing specific on which to criticize General Pleasonton, Grant called Gen. Philip H. Sheridan from Chattanooga and put him in charge of the Union cavalry. From Knoxville, General Burnside was directed to Annapolis, Maryland, where he took over the 20,000-man 9th Corps, in support of the Army of the Potomac. As for General Meade, he remained commander of the Army of the Potomac. Grant would, however, travel with the army and direct the movements of General Meade's command, a somewhat strange and at times embarrassing arrangement for both generals.

With his administrative and organizational tasks completed, in mid–March Grant met with General Sherman in Nashville, where they discussed plans for coordinating Sherman's movements in the west with those of the Army of the Potomac in the east. Their adversaries were Lee's Army of Northern Virginia, still on the southern bank of the Rapidan River in Virginia recovering from the defeat at Gettysburg, and Bragg's Army of Tennessee, now at Dalton, Georgia, 38 miles south of Chattanooga.

In the Confederate camp, an organizational shuffle also took place. President Jefferson Davis finally acceded to the demands of his commanders and relieved General Bragg from his command of the Army of Tennessee. Oddly enough, in a letter to Davis, Bragg himself admitted that, considering the uproar over his leadership, retaining him as commander of the Army of Tennessee would have been a mistake. Bragg was called to Richmond to serve as a military advisor to the president. In his place Davis transferred Gen. Joseph E. Johnston, currently idle in Tennessee, to assume command of the Southern army camped at Dalton, Georgia. Meanwhile, General Longstreet, after failing to dislodge Burnside, withdrew from Knoxville and marched his men through the mountains to rejoin Lee and the Army of Northern Virginia on the south bank of the Rapidan River.

At this time, the Confederate government was very much aware of the strain the war was having on Northern resources, and of the influence that strain could have on the upcoming presidential election.

The Davis administration gambled that a possibility existed, however remote, that a war-weary North would nominate and elect a Democratic peace candidate. They also speculated that this peace candidate could be inclined toward negotiating a treaty agreeable to Southern interests. With this rationale in mind, the Confederate armies were instructed to maintain a defensive posture and to continue fighting from behind entrenched fortifications. The military needed to make every effort to hang on until the election of 1864 in hopes that this speculation would prove correct.

General Grant refused to allow any political considerations to influence his actions. His grand plan was to engage the enemy simultaneously on five different fronts and end the rebellion before election day. To assist him in this aggressive endeavor he would employ the services of five generals: William T. Sherman, George G. Meade, Nathaniel P. Banks, Franz Sigel and Benjamin F. Butler. By keeping each Confederate sector under attack at the same time, reinforcements from one Rebel army to another would be held to a minimum. In addition, the inherent diversionary character of the operation would create enough confusion to keep the enemy off guard, and would weaken the fighting capability of the Confederacy.

The primary objective of Grant's campaign was to defeat Lee's Army of Northern Virginia and to march triumphantly into the Confederate capital of Richmond, a feat unattainable by the Army of the Potomac for nearly three years. To accomplish this goal, Grant, along with General Meade and his magnificent army, would march south and cross the Rapidan River to initiate the decisive confrontation with General Lee's forces. In his orders, Meade was told, "Wherever Lee goes, there will you go also." Grant also realized that this final effort would require massive and widespread fighting with a commensurate toll of extremely heavy casualties.

At last the battle plans were finished and the commanders briefed. Four thousand wagons were loaded with rations, forage and ammunitions. With three days' rations distributed to each soldier, along with 50 rounds of cartridges, the first fully coordinated military operation of the Civil War was set to go forward on May 4.

While the Army of the Potomac marched to the Rapidan, General Sherman would advance his massive army from Chattanooga to press an attack on Joe Johnston's Army of Tennessee, presently defending Dalton on the outskirts of Atlanta. At the same time, to support

Sherman, Gen. Nathaniel Banks, in Louisiana commanding the Army of the Gulf, would attack Mobile and prevent reinforcements from reaching General Johnston.

To support the Army of the Potomac, Gen. Franz Sigel, commanding 6,500 troops in the Shenandoah Valley, was assigned to cut off Lee's communications as well as his food, materials and reinforcements from that sector. Finally, Gen. Benjamin Butler would lead his 30,000 soldiers of the Army of the James up the James River from Fort Monroe. His role would be to destroy railroad connections between Petersburg and Richmond and then to threaten the Confederate capital itself.

Grant's strategy concluded that without reinforcements, Johnston's army would be unable to sustain Sherman's assault. The Army of Tennessee would be destroyed, and Atlanta, a strategic Confederate railroad depot, would fall into Union hands. General Sherman would then have unchallenged access to the Deep South. In the East, with Lee cut off from reinforcements, food and supplies, he would be unable to save Richmond, the Confederate seat of government. On the other hand, if Lee sent additional troops to Richmond from his own command, manpower he could not afford to lose, he would have been committing his army to a swift and bloody defeat and the Confederacy would lose the war.

The Union command prepared to break camp, fully confident that their plan put the Confederacy in a hopeless dilemma.

Shortly after midnight on May 4, the men of the Army of the Potomac began their journey to the Rapidan River. Marching south along two parallel roads, they arrived at the river in the early morning twilight, and within minutes the arduous task of stringing pontoons across the river began. Within a few hours the men and artillery of this huge army crossed the Rapidan at Germanna Ford and at Ely's Ford, six miles farther east, to begin their trek through the Wilderness.

The Wilderness through which the Union army now moved was a 70-square-mile area of extremely dense forest. An almost inaccessible tangle of scrub-oak, pines and cedar surrounded a maze of poor and narrow roads. In this vicinity General Hooker had been shamefully defeated a year earlier at Chancellorsville, approximately 15 miles to the east. As the men in blue advanced, skulls and bones of countless unknown soldiers from that battle were still found scattered in the brush.

Before Grant's arrival from Tennessee, the Army of the Potomac, 134,000 strong, was consolidated from five to three infantry corps, the 2d, 5th and 6th. Remaining as commander of the 2d Corps was Gen. Winfield S. Hancock. Gen. Gouverneur K. Warren now led the 5th Corps; the 6th Corps was still under Gen. John Sedgwick. Included also was the cavalry corps commanded by Gen. Philip H. Sheridan, and the artillery under Gen. Henry J. Hunt. On April 27, General Burnside's supporting 9th Corps had been called from Annapolis and now guarded the railroad line from Bull Run Creek south to the Rappahannock. Burnside's corps would join the others when word reached him that the army was safely on the south side of the Rapidan.

Since Lee's army was only 10 miles west of Germanna Ford, Grant was somewhat surprised that his army went unchallenged, and assumed that Lee was unaware of the crossing. The wily Confederate general was well aware of Grant's movements. Watching the Union troops through field glasses from his signal-station on nearby Clark's Mountain, Lee intentionally allowed the Army of the Potomac to cross the river unopposed. Lee thought that once clear of the Wilderness, Grant intended to draw the Rebel army south, away from their fortifications. At that point Lee suspected that Grant would swing around and cut his army off from Richmond, trapping the Army of Northern Virginia between the Union army and the river. With Lee's army in the open, Grant would then attack in full force. Lee had ideas of his own that involved using the thick growth of the Wilderness to his advantage. For the moment, Lee patiently watched as the Union forces crossed the river. When the Union army was thinly strung out and highly vulnerable in the Wilderness, he would launch a two-pronged attack on their right flank. Operating under this strategy, Lee anticipated that both Grant's superiority in numbers and his own weaknesses would be minimized.

Leading the Union advance on the road from Germanna Ford was a division of cavalry followed by Warren's and Sedgwick's corps. On the road from Ely's Ford, another division of cavalry, Hancock's 2d Corps, and the artillery followed. Approximately 10 miles farther south, these two roads met to form the Brock Road, the road south to Spotsylvania and the direct route into Richmond. Approximately a half-mile north and a half-mile south of this juncture were the Orange Turnpike and the Orange Plank Road, respectively, both transversing at right angles to the Union army. Along these two roads the Army of

Northern Virginia quietly marched east to attack the unsuspecting Federals.

In stark contrast to the well-dressed and superbly-equipped Union army, the men of the Army of Northern Virginia resembled a ragged and half-starved bunch of unsightly ragamuffins. Intensely loyal fighters in spite of their hardships and suffering, their morale and positive attitudes never seemed to waiver. Composed of only 61,000 men, the "elite" of the Southern military establishment consisted of three corps, under the leadership of Gens. James Longstreet, Richard S. Ewell and Ambrose P. Hill. Included in the force was the cavalry, commanded by Gen. J.E.B. "Jeb" Stuart, and the artillery under Gen. William N. Pendleton.

General Ewell's 2d Corps was advancing along the Orange Turnpike, quickly approaching the Union right flank. General Hill, marching east in parallel with Ewell, was also closing in on the Union forces crossing the Orange Plank Road. General Longstreet was 20 miles away at Gordonsville and would follow Hill.

On the night of May 4, the Union army camped along a line extending three quarters of a mile from the Orange Turnpike south through the woods and across the Orange Plank Road. The Confederates camped out of sight several miles to the west.

In the morning of May 5, both sides resumed their marches, General Warren's corps to the south across the Orange Turnpike and General Ewell's corps advancing along the same road toward them. Around 6 A.M., the silence of the woods was abruptly shattered as gunfire erupted seemingly from everywhere. On the adversaries' mutual sighting, the Battle of the Wilderness was underway.

For the entire day, both sides endured a severe and bloody fight, firing blindly at musket flashes of an often-unseen enemy. Following an initial setback, Warren's corps, now supported by a division from General Sedgwick's command, held off the three divisions of General Ewell's 2d Corps led by Johnson, Rodes and Early.

At the same time, Gen. A.P. Hill's corps, marching parallel to Ewell, also engaged with other troops of Warren's 5th Corps crossing the Orange Plank Road, as well as Union Gen. George W. Getty's division from Sedgwick's corps sent in as reinforcements. Around 4 P.M., as Getty's men began to waiver, General Hancock's 2d Corps arrived to support them. When darkness halted the fighting, both sides found themselves in much the same positions from which they started.

On May 6, fighting resumed at the first light. Across the Orange Plank Road, opposite the Confederate divisions of Cadmus Wilcox and Henry Heth of Gen. A.P. Hill's corps, General Wadsworth's division from Warren's corps now supported Hancock's troops. General Burnside was also ordered to support Hancock but was prevented from getting into position on time by the density of the woods. While the fighting continued on the Orange Plank Road, the Union forces near the Orange Turnpike, Warren and Sedgwick, would continue pressing their attack to prevent General Ewell's men from reinforcing Hill.

Back on the Union left, the murderous hail of gunfire from the combined forces of Hancock and Wadsworth (30,000 men), was devastating. Hill's troops were heavily outnumbered as well as outgunned. Forced backwards in a scrambling withdrawal through the woods, Hill's men retreated in wild confusion as Hancock's men fired relentlessly in pursuit. Meeting the retreating Rebels was General Longstreet with his 12,000 troops, arriving from Gordonsville. Combining his forces with the retreating men of Hill's corps, the Confederate general resumed his march east along the Orange Plank Road. Soon, Longstreet's veteran Texas Brigade, eager for more frontline action, charged headlong into Hancock's advancing line. Filling the woods with their shrieking Rebel yell, the new Confederate attack surprised Hancock's troops and drove them back to their earlier position.

To the raw troops in battle for the first time, the battlefield presented a grim scene. The dead and the dying were scattered everywhere, their blue and gray forms barely visible through the swirling gunsmoke and dense, shadowy underbrush. In this assault, General Wadsworth, one of Warren's four division commanders, sustained a mortal wound and was captured, and General Longstreet himself was carried from the field.

The Confederate commander had been partially hidden in the gunsmoke and thick foliage of the Wilderness. While preparing his troops for another attack, Longstreet had been shot and wounded just below the neck by his own men. Ironically, Longstreet's comrade-in-arms, Stonewall Jackson, had been shot and killed in the same woods and in the same manner a year earlier. For Lee, it was a devastating turn of events, a loss he could ill afford, but one he would have to accommodate the next five months.

Pushed back to his original position by the Texas Brigade, Hancock urgently called for infantry support. It was about 9 A.M., and as reinforcements worked their way through the woods to Hancock's position, General Lee arrived to command personally his right wing, now absent their beloved commander. With the absence of Longstreet, the men were suddenly dispirited and the impetus to fight lacking. Unable to rally his men to continue their attack, Lee ordered them to withdraw. Sensing the tide turning, Hancock renewed his attack and drove forward with an additional brigade to repel all remnants of Hill's and Longstreet's forces from the Orange Plank Road. Around 4 P.M., Lee's forces returned and temporarily regained the previously lost ground, but were savagely repulsed with heavy losses by another brigade from Hancock's 2d Corps.

Meanwhile, on the Orange Turnpike, with the exception of a small attack by Gen. John B. Gordon on the extreme Union right, the situations was relatively quiet. In the sporadic fighting in that sector, Gens. Warren, Sedgwick and Burnside successfully foiled the Rebel attempts to reinforce the Confederate right.

As darkness overtook the battleground, Lee's men withdrew from the field and retreated to their camps.

As Grant had predicted, Union losses were terribly high. Merely fighting a battle in the thick, dank environment of the Wilderness itself brought inherent difficulties for survival. Visibility was poor, friendly fire commonplace, artillery useless and troop movements difficult, if not impossible. At one point, the fury of flashing gunfire ignited the underbrush, setting off a blazing fire that agonizingly consumed many wounded soldiers, Rebel and Yankee, who were too badly injured to escape its deadly path. In two days, nearly 2,500 Union men were killed, 12,000 wounded, and over 3,000 captured. As one Union soldier related, "This battle of the Wilderness was simply bushwhacking on a grand scale."

Confederate losses amounted to about 13,000 men killed, wounded, and captured. Casualties were harder for the South than the North to replace. With each battle, the Confederate army and its fighting capacity gradually diminished.

On May 7, puffing on his ever-present cigar, Grant received a dispatch informing him that "Sherman had probably attacked Johnston" and that Butler was now safely at City Point, seven miles northeast of Petersburg. As Grant's campaign unfolded, it would become apparent to Grant that the supporting characters were not performing their vital roles. Gens. Banks, Sigel and Butler would all fail to carry out their assignments, leaving Grant and Sherman to meet the challenge without their assistance. General Banks, previously diverted by Washington to another mission in Louisiana, did not return in time to carry out his part in the campaign. General Sigel, when assaulted by a Confederate force in the Shenandoah, retreated. General Butler would soon be trapped between the James and Appomattox Rivers, crippling any further efforts of the Army of the James in the campaign. As a result, General Johnston received his 15,000 reinforcements, Richmond went unmolested, and General Lee's concerns of being isolated did not materialize.

With Butler so close to Richmond, General Grant suspected that Lee would advance south to smash the Army of the James. With no time to lose, Grant ordered Meade to break camp that night for Spotsylvania, a 12-mile march. By moving quickly, the Army of the Potomac would be positioned squarely between Lee and Richmond, and could reach General Butler first. As the Union army moved out, cheers for their new general-in-chief filled the night. Grown accustomed to withdrawing to a safer position after a battle, the Union troops were elated to find themselves marching south and still advancing. Moving out on the road to Spotsylvania, they voiced their approval of Grant's decision to keep moving forward.

Again, Lee was not to be outfoxed. Informed by J.E.B. Stuart that Union wagon trains had been seen rolling south that afternoon, and hearing the Union army moving down Brock Road that night, Lee also ordered his forces to Spotsylvania, but via a parallel route that would approach the town from the west. The race to Spotsylvania was on.

Unwittingly, Lee got the jump on the Union army. Gen. Richard H. Anderson, Longstreet's replacement, was ordered at 7 P.M. to start moving his 1st Corps by 3 A.M. the next morning. Anderson obeyed the orders promptly and began moving his corps that very night. With a little help from General Stuart's cavalry, who successfully blocked the Brock Road, Anderson's men won the race and reached Spotsylvania first, at 8 A.M. on May 8, much to the chagrin of General Grant.

By the morning of May 9, the entire Confederate army had reached Spotsylvania. Refraining from battlefield engagements, both sides used the day to build new front-line breastworks and to reconnoiter the land. The three infantry corps of the Confederate army were well positioned along a semicircular line on the outskirts of

Spotsylvania. General Anderson was on the Confederate left, General Ewell defended the center and General Early took on the extreme right. (General Early had assumed temporary command of the 3d Corps when Hill had become sick).

On the other side, the Union line formed with Warren on the right, opposite Anderson; Sedgwick to his left in the center, and Burnside occupying the Union left. When he arrived, General Hancock would occupy a position next to Warren's corps on the extreme right.

As quiet as the front lines were that morning, tragedy struck the Union camp when General Sedgwick, announcing to his men that snipers "couldn't hit an elephant at this distance," was shot and killed by a Rebel sharpshooter. Gen. Horatio G. Wright was named as his replacement.

On the night of the ninth, shortly after his arrival, Hancock moved his corps forward on the extreme right, and placed three divisions on Anderson's flank to threaten the Confederate rear. To counter this Union move, Lee quickly shifted two divisions from Early's corps over to Anderson's left to reinforce the Confederate defenses opposite Hancock. As the sun rose on May 10, Hancock tried to advance directly on the rear of Anderson's corps, but found the Rebels too strongly entrenched there and was immediately repulsed. Grant reckoned that Lee had severely weakened his line when he had shifted reinforcements to his left. To take advantage of this opportunity, Grant ordered an assault on the Confederate center by men of Warren's and Wright's corps.

With four lines of troops ready for battle, the 9 A.M. attack commenced on the mile-wide Confederate center. The Union front line met stiff Rebel resistance and was handily turned back. After the Union lines reorganized, they made another drive on the Confederate front at 3 P.M. This attack also failed. Not easily discouraged, later that afternoon the Union assault was renewed, and this time succeeded in breaking the Confederate center, driving the disorganized Rebels to the rear. At this point, fighting desperately to regain a foothold, the dauntless Rebels fended off the Yankees with bayonets and rifle butts. Reinforcements came on the double-quick from Anderson's corps, who steadily pushed the Union men back to their own lines. In the end, the Union attackers lost a quarter of their men.

The troops were rudely awakened on the morning of May 11 by the staccato of pouring rain. It was a depressing and foggy day, as the

CHANCELLORSVILLE TO PETERSBURG

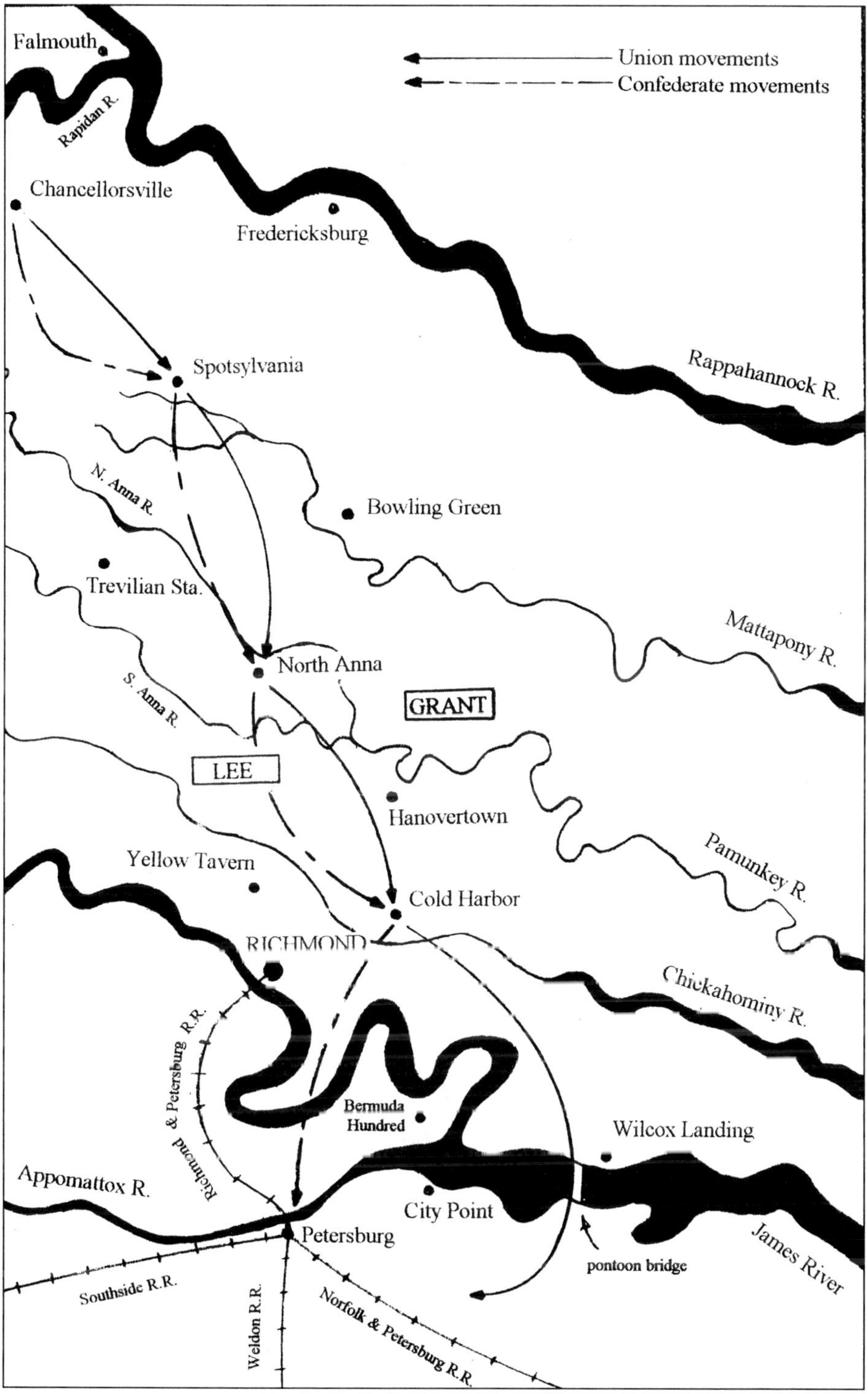

weather would be all week. From over the tree tops, the familiar clatter of teamsters and muffled voices was easily detected in the stillness of the early dawn. Confederate scouts told Lee that large numbers of Union soldiers had been seen shifting to rear positions within their lines. Lee instinctively interpreted these Union troop movements as preliminary to another flanking attack. Responding to this new crisis, the Confederate general ordered his men to shift the 22 pieces of artillery from their front lines to their flank to counter the attack expected in that sector.

The next morning, half obscured by the rising fog, General Hancock's 15,000 troops came charging from the woods straight for the Confederate center, at the defensive works in a salient commanded by Gen. Edward Johnson, a division commander in Ewell's 2d Corps. Without their artillery support, Johnson's men had no chance against the swarming invaders as Hancock's corps quickly overran the Rebel breastworks. The Union assault moved so quickly that the retreating Rebels had no time to reload and were forced to fight back in savage hand-to-hand combat. In the end, General Johnson and over 3,000 of his gallant men were captured.

That evening, while Hancock's men reformed their lines for a sweep deeper into the Confederate works, Gen. John B. Gordon, commanding Early's old division held in reserve, took up the fight to reclaim the lost ground. With his center broken, Lee knew his army was in serious trouble, and ordered three brigades from Early's corps to reinforce General Gordon's effort to carry out his Herculean task. The renewed battle proved a test of endurance as both sides fought the entire day and well into the night. When the fighting abated well after midnight from the combatants' sheer exhaustion, the sides withdrew with nothing accomplished but the heavy toll of casualties imposed on each other.

The next day's light brought a strange silence to the air. All was quiet. There would be no fighting this day. The worn-out soldiers remained in their respective camps, resting or nursing wounds. Others spent the day under a flag of truce, recovering their dead comrades. Some Confederates, without food for days, rifled through the haversacks of dead Union soldiers for edibles and coffee, a luxury in their meager existence.

On May 18, Grant received about 8,000 fresh troops to reinforce Hancock's corps. Together with the men of Wright's corps, they made another attempt at breaking the Confederate line. It failed miserably. Hunkered down within their new entrenchments, the Rebels were ready and waiting to do battle, and systematically slaughtered the onrushing bluecoats with volley after volley of canister, grape and minié balls. Again and again the Union troops rallied against Lee's works, but the results remained the same as the casualties grew.

Northerners were delighted by what they read of the war. Northern newspapers printed glaring banner headlines predicting, "The End Draws Near" or "Lee Terribly Beaten," and exaggerated stories of Lee's terrible defeats. The public's response to this press coverage worried Lincoln. The president thought that too much optimism was bad when so much was yet to be accomplished. When Union casualty figures begin to trickle in, the public's mood changed dramatically. Incensed over the staggering loss of life, the people and politicians began to criticize what they saw as Grant's reckless disregard for Union lives. In one week, May fifth through twelfth, 32,000 young Union men were killed, wounded or missing. These casualty figures surpassed those of any previous week of the war, even with all the Union armies combined.

On the Southern side, matters were also grim. Again, General Lee received bad news. Lee's highly respected cavalry commander, General J.E.B. Stuart, was dead. The general's death resulted from a gunshot wound to the stomach, received on May 11 at the small town of Yellow Tavern, Virginia. The fatal wound occurred in a gunfight about six miles from Richmond, where half of Stuart's cavalry forces were engaged in a battle with General Sheridan's 10,000 horsemen, on a mission to destroy 20 miles of railroad. For the Confederate commander, it was a trying time. On losing Stuart, Lee said, "I can scarcely think of him without weeping." In one week, Lee had lost 18,000 men and 20 of his 57 commanding officers.

From May 18 to May 22, both armies engaged in a "sidling" movement to the southeast, as if playing a game of chess. One side moved first, with the other side making a corresponding counter-move.

On May 22, Lee's army was securely dug in on the south side of the North Anna River, 25 miles from Spotsylvania. The Army of the Potomac arrived on the north side of the river the following day. General Lee, always the supreme tactician, formed his battle lines parallel to the river. His defending army was strategically positioned to thwart any attempt by Grant to cross the river from Jericho Ford to the Chesterfield Bridge. While maintaining a strong hold on his center,

Lee cleverly angled back his two wings to form a "V," allowing the Union forces unimpeded access to cross both at the ford and over the bridge. Patiently drawing in his prey, Lee watched and waited. General Warren's corps crossed the river at the Jericho Ford on May 23, as did General Wright the following morning and Hancock, over the Chesterfield Bridge, also on May 24. When General Burnside, the commander of the Union center, tried to cross the river in the middle, between the ford and the bridge, the waiting Confederates attacked. Lee's strategy paid off. Both Union corps that had been allowed to cross the river earlier were now split apart. They could not send reinforcements while Lee's center kept them disconnected. At that point, Lee ordered the wings to close their ranks around them. Burnside's men were sent reeling back across the river, but there was no Confederate pursuit. Lee fell ill with a terrible fever and bouts of delirium, and did not issue any follow-up orders.

During this period, Lee was finally sent reinforcements. About 8,500 men were transferred from Richmond and North Carolina to help replenish his depleting ranks. Coincidentally, General Grant was also expecting additional troops from Drewry's Bluff. The 18th Corps, commanded by Gen. William F. Smith, was transferred from Butler's command and received its marching orders to join the Army of the Potomac.

For the next two days, Grant was severely challenged as he tried to figure a way to break through Lee's position. As Grant related, "We were, for the time, practically two armies besieging."

Suddenly on the 27th, the Confederate troops awakened to find the Army of the Potomac gone. The army had folded its tents and silently stolen away. In actuality, Grant had withdrawn his forces to the north side of the river during the night, and by morning was crossing the Pamunkey River, near Hanovertown. Alerted to Grant's disappearance from his front, Lee ordered his army to break camp for Cold Harbor, and once again the race was on.

On May 31, General Sheridan and his cavalry were the first of Grant's forces to reach Cold Harbor, a village of three churches, a hotel, store and a few county buildings 11 miles southwest of Fredericksburg. Finding a contingent of Confederate cavalry and infantry already entrenched there, Sheridan managed to drive them out after a difficult fight. Lee did not intend to give up Cold Harbor that easily. During the night, the Rebels struck Sheridan's smaller force twice more, but each time failed to dislodge the troopers from their own works.

Notified of Sheridan's dilemma, Grant quickly dispatched General Wright's 6th Corps to reinforce the cavalrymen. They reached Cold Harbor around 9 A.M. on June 1. At the same time, General Smith's marching orders were revised and he was directed to rendezvous with the Army of the Potomac at Cold Harbor. Smith's 18th Corps also reached the Union lines on June 1.

Meanwhile, the armies resumed their sidling movements, the lead elements of the Union column reaching Cold Harbor at 6 A.M. on June 2. No serious fighting occurred that day thanks to General Hancock's late arrival, which postponed Grant's battle plans. The Union fine-tuned its assault strategy and the Confederates improved their works for the battle expected the next day.

Although the Union army was nearly twice the size of Lee's and the men supremely confident of the following day's outcome, many Federals, perhaps hundreds, pinned slips of paper to their clothing with their names and addresses written down so their bodies could be identified after the battle.

At 4:30 A.M. on June 3, the lines of Hancock, Wright and Smith moved forward to engage the Confederate forces entrenched before them. Warren and Burnside would act as support, but would attack only if an opportunity occurred. The Union soldiers soon found the territory to their front extremely difficult to cross because of the swamps, thickets and ravines. On the other hand, the Confederate troops were waiting with their muskets ready, secure behind the safety of their works. Advancing straight-on into the Confederate line of fire, the Union army was mercilessly gunned down and captured only the outer or picket rifle pits before being turned back. For this small accomplishment, the Army of the Potomac paid dearly, with around 7,000 casualties. It was a battle Grant would always regret ordering.

The Union commander was usually found relaxing outside his headquarters, whittling sticks and smoking his favorite cigars. But this day, the general-in-chief was frustrated over the fact that it was proving nearly impossible to flush Lee out of his trenches, to fight him in the open where Grant's superior numbers would have a tremendous advantage. Lee's defensive strategy was costing Grant twice as many casualties, which in turn was causing political and civilian resentment in the North. This resentment focused specifically on Grant, now called a "bull-headed Suvarov" by the Democrats. As Mary Lincoln lamented, "Grant is a butcher and not fit to be at the head of an army. He loses two men to the enemy's one. He has no management, no regard for life.... I could fight an army as well myself."

Much of the Union dilemma owed to recent Confederate strategy, in both theaters, that maintained a defensive posture at all costs, to "only subsist" until the Northern election. Consistent with that policy, Rebel forces became masters at building strong, state-of-the-art fortifications, and extremely adept at stalling and outmaneuvering the larger and more powerful Union armies. In time, this policy proved frustrating to both Sherman and General Grant. Time and again, both commanders failed to flush the elusive Confederates from their works, to fight in the open. Instead, the Union generals only suffered higher and higher numbers of frontline casualties.

To counter this problem, in the second half of 1864 the Union military launched a new phase of offensive tactics. Over the course of the rebellion, the Union strategy had been always to attack the Rebel armies directly, and to assault and occupy the captured cities. Now, the Union army would concentrate more and more on destroying the resources that both the Army of Northern Virginia and the Army of Tennessee needed to continue waging war. This new phase would include destroying not only food and materials, but also the farms that grew the food and the railroads that transported these resources to the front lines. Eliminating the capacity of the Southern people to support the war effort would become the North's main strategic principle. As cavalry brigade commander Gen. James H. Wilson wrote, "the smash-'um up policy was abandoned about that time and never again favored at headquarters."

In another effort to drive Lee's army from their trenches, and consistent with his new strategy, Grant devised a three-prong coordinated operation aimed at destroying Lee's meager cache of supplies at Lynchburg and laying waste his food source in the fertile Shenandoah Valley. He ordered to Lynchburg Gen. David Hunter, who had replaced Sigel after Franz Sigel's disappointing retreat in May, and cavalry commander Gen. Philip Sheridan into the Shenandoah Valley. With Lee's attention now focused on the attacks to his rear, the Army of the Potomac quietly disengaged from Cold Harbor and marched south toward Wilcox's Landing on the James River. Once across, Grant would seize the all-important railway hub, Petersburg.

XIII
The Battles for Atlanta
(May–September 1864)

One of 11 children, 44-year-old William Tecumseh Sherman was born in Lancaster, Ohio. Named after the famous Shawnee chief, Sherman was educated at the U.S. Military Academy, graduating sixth in the class of 1840. After a mediocre 13 years in the military, Lieutenant Sherman resigned his commission, and in 1853 went into banking. Following his bank's failure in 1859 due to the outbreak of the war, he held a position as superintendent of a Louisiana military academy, now Louisiana State University. When Louisiana seceded in 1861, Sherman rejoined the Union army, and was promoted to brigadier general for his gallant duty in the first Battle of Bull Run. Following the Battle of Shiloh, Grant promoted Sherman, by then his most trusted commander, to major general in command of the 15th Corps. Later, when Grant was sent to rescue the Army of the Cumberland at Chattanooga, he put his friend in charge of his old command, the Army of the Tennessee. "[Grant] stood by me when I was crazy," Sherman once explained, "and I stood by him when he was drunk; and now we stand by each other always." As general-in-chief, one of Grant's first actions was to promote his military chum to the command of the Military Division of the Mississippi, still bivouacked in Chattanooga.

The army that Sherman now commanded boasted a troop-strength of about 100,000 men. It included three army commands: The Army of the Cumberland, four corps of 50,000 men commanded by the "Rock of Chickamauga," Gen. George H. Thomas; the Army of the Tennessee, three corps of 35,000 troops now under the young and brilliant Gen. James B. McPherson; and the 15,000 men of the Army of the Ohio, commanded by Gen. John M. Schofield, a New Yorker who would later become President Andrew Johnson's secretary of war. Gen. George Stoneman commanded the cavalry.

Overwhelming responsibilities inherited by the victorious Union army were the needs to occupy vast expanses of territory now back in Union hands, and to provide protection from hostile civilian and Rebel raiding parties. Grant faced problems of manpower constraints as the Union army stretched to its very limits. The strain on military resources, regarding human and material readiness, also weakened the capacity for the Union to wage war on the front lines. Assigned to this daunting task, General Sherman's mission was to provide for the security of over 100,000 square miles of captured territory. Particularly important were the many supply routes, covering hundreds of miles, used for transporting food and materials to his three armies.

Coordinating his movements with General Grant's drive toward the Rapidan, Sherman ordered his western army out of Chattanooga on May 6. His target was Confederate Gen. Joseph E. Johnston, commanding the Army of Tennessee, 38 miles to the south at Dalton, Georgia. Anticipating the magnitude of the campaign into Georgia, and the inherent difficulties of protecting and maintaining the depots and trains, part of Sherman's plan was to have his army travel as lightly as possible. To this end, he restricted the number of wagons carrying such supplies as rations, clothes and tents. This move minimized his army's dependency on its trains and increased the mobility of his forces. At the same time, Sherman had to carry out his prime objective, that of marshaling his forces in a drive to defeat his enemy, the Army of Tennessee.

Leading an army approximately half the size of Sherman's, Johnston planned to fight defensively, from behind breastworks at all times. The only exceptions came when holding an inferior position made it necessary to attack, or when Union forces were found separated from one another. From Johnston's experience, this strategy would minimize Confederate casualties, and as Union lines lengthened, their numerical superiority would also be reduced.

The Army of Tennessee, about 60,000 strong, comprised of three infantry corps and the cavalry. The respective commanders were Gens.

William J. Hardee, John B. Hood, Leonidas Polk and Joseph Wheeler. (General Hood had been transferred from the Army of Northern Virginia following his promotion to corps commander).

As the Union army moved steadily south along the Western & Atlantic Railroad, Johnston prudently evacuated his works at Dalton on May 11 for Resaca. By May 15, the Confederates were again forced to retreat, this time to Adairsville, and then to the vicinity of Cassville on May 19. Evidently, each time Johnston's communications were threatened, he ordered a general retreat south, moving to another location where his communications could be reestablished. Military dispatches of Johnston's continuous retreats were not well received by President Davis, and only served to reinforce his long-standing personal disdain for the general. Soon, Johnston became the butt of sarcasm and dinner-party jokes as Southern newspapers incited questions on his military competence.

Johnston's rank-and-file troops held a different point of view, as a private in the 1st Tennessee Regiment explains: "When Johnston took command, men returned to their companies and order was restored. He ordered his soldiers new suits of clothes, shoes and hats. He allowed us what General Bragg had never allowed — a furlough. He passed through the ranks, shaking hands with everyone. He brought the manhood back to the private's bosom. He was loved, respected, admired. I do not believe there was a soldier in his army but would gladly have died for him."

On May 20, the Army of Tennessee withdrew again, to Allatoona and then to New Hope Church on the 25th. With each Confederate retreat, the Union army made a commensurate advance, step by step, mile by mile.

The first serious engagement between the two armies occurred at New Hope Church, when three divisions of General Hooker's 20th Corps tried to secure the town. Johnston's troops delayed the advancing federal columns with sharp and bloody fighting as well as heavy concentrations of artillery fire. Hooker's men fought far into the night, but were eventually forced back. Two days later, O.O. Howard's 4th Corps pushed to the front; they, too, were blasted back. For one week the skirmishing and sniping continued in the dense woods, now called "Hell Hole" by the Union troops. Firing from behind trees, boulders and fallen logs, neither side could see the enemy except when an occasional soldier darted from one cover to another.

On June 1, the rains began. It rained in torrents, and it rained again the following day. It rained for the next 19 days. The roads, if indeed they could have been called roads at all, were transformed into pools of mud, making travel very difficult for both sides.

Despite the poor roads and inclement weather, Johnston persevered, and his army kept retreating toward Atlanta, now only 30 miles to his rear. By June 10, the Army of Tennessee was securely concealed behind their breastworks around and on the summit of the 700-foot Kennesaw Mountain. Tracking Johnston's movements every step of the way, Sherman's army moved near Big Shanty, a station on the Western and Atlantic Railroad, in plain sight of Kennesaw Mountain. On the morning of June 14, Sherman reconnoitered the mountain slopes through his field glasses and was surprised to discover a small group of Confederate officers standing in the open spying on the Union army through their field glasses. The sight of the Confederate officers standing in plain view outside their protective fortifications, as if taunting Sherman, highly irritated the Union commander. Sherman ordered three artillery volleys at the group of onlookers to teach them to stay behind their works. The accuracy of the shots must have surely impressed Sherman. One officer in this small group of spectators was General Polk, who was hit in the chest by the second cannonball and killed instantly.

Sherman met with his commanders and disclosed his plan to attack Johnston's army, by then fully concentrated across Kennesaw Mountain, 20 miles northwest of Atlanta. The Confederate works presented a formidable challenge. Johnston's men were strongly positioned in rifle pits on the mountain slopes and behind fortifications on the crest; they had also deployed artillery cover over a 10-mile front. In spite of this display of resistance, Sherman considered the Rebel line thinly stretched, and found the possibility of breaking through the Confederate center quite feasible. Once the Rebel center was breached, Sherman estimated that his men could sweep around and overwhelm both of Johnston's flanks.

At 9 A.M. on June 27, the attack opened along a 10-mile front. Charging into a thunderous artillery barrage of grape and canister and unrelenting musket fire, the Union forces of Gen. John A. Logan's 15th Corps were stymied in their attempt to break through the stiff Confederate resistance. Union soldiers ran headlong over Rebel rifle pits, some without firing a shot to save ammunition for the encounters expected on the crest. Many never survived to achieve that goal. At every point of attack Sherman's army was repulsed, and was forced to quit the field at 11:30 A.M., with 2,300 casualties. The Confederates lost 800.

The Union commanders understood now more than ever how punishing and futile a direct assault on entrenched lines could be. One Confederate soldier taking part in the onslaught related, "All that was necessary was to load and shoot. In fact, I will ever think that the reason they did not capture our works was the impossibility of their living men to pass over the bodies of their dead."

While Johnston was occupying Kennesaw Mountain, he had the foresight to establish his next stand of fortifications. Employing hundreds of slaves, Johnston prepared five miles of redoubts (protective barriers) and abatis (barriers formed of felled trees with sharpened branches pointed toward the enemy) several more miles to his rear, at a point where the railroad crossed the Chattahoochee River. Following his victory on the 27th, the Confederate general quietly abandoned Kennesaw Mountain and withdrew his army to his new fortifications at the Chattahoochee.

On July 3, Sherman discovered Johnston's army gone, and ordered his three corps into a "right-wheel" maneuver in pursuit of the Rebels. Thomas' Army of the Cumberland, acting as the pivot, advanced directly behind Johnston, and confronted the Confederate breastworks at the Chattahoochee River. At the same time, Gen. Schofield also headed for the river by wheeling to the right in parallel with Thomas but at some distance to his left. After bluffing a move toward Johnston's front, McPherson marched east to Roswell. Circling to the right in parallel with Schofield's left, McPherson's corps would then cross the Chattahoochee and begin sweeping around Johnston's right flank to the Georgia Railroad, a line leading directly into Atlanta.

With McPherson nearing the river at Roswell, General Schofield's army crossed the Chattahoochee at its junction with Soap's Creek, several miles from Johnston's works on July 9. Meanwhile, General Thomas had his hands full fighting a determined enemy firing from behind well-prepared breastworks. Informed that Schofield and McPherson were about to cross the river and could easily threaten either his rear or the city of Atlanta, General Johnston burned his pontoon bridge, as well as the railroad bridge, and retreated to a ridge behind Peachtree Creek, only six miles from Atlanta.

Eight days later, the Union army began its final drive toward the

"Gate City of the South." With very little interference, the Army of the Cumberland approached Peachtree Creek on the 18th. The Army of the Ohio remained to Thomas' left and on the extreme left, the Army of the Tennessee was tearing up the Georgia Railroad between Stone Mountain and Decatur.

Inside the city, the trains that still ran were inundated each day with the citizens of Atlanta, frantically trying to escape a Union invasion. For those inclined to stick it out, underground shelters were built to protect the non-combatants from the expected shelling.

In the Confederate camp that day, a different sort of struggle took place. Monitoring the movements of the Confederate army closely, President Davis was extremely concerned about Johnston's unbroken string of retreats, and tried to get assurances from the general that a determined fight by the Confederate army would be waged if the city of Atlanta were threatened. Johnston's telegraphed response to Richmond: "We are trying to put Atlanta in condition to be held by the Georgia Militia, that army movements may be freer and wider." Whatever his intent, Johnston's reply was interpreted by the Confederate president as being too "evasive." Now lacking all confidence in his commander, Davis felt he had no choice but to relieve Johnston of his duties as commander of the Army of Tennessee.

Replacing Johnston was John Bell Hood, a 33-year-old Kentuckian who graduated from the U.S. Military Academy in the same class as Union Gens. Schofield, McPherson and Sheridan. Chafing over Johnston's failure to bring the fight to the enemy, Hood's design since the campaign had begun was to take over the command. Despite his left arm being crippled from a wound received at Gettysburg and his right leg lost at the Battle of Chickamauga, Hood remained a bold and fierce fighter, exactly what Davis wanted. Not a strong supporter of General Johnston's style, Hood, to the satisfaction of Johnston's critics, was an ardent advocate of the Lee and Jackson school. Replacing Hood as corps commander was Gen. Benjamin F. Cheatham, a division commander from Hardee's corps.

After carefully plotting his map with the positions of his enemy, Hood was astounded to find that Schofield and McPherson were a considerable distance from Thomas' Army of the Cumberland. Because of this long distance, it would have been nearly impossible for them to send Thomas reinforcements. To Hood's delight, the Army of the Cumberland was effectively isolated.

Only two days after receiving his new command, Hood determined to make a bold attempt to surprise General Thomas as he crossed the Peachtree Creek. Hood ordered the Army of Tennessee on an offensive to commence at 1 P.M. on July 20. Taking part in the attack would be Hardee's corps and the five divisions of Polk's old corps, now commanded by Gen. Alexander Stewart. At the appointed time, however, General Hardee's forces had not moved into position. This delay caused the opening salvo to occur at 4 P.M. Almost immediately, the combined strength of both Confederate corps had Thomas' men in serious trouble. Because of the late start, darkness soon obscured the field, and the Rebels were forced to pull back, their assault a failure. Although General Hood believed Hardee's delay had no serious impact on the outcome, he did blame the loss on Hardee's troops, who failed to fight aggressively. As Hood wrote later, the troops "did nothing more than skirmish with the enemy." Regardless of fault Hood lost 3,000 troops. As later historians would agree, most of the fault was Hood's alone, for ordering such a foolhardy attack.

That same night, Confederate headquarters received a report from cavalry commander Wheeler informing Hood that General McPherson's left flank, camped along the Georgia Railroad line, was found completely exposed, without the protective support of Union cavalry. Deeming it essential to protect the railroads leading into Atlanta to save the city, General Hood triggered the Battle of Atlanta on July 22.

As a result of the previous day's poor showing, Hood ordered Hardee's relatively fresh troops and Stoneman's cavalry on a 15-mile circuitous route to McPherson's exposed left flank. The march began on the night of the 21st, with Hardee assigned to attack McPherson's unprotected flank and rear the following day. While McPherson's forces were being turned and driven back to Peachtree Creek, General Cheatham, posted on the Confederate right, joined the attack and continued rolling the federal line back to the creek. Gen. G.W. Smith, commander of the Georgia State troops, on Cheatham's left, followed suit. General Stewart was on the Confederate left, opposite Thomas, and tried to occupy the Army of the Cumberland sufficiently to prevent reinforcements from reaching McPherson, and to maintain the general movement from right to left.

Around noon, on a very hot and humid July 22, General Sherman and General McPherson were found enjoying the peaceful, cool shade of the woods. With their maps spread before them, the two generals were busy discussing their plans for continuing the destruction of the railroads entering and leaving Atlanta. Of particular concern was the only one still untouched, the Macon & Western from East Point, on the Union extreme right. Suddenly, a flurry of musketry and the deep roar of artillery came from the distance. Startled by this unexpected attack, General McPherson rode out to investigate and within minutes was killed while directing reinforcements to his harried flank. While riding at full gallop along a wagon-trail in the woods, McPherson ran directly into a Confederate division. Refusing to heed an order to surrender, McPherson tried to escape but was shot in the back as he sped away.

The sudden Confederate attack on their flank indeed surprised the Yankee troops. Caught completely off guard, the Union men were driven back, repulsed by the heavy Confederate fire from Hardee's four divisions. The fighting was intense and bloody, lasting through the afternoon and into dark. As one Union soldier wrote, "Soldiers were wounded and knew it not, so intense was their excitement. Men with shattered fingers changed their muskets to their left hands." As Union reinforcements joined the fray and connections were made with other Union forces by the retreating Federals, the momentum clearly shifted to the Northern side. Around 4 P.M., General Cheatham's corps received the signal to advance as Hardee's attack stalled. Charging headlong into the 15th Corps under Gen. Morgan L. Smith of the Army of the Tennessee, Hood's army was severely rebuffed by a massive counterattack from 20 pieces of artillery and a concentrated force of seven brigades.

General Hood's aggressive tactics were in clear contrast to those of his predecessor, and the Confederate army paid a high price for it. After only two battles, Hood's 8,000 casualties exceeded Johnston's losses over a 10-week period.

Following a discussion with his commanders, General Sherman chose O.O. Howard to replace General McPherson as commander of the Army of the Tennessee. General Hooker, commander of Thomas' 20th Corps, was incensed over Sherman's selection. Hooker believed Howard inferior in seniority; because of Howard's promotion, Hooker tendered his resignation, which General Thomas gladly accepted.

Still number one on Sherman's priority list was the destruction of the Macon & Western Railroad from East Point. This would be his next objective. Destroying this railroad would sever the last conduit for getting supplies to Hood's army entrenched inside Atlanta. This accomplished, Atlanta would be in the jaws of a siege that Sherman hoped would force the Confederates out in the open to fight. For this important mission, Sherman believed the cavalry best suited, and sent his crack horsemen under Gen. George Stoneman.

At the same time, the entire Army of the Tennessee moved to the rear and shifted over from the extreme left of Atlanta to the extreme right, near a rural meeting house, the Ezra Church. As Howard's men hiked to their new position on July 28, gunfire from the woods scattered General Logan's 15th Corps, who instinctively ducked for cover. Coming from the vicinity of the meeting house, the shooting compelled Logan's men quickly to construct crude breastworks from logs and church pews found in the immediate area. General Hood's evident intent was to drive Howard's corps from the east side of Atlanta by dispatching four divisions to attack the unsuspecting Yankees. Firing back from behind their makeshift works, Howard's men won the day, and Hood suffered 5,000 more casualties.

With his three armies in position, Sherman entrenched before Atlanta, with Schofield on the left, Thomas commanding the center, and Howard's army on the right. A direct attack on Atlanta was not even considered as an option. The strength of Rebel fortifications such as abatis, redoubts and chevaux-de-frise (lines of spikes) would require months to take and would incur immense casualties. For the next several days an attempt was made to flush the Rebels out into the open. Union batteries lobbed shells into the streets and buildings of Atlanta all day and into the night, but to no avail. The Army of Tennessee remained in their fortifications, and the citizens cowered in their underground bunkers. Sherman then decided to use strategy instead of force.

In the first week of August, several of Stoneman's cavalrymen returned to the Union lines with bad news. Disobeying his orders to destroy the Macon & Western Railroad, General Stoneman had altered his mission, and had ridden to Andersonville first. In so doing, Stoneman had been unexpectedly confronted by a strong contingent of the enemy and had been captured along with 800 of his men without reaching the railroad. Frustrated over the cavalry's lack of responsibility, Sherman was now determined more than ever to destroy the railroad. Taking matters into his own hands, Sherman decided to march personally his main army south to the Macon line. Obsessed with this objective, during the night of August 25, Sherman moved his troops from their entrenchments around Atlanta and slipped south. The following day, Confederate infantrymen discovered the Union army missing from their trenches. Learning that Sherman had evacuated their front, the people and troops in Atlanta celebrated their good fortune and their startling victory. The celebration was premature.

When Sherman's whereabouts became known, it was evident to Hood that the Union troops were moving south for one reason: to destroy his lifeline, the Macon Railroad. This was a critical time for Hood, because he knew if the railroad was lost, so was Atlanta, a city vital to the survival of the Southern war effort as a home of foundries, factories, munitions plants and supply depots. To Hood, one thing was certain: Sherman's men had to be stopped. Hood mistakenly believed that Sherman had dispatched only two corps south, while the rest of the army withdrew to the north from lack of supplies. Consequently, to handle this mission, he sent out only General Hardee's corps on a 30-mile march south to Jonesboro.

Howard and Thomas were the first to reach the Macon tracks, arriving at a section of rail lines extending from East Point to Red Oak and Fairburn. Setting to work immediately, the soldiers began a well-conceived program of destruction, an exercise they would continue to perform right across the state of Georgia in the months ahead. As Sherman related, "The track was heaved up in sections the length of regiments, then separated rail by rail; bonfires were made of the ties and of fence rails on which the rails were heated, carried to trees or telegraph poles, wrapped around and left to cool." Eventually the thousands of twisted and contorted rails become known as "Sherman's neckties," or "Sherman's hairpins."

Shortly, the Union army was strung out along many miles of the Macon & Western Railroad, having a grand time tearing up the tracks and destroying the stationhouses. General Schofield was at Rough & Ready, Thomas between Schofield and Jonesboro, and Howard at Jonesboro, where he found Hardee's 24,000 troops lying in wait. At that point, the Confederate commander was instructed to attack vigorously with all his forces on August 31. In this desperate hour, Hood would rest the success of this critical assault and the fate of Atlanta on Hardee's shoulders. As soon as Hardee's whereabouts was known, orders were dispatched to Thomas and Schofield to report to Jonesboro on the double-quick. Overwhelmed by the sheer numbers of opposing troops and guns, Hardee's attack failed, and on September 1 Sherman's forces moved in to encircle Hardee's entire corps. Hardee was spared. The coming of darkness prevented the Union army from completing the encirclement, and the Confederate forces escaped south to Lovejoy's station through the only remaining opening in the woods.

With the Macon Railroad out of service, Hood knew by now that Sherman's huge army was within striking distance of Andersonville, the infamous Confederate prison housing over 34,000 Union soldiers. It was imperative, therefore, that the Army of Tennessee position itself to prevent Sherman from releasing the thousands of starved and emaciated prisoners. Postponing his march north to break up the Union communications and supply depot at Marietta, Hood's army travelled south to rendezvous with Hardee at Lovejoy's Station.

The following day, Sherman received a note from one of his corps commanders who had been left behind to monitor the enemy in Atlanta. Gen. Henry W. Slocum sent a message from within Atlanta itself informing Sherman of Hood's departure from the city. As General Sherman had predicted, the futility of remaining in Atlanta, particularly with his supplies cut off, forced General Hood to evacuate his entrenchments and march out into the open. Sherman's grand army was miles away and could not take advantage of this propitious occasion. At the time, Sherman was unaware that Hood was marching toward him to connect with Hardee's corps at Lovejoy's Station.

Following receipt of General Slocum's message, Sherman wired Washington, "Atlanta is ours, and fairly won."

Instead of marching to Andersonville, on September 6 Sherman ordered his men to withdraw north, back to East Point, Atlanta and Decatur, effectively ending the Atlanta campaign.

Both armies remained in place for the rest of the month, recovering from this long and painful campaign.

XIV
The Siege of Petersburg
(June–December 1864)

It was a marvel of Union engineering: 101 pontoons lashed together, gently twisting and bobbing in the current like a huge snake in slow motion. Started at 4 P.M. on June 14, the longest pontoon bridge ever assembled was ready to cross seven hours later. With the aid of several improvised ferries, by midnight of June 16, the entire Union infantry, with its artillery, cavalry and hundreds of wagons were safely across the 2,100-foot James River.

Stung by the harsh criticism of recent weeks over his mounting casualties, Grant had grown wary of attacking Lee's entrenched and well-fortified troops. Therefore, applying his new offensive strategy of attacking Lee's support infrastructure, Grant broke away from the Army of Northern Virginia and focused on luring Lee out of his works with a three-pronged offensive. Grant would attack Lee's supply depot at Lynchburg using General David Hunter's army; his food sources within the Shenandoah Valley with General Sheridan's forces; and with the Army of the Potomac, Grant would threaten the Confederate capital itself. While the Union troops crossed the James, Grant was at Bermuda Hundred, finalizing plans with General Butler on the details of the attack his 18th Corps would make on Petersburg, the key to Richmond and its lifeline to the South.

Petersburg, 22 miles south of Richmond, was the main conduit for all material, troops, food, medical and other supplies and communications between Richmond and the rest of the South. Nearly all the railroads to Richmond from the South connected through Petersburg first. These lines included the Weldon and the Norfolk railroads coming from the Carolinas and the Southside Railroad from the farms of the Shenandoah Valley through Lynchburg in the west. If the Confederacy lost these railroads, Richmond could not survive, and without Richmond, the rebellion would certainly die.

Even now, Richmond was suffering immensely from the lack of food and other commodities. Southern refugees by the thousands were pouring into the city and exacerbating the difficulties there by helping to consume whatever food was left. Chaos ruled the streets of the capital as people fought among themselves for the basic necessities.

The commanding general at Petersburg was General Pierre G.T. Beauregard, who together with a scratch force of only 2,200 troops constituted the entire garrison defending this all-important city. Although heavily fortified with abatis, shielded redans (triangular projections open in the rear and designed to allow for both frontal and flanking fire), and 10 miles of interconnecting rifle pits, the gross disparity between the Rebel defenders and the approaching Yankees concerned Beauregard immensely. Petersburg was so lightly garrisoned that four-and-a-half miles of the city's perimeter lay wide open and completely defenseless. Quickly responding to the unfolding events, on June 14, Beauregard wired Richmond several times, and also General Lee himself, twice, urgently requesting reinforcements. No reply came from either of them. In desperation, Beauregard sent a courier from his own staff to notify General Lee personally of the advancing Union forces and to appeal for additional troops, specifically Beauregard's own forces on loan to the Army of Northern Virginia.

Surprisingly, in a rare turn of events, Grant's move toward Petersburg completely fooled General Lee. The battle by Hunter at Piedmont on June 5 and the cavalry engagement by Sheridan at Trevilian Station on June 11 drew Lee's attention away from the Army of the Potomac. With the Confederate cavalry chasing Sheridan instead of monitoring Union troop movements, Lee lost track of Grant's location. Beauregard was astonished not only by Lee's ignorance of the whereabouts of Grant's army, but also by his failure to accept Beauregard's contention that the Army of the Potomac had crossed the James and that a Union corps was preparing to attack Petersburg.

The first confrontation between the two sides occurred around 7 A.M. June 15 between City Point and Petersburg. Marching his 18th

Corps toward Petersburg, Gen. William F. "Baldy" Smith encountered a small force of Southern cavalrymen. Reinforced with additional troops from the Army of the James, Smith's 18,000 men easily repulsed the Rebel contingent and proceeded on to Petersburg, arriving there around noon.

For most of the day, Smith's forces reconnoitered the Confederate center, hesitantly probing for weaknesses in the strong man-made defenses. The outnumbered Rebels fought back, however, keeping the seemingly timid Union troops at bay while trying desperately to hold on until reinforcements arrived. Finally, around 7 P.M., the sheer number of Union troops overwhelmed the Confederate outer perimeter, and in two hours a good portion of Beauregard's redans fell to the Union invaders. The sudden onslaught drove the Southerners back to the rear and into newly built breastworks, wisely prepared beforehand for such a predictable eventuality.

During the night, Confederate reinforcements came (a division of Beauregard's own troops loaned to Lee's army), and began building additional breastworks to protect themselves during the battle expected in the morning. The advance forces of Meade's Army of the Potomac, composed of two divisions of General Hancock's 2d Corps, also reached Petersburg, as did General Burnside's 9th Corps, bringing the Union front line strength to some 66,000.

Finding his predicament worsening by the hour, on June 16 Beauregard ordered Gen. Bushrod R. Johnson and his troops to evacuate the immediate front of Butler's Army of the James at Bermuda Hundred to assist in defending Petersburg. With General Johnson's forces present on the Rebel line, Beauregard was somewhat comforted by having about 10,000 troops sparsely drawn out along the perimeter of Petersburg. The defenders' numbers were still far from the strength of the approaching attackers.

As the Union troops tramped in from the James River, Beauregard continued his efforts to convince Lee of his dire straits. Inexplicably, Beauregard was unable to convince General Lee that the Army of the Potomac was at Petersburg. Meanwhile, the fight on the 16th was fierce and swift. In a battle lasting only three hours, Union forces stormed the outer works and captured several more redans and rifle pits. By nightfall, the corps of General Warren and General Wright were also on the front lines, bringing the Union forces to approximately 90,000 men, a nine to one advantage over the Confederate forces.

On June 17, the fighting raged on for the entire day and into the night. The Union army, although numerically superior, would not commit to an all-out assault. Instead, the Federals continued to fight against an unseen enemy lurking behind strong defensive barriers. Despite their cautious and limited assault, the bluecoats suffered extremely heavy losses at the hands of a very combative and gallant Rebel force. Eventually, at 11 P.M., Beauregard's hungry, exhausted men could not hold off the overwhelming numbers any longer and were forced to retreat to a new line several miles to the rear. With a late-hour telegraph exchange, General Lee, still not entirely convinced, finally agreed to move his army to Beauregard's assistance. As Lee's message said, "Am not yet satisfied as to General Grant's movements; but upon your representations will move at once to Petersburg."

The first 5,000 soldiers of the Army of Northern Virginia began to arrive by noon of June 18. Even General Lee himself was there to face Hancock, Warren, Burnside, and Wright's corps, with the entire Union artillery force.

At Petersburg, as General Lee scanned the Union line in his front, he may have thought about his three years of defending the Confederate capital, and how he had done the best he could by keeping Union forces away from her borders. Suddenly, everything seemed to be falling apart. Southern troops, predicting the end was near, were deserting in record numbers, recruiting programs for new soldiers no longer existed, weapons and ammunition had to be scavenged from the battlefield, rations were meager, Lee's supply depot was under attack by General Hunter at Lynchburg, his food source was threatened by General Sheridan in the Shenandoah Valley, and the remaining Confederate troops were exhausted, ragged and half-starved. Now the huge Army of the Potomac was at the gates of Petersburg, the "Cockade City," and Lee knew very well that this could be the defining hour for the Confederacy.

As Lee's forces began to arrive, Hancock's troops renewed the assault but were repulsed. At 4 P.M., a second attack by all three corps was made; even this was set back by the tenacious Southern fighters. Later a third try with the 5th and 9th Corps also failed. An example of the terrible losses experienced by the Union forces that day can be illustrated by the 1st Maine Regiment. In 10 minutes, the 1st Maine suffered 632 killed or wounded out of 900 men. This was the greatest loss of any Union regiment in one single engagement.

General Grant was greatly disappointed by the results of the Petersburg assaults. Considering the huge disparity of men and firepower, Grant was highly critical of General Smith's failed effort to take Petersburg on June 15, or even with the support from General Hancock's additional forces the following day. Perhaps the Union's lack of aggressiveness was part of the so-called "Cold Harbor syndrome," the growing fear of storming Confederate breastworks which, based on past experiences, meant certain death for the soldier or failure for the commander; or perhaps the Union commanders were unconvinced of the magnitude of disparity between the two sides. General Smith, responding to his critics, "Deeming that I held the important points of the enemy's line of works, I thought it prudent to make no further advance."

In spite of the Union's new tactical strategy of limited attacks on entrenched forces, this was one frontal assault that should have been made and one that certainly would have succeeded.

Following Grant's abortive attempt to take the Weldon Railroad on June 22, matters began to take on a different tone. Having already suffered 12,000 casualties, there was little left for the Federals to gain from additional assaults on the entrenched Rebels, except more casualties. Accordingly, the Union settled in for a siege. Burnside's 9th Corps took the right, Warren's 5th and Birney's 2d the center (David Birney was temporarily filling in for Hancock, who had been taken from the field suffering from a reopened wound received at Gettysburg), and Wright's 6th Corps was on the left. Here would be decided the fates of Richmond, the Confederacy and perhaps the rebellion itself.

When Lee dispatched reinforcements to assist General Early, then in the Shenandoah Valley advancing toward Washington, Grant immediately capitalized on the Confederates' reduced manpower by extending the Union lines farther around Petersburg. It was also during this time that a bizarre scheme was devised in which Grant and Meade half-heartedly acquiesced. It was an outrageous idea, but one that might have broken the standoff and enabled the Union to carry Petersburg. The plan was to dig a tunnel under the Confederate line, charge the tunnel with explosives, and, following the detonation, overrun the rebel works and the defenders, and take Petersburg.

The idea belonged to Lt. Col. Henry Pleasants, a mining engineer with the 48th Pennsylvania Volunteers. Colonel Pleasants' division commander presented the scheme to General Burnside, who approved it and began outlining the post-detonation assault strategy.

In spite of criticism contending that the tunnel would cave in, or the rebel artillery on the surface would be too heavy, or that something like this just could not be done, plans for the project went forward. A regiment of Pennsylvania coal miners, mostly from Schuylkill County, was rounded up and began digging the tunnel on June 25. Pleasants first had to overcome the enormous difficulties he met from the support and lack of materials. Refused lumber, he went to a sawmill outside Union lines. Denied mining picks, he redesigned standard picks to his own specifications, and for wheelbarrows, he equipped cracker boxes with iron hoops from discarded barrels to carry out the dirt. He even used an obsolete surveying tool, a theodolite, borrowed from a civilian, to plot distance and direction coordinates.

Finally, on July 23, the massive tunnel was ready. The main shaft was 510 feet long, the longest military tunnel in history. Extending from the sides of the main tunnel were two additional chambers, one to the left and one to the right, each around 38 feet long, that would hold the explosive charge: four magazines of gunpowder in each chamber totaling four tons of explosives.

Following the blast, the initial charge to the Confederate lines would be carried out by a division of black troops, who were specifically trained for this operation, from General Burnside's 9th Corps, commanded by Gen. Edward Ferrero. Quickly following them would be several brigades, also from Burnside's corps, from divisions under Gens. James H. Ledlie, Orlando B. Willcox and Robert B. Potter, and finally the entire 5th and 18th Corps. Everything sounded fine and promised to be a rousing success. At the last minute the plans changed. The black soldiers were removed from the lead assault. General Meade evidently had second thoughts about the advisability of sending black troops in first. Because they lacked combat experience, Meade did not trust their ability to hold up under fire. In addition, if he was proven correct and the charge went awry, Meade feared it would appear that he had knowingly sacrificed hundreds of black men to save white lives. Therefore, by a draw of straws, General Ledlie's brigades under Col. E.G. Marshall and Gen. William F. Bartlett would go in first.

At 3:30 in the morning, on July 30, as Ledlie's troops stood by, the fuse was lighted. For these Union troops, the strain and anxiety were made even more unbearable by the long, silent wait as the fuse slowly burned toward its target. Eagerly anticipated for over a month, the time for the explosion had finally arrived.

After waiting for an hour, a check in the tunnel disclosed that the 90-foot fuse had burned out at a splice. With the fuse relighted, the mine soon exploded in a thunderous roar of fire, earth, rocks, wood, guns and men. The Confederate fortifications at ground zero were completely destroyed, along with an entire Confederate regiment and one artillery battery. In the immediate vicinity, the surviving Rebels fled for their lives, terror-stricken at the sight of the mushroom cloud. Even the Union soldiers, terrified by what they had just witnessed, abandoned their positions and ran for cover. By the time the cloud of dirt, debris and mangled bodies had settled back to earth, the Union line had reformed. At a given signal, Colonel Marshall's brigade was on its way, charging over the 130 yards to the crater through the white smoke and dust still lingering in the air. The massive crater created by the huge explosion was about 200 feet long, 60 feet wide, and 30 feet deep.

The Union advance was not sustained. Marshall's brigade, in awe, stopped to gape into the huge hole, impeding the advance of Bartlett's troops who were right behind them. When the order came to resume the charge, instead of going around the hole, Marshall's men went directly into the crater, as did the troops in Bartlett's unit. Worse, once inside the crater, the men found it almost impossible to climb up the steep 30-foot walls of soft dirt without falling back to the bottom.

For the few who did climb out, another disaster waited. By this time, the Confederate troops had regained their composure, and several manned a battery redan to the left of the crater; a Rebel infantry contingent was also poised to attack from a depression a short distance away. As the Union men climbed from the crater, volley after volley of deadly canister was fired, killing them on the spot.

At this point, a third brigade, commanded by Gen. Simon G. Griffin, was directed from the Union lines to continue the attack. Upon nearing the crater, Griffin's men were also exposed to the heavy barrage of canister from the Confederate battery. Running for the nearest cover, Griffin's brigade likewise entered the crater and was trapped in the hole along with the rest of the Union troops.

It was now around 7 A.M. The order was given for Ferrero's black division to enter the battle. Disappointed over not leading the charge, the black troops were nevertheless determined to show the white soldiers what they could do. When Ferrero's men charged across the open ground, Confederate orders were barked out to take the white men, but kill the blacks. Under a steady barrage of artillery, musketry, and canister, the Southerners were hell-bent on slaughtering each and every black on the field. In spite of the horrific Confederate fire, Ferrero's division advanced around the crater and captured over 200 men from the infantry force firing from the depression. After about 20 minutes of this deadly exposure, without reinforcements or protective cover, the black troops broke and quickly retreated to the Union lines. Taking advantage of the mass confusion, a large number of troops ran from the crater and made their own escape. In the end, Ferrero's division lost 913 gallant soldiers.

During a lull in the fighting, the Union commanders reviewed their options for rescuing the thousands of Union men still trapped in the crater. The decision was made to wait it out for the rest of day, that the best opportunity for success would be under cover of darkness. Suddenly, the sound of gunshots came from the crater. During the inactivity, the Confederate soldiers, under Gen. William Mahone, of Bushrod R. Johnson's division, had reorganized. Now, with fixed bayonets, they advanced into the crater to engage in hand-to-hand combat. The bloody confrontation was mercifully short, because the Union troops were relatively defenseless and could offer only feeble resistance. Those who did resist were shot or bayoneted; the rest were taken prisoner.

The Battle of the Crater was a bad episode for the Army of the Potomac. The Union lost 4,000 men—killed, wounded or captured. Embarrassed over this tragic fiasco, Grant called it "a stupendous failure" and "the saddest affair I have ever witnessed in the War."

The immediate commander of the operation, Gen. James H. Ledlie, was not present on the field to control the assault. He was found hiding in a bombproof, drunk on rum while his men were being killed. Following a hearing by a court of inquiry, Ledlie was dismissed from the Army in disgrace. Once the commander of the Army of the Potomac itself, Gen. Ambrose E. Burnside, whose corps conducted the attack Burnside thought would capture Petersburg and end the war, resigned from military service.

After the disaster of July 30, the adversaries settled back into their siege mentality, although they did conduct a series of small confrontations, frequent skirmishes, and bold raids. Carried on over a 10-month period, these actions were seemingly designed on one side to wear down the opponent through attrition, versus a commitment by the other side to resist at all costs. Commanders in both camps closely monitored the movements of their opponents, looking for signs of weakness where they could themselves shift troops for an advantage of their own, only to be counter-moved. It was a daily battle of maneuvers and tactics with one general always trying to outwit the other.

Fighting conditions at Petersburg were in some sense a prelude to World War I trench warfare. The Confederates by this time had become master builders of fortifications. Their defenses included redans, redoubts, trenches, bombproofs, abatis, gabions (a cylinder of wicker filled with dirt and rocks), infantry parapets (small walls in front of trenches to protect the infantry therein), stakes and chevaux-de-frise. General Lee's line was thinly stretched over a distance of 35 miles; these defensive measures maintained the standoff and safeguarded that thin line.

On the Union side, miles of trenches, tunnel-like covered trenches known as covered-ways, and bombproofs were the order of the day. Although their fortifications were not as sophisticated as the Confederate works, the Union troops were not on the defensive. The dank conditions in these works, marked by fly infestation and exposure to the searing sun, forced such improvisation as described by one Union private: "The bombproofs were damp and unhealthy, so we had our tents out in the open air and fled to the bombproofs when danger threatened us."

For the balance of 1864, several small battles did break out that kept both sides fairly active. The railroads that Lee depended on for his supplies were General Grant's primary targets, and because the Confederate supply routes were so limited, Lee was expected to fight hard to protect them from capture. And fight he did. But on August 18, General Warren's 5th Corps captured the Weldon Railroad. Far from giving up, Lee tried repeatedly to dislodge Warren from his new trenches, but each time the Confederates were repulsed. With the railroad in Northern hands and the bridges destroyed, Lee was forced to use wagons to transport materials the 30 miles from the coast to his camp.

In September, the 18th Corps, now under Gen. Edward O. Ord,

the 10th Corps under Gen. David B. Birney, and a cavalry force under Gen. August V. Kautz from the Army of the James, were sent to threaten Richmond. Meant to create a diversion to prevent Lee from sending more troops to the Shenandoah Valley, the Union troops overpowered the strong Confederate lines and captured Fort Harrison. In the afternoon the Union attempts to continue their drive failed. Grant's casualties exceeded 2,000 killed, wounded or missing, including General Ord, who fell badly wounded and was replaced by Gen. Godfrey Weitzel.

With the Weldon Railroad safely in Union hands, General Meade tried to take the South Side Railroad on October 27. Again, the Confederate fortifications were so strong that Grant saw the futility in further expenditure of young lives. Unable to come closer than six miles to the railroad, the Union troops were withdrawn the same day.

While Grant and Lee waited out the siege at Petersburg, in Missouri Confederate Gen. Sterling Price and 12,000 troops threatened St. Louis, Jefferson City and Kansas City. Challenging Price on October 23 was Gen. Samuel Curtis. Fighting the Confederates with the help of Alfred Pleasonton's cavalry at Westport, Missouri, Curtis turned back the Rebels, driving them into Arkansas. This small battle represented the last Confederate offensive west of the Mississippi.

President Lincoln proclaimed the last Thursday in November a National Day of Thanksgiving. It was a great day for the Army of the Potomac. The Union cooks served 120,000 turkey and chicken dinners while the Confederates sat it out peacefully in respect for the Union holiday. Gen. Winfield S. Hancock, recovered from his Gettysburg wound, was relieved in November from command of the 2d Corps. Called to Washington, Hancock would organize and lead a new and larger command, the 1st Corps. Comprising mostly veteran troops, Hancock's new command was expected to be ready in time for the spring offensive. The new commander of the 2d Corps was Army of the Potomac Chief of Staff Gen. Andrew A. Humpreys.

In Washington, meanwhile, the presidential election of 1864 was over. Abraham Lincoln easily won his reelection bid for the $25,000-a-year post. The president's Democratic rival, former Gen. George B. McClellan, was a popular candidate and a significant rallying point for those opposed to Lincoln's war policies. Many Northerners were war-weary, and represented a voting constituency highly in tune with the Democratic platform. Trying to appeal to the "doves" of that day,

McClellan consistently highlighted in his speeches his preference to end the rebellion by peaceful means, rather then by war. For the first time, 19 states enacted legislation that permitted their Union soldiers to vote in camp via absentee ballots. The troops unable to cast their ballots in camp were furloughed home to vote. The Democratic Party, convinced that the Union army was heavily Republican, failed in its efforts to block the new provision from passing in a majority of states. As a result, for the 12 states that counted the soldiers' ballots, Lincoln received almost 80 percent of their votes, significantly influencing the outcome of the election. Lincoln won all the states except Kentucky, Delaware and New Jersey, and gathered an electoral count of 212 to 21.

With 1865 quickly approaching, General Grant's plans for the spring offensive were designed for only one purpose: to end the war. General Hancock's army would be either in the Shenandoah Valley or in the Lynchburg area. General Sherman's forces were expected to arrive from the South, General Meade and the Army of the Potomac would still be covering the outskirts of Petersburg and Richmond, and General Thomas, presently in Tennessee, would move into Western Virginia. Grant hoped that his calculated movements, designed to encircle the Army of Northern Virginia, would cut off Lee's supplies. Without his supplies, Lee would be hard pressed to support his army.

As the armies went into winter quarters, Grant said, "I could not see how it was possible for the Confederates to hold out much longer where they are. Desertions were taking place throughout the whole Confederacy. It was my belief that the enemy were losing at least a regiment a day by desertions alone. It was a mere question of arithmetic to calculate how long they could hold out."

XV
Fight for the Shenandoah Valley
(June–October 1864)

Two days before the Union army crossed the James, Gen. Jubal A. Early received an order to prepare Ewell's 2d Corps for a march from the outskirts of Cold Harbor to Lynchburg. Concerned over General Hunter's foray to his rear, Lee's instructions to Early were to stop Hunter in his tracks and then to march his 10,000 men north through the Shenandoah Valley, cross the Potomac and threaten Washington. With Early's threat drawing attention, Lee anticipated Grant weakening his army by sending reinforcements to shore up the outer defenses of Washington.

The 47-year-old Early, a grizzled and cantankerous veteran of Chancellorsville and Gettysburg, was a native of Virginia, born in Franklin County. Called "Old Jube" by his troops, Early was also a graduate of the U.S. Military Academy and was highly regarded by General Lee. Supporting Early would be Gen. John C. Breckinridge, who was leading a ragtag army recently thrown together and currently behind breastworks at Lynchburg.

Arriving at the Rivanna River on June 16, near Charlottesville, Early was able to board only half of his troops on the few trains available for the trip to Lynchburg on the 17th. Following their arrival that afternoon, the trains returned for the remainder of the army.

At Lynchburg, Early dispersed his troops along a defensive line on the outer edge of Breckinridge's works. The defenders, besides Breckinridge's infantry, included patients from the nearby Confederate hospital considered well enough to carry a musket, and even the young cadets from the Virginia Military Institute at Lexington. As soon as Early's remaining troops arrived on the 18th, plans were made to attack Hunter the following morning. At daylight, the Confederates were surprised to find that Hunter and his 15,000 men had withdrawn from Lynchburg.

A 61-year-old political appointee, Hunter relished his first command since being wounded in the first Battle of Bull Run. Leading his Army of West Virginia into the valley, Hunter had swept aside a smaller Confederate force after killing its commander, Gen. William E. "Grumble" Jones, and capturing about 2,000 of his men at Piedmont, Virginia, on June 5. After a number of devastating attacks on his supply trains by the notorious ex–Confederate cavalry scout John Singleton Mosby and his Rebel band of guerrillas, Hunter had become preoccupied with a violent obsession against everyone and everything Confederate. Acting like a band of guerrillas themselves, Hunter and his army had left a trail of reckless destruction and unjustifiable cruelty along their march from Piedmont to Lexington. Terrorizing and foraging from Southern civilians took on a whole new dimension, as well as did the spiteful and wholesale destruction of personal property. Even the governor's residence and the Virginia Military Institute had not been spared the wrath of Hunter's army. As one of Hunter's men explained, "We feel the South brought on the war and the State of Virginia is paying dear for her part." Leaving Lexington in flames, Hunter had arrived at Lynchburg with very little ammunition left to fight the now reinforced Confederate defenses there. Consequently, that night, Hunter had decided to withdraw his army toward the Blue Ridge Mountains in West Virginia, a mistake in judgment that would eventually cost Hunter his command. Because he retreated west, Hunter left the Shenandoah Valley free and clear to the Confederate forces, and opened the way for Early to carry out the second phase of his mission: advancing on Washington.

Immediately ordered in pursuit, on June 21 Early's men, along with the troops of Breckinridge's army, caught up with Hunter at Buford's Gap in the Blue Ridge Mountains. Having eaten little during the 60 mile, three-day chase, Early called off the hunt and gave his hungry and exhausted troops a day to rest.

His tactics reminiscent of Jackson's march down the valley in 1861, General Early broke camp on June 23 and began his advance toward Washington. When Early reached Staunton on the 27th with nearly half of his men without shoes and only seven days' rations, his dedicated troops faithfully went on, eager to reach their prime objective. Burning all the bridges in their wake, the Confederate force reached Martinsburg on July 3, and when Union Gen. Franz Sigel evacuated the town, Early took possession of the abundant supply of rations left behind. Finally, on the afternoon of July 5, General Breckinridge's command crossed the Potomac at Shepherdstown, followed by Early's troops the next day. By July 8, Early's entire force was moving through the South Mountain passes over a wide swath from Crampton's and Fox's Gaps to Boonsboro's Gap. As the Rebel army steadily advanced toward the Monocacy River, the Confederate cavalry north of Frederick created a great deal of havoc themselves, destroying the railroads connecting Baltimore to Harrisburg and Philadelphia and the rail line between Baltimore and Washington. While occupying Frederick, Early persuaded the distressed town fathers to "contribute" the tidy sum of $200,000 to his cause.

In the Union camp meanwhile, General Grant was fully briefed on the seriousness of Early's successes and of the extremely limited manpower on hand for protecting the nation's capital. In response to this latest crisis, Grant instructed General Meade to dispatch two infantry corps to Washington. The 19th Corps under Gen. William H. Emory was directed to proceed from Fort Monroe, and the 6th Corps, General Wright's command, was sent to reinforce Fort Stevens.

At the Monocacy River near Frederick, Maryland, 30 miles from the capital, a small army commanded by Union General Lew Wallace, although vastly outnumbered, anxiously waited to confront the wayward Confederates. With the Shenandoah Valley lying in his district, Wallace and his men were responsible for its defense. Mostly recruits with little combat experience, the young soldiers took a stand on the east bank of the river. Their mission was to protect the railroad bridge as well as the bridge on the Georgetown Pike. The fighting was savage, and Wallace's little army was severely tested. By sunset, even with the reinforcements from General Wright's corps, who had been diverted from their march to Fort Stevens, Wallace found it impossible to hold off his enemy any longer. The Union army was driven back, and about 650 bluecoats taken captive. Early's troops crossed the river the night of the 9th, and the road to Washington was open and free of Union resistance.

At daylight, the Confederate troops began their march toward the Union capital. Excited over the success of their campaign and the prospect of capturing Washington, Early's men stepped off on the Georgetown Pike with a bounce in their stride indicative of their pride in their accomplishment and the high expectations for the day ahead. Within a few hours, the steamy, hot and humid July weather caused many to fall out by the roadside, too weak to continue. Finally, around noon on July 11, the exhausted Rebels reached the outskirts of Washington, in sight of Fort Stevens and the white dome of the Capitol in the distance.

In Washington, people talked in fear of nothing but the approaching Confederate troops. As anxiety mounted, roads leading north and south were thronged with Washingtonians, fleeing from this totally unexpected incursion into their lives. To shore up the weakened defenses, the governors of Massachusetts, Pennsylvania and New York were urged to recruit "hundred-days men" to help defend the city against Early's invasion. In near panic, shops closed so that clerks could help man the some-900 guns surrounding the capital. A number of convalescent soldiers considered fit enough to leave their hospital beds were also pressed into service. Even President Lincoln himself went to Fort Stevens to survey the battlefront.

As he gazed out toward his enemy, Early's first priority was to reconnoiter the fort to determine its strength and to assess the feasibility of assaulting the Union works. Early found the fortifications of heavy artillery, protected by ditches, palisades (fences of stakes), and abatis much too strong to carry by assault. To intimidate Early even more, Gen. Horatio G. Wright's 6th Corps also arrived on the 11th and was seen filing into Fort Stevens by the Confederate troops that very afternoon. Considering the poor condition of his troops and the formidable defenses confronting them, Early decided to withdraw before the South Mountain passes were closed to his retreat.

This decision did not satisfy his troops, however, as one complained later, "A volley, a Rebel yell, and a vigorous charge would have given us Washington." Even the Union press was surprised that the Confederates failed to attack. A *New York Herald* reporter later wrote, "I have always wondered at Early's inaction. Washington was never more helpless. Our lines in his front could have been carried at any point."

If General Early had arrived on July 10, just one day before Wright's corps, he would have attacked the outmanned fortification without hesitation, and possibly even the Union capital itself. In this regard, Grant considered General Wallace's loss at the Monocacy River a tremendous victory in disguise, because in effect Wallace's valiant and stubborn resistance against heavy odds delayed the Confederates that one day and gave Wright the time to reach the fort and save Washington from attack.

That night, after consulting with his generals, Early and his Confederate army withdrew from the gates of Washington. Marching by way of Rockville and Poolesville, they crossed the Potomac at Leesburg and reentered the Shenandoah Valley through Snickers Gap to Berryville, Virginia.

Badly shaken over the near disaster to the Union capital, and with Early still at large in the Shenandoah Valley, Grant's attention shifted from Petersburg. Grant now focused on stopping this wily old Rebel and on destroying once and for all the Southern farmlands the Confederates depended on so dearly. At his headquarters outside Petersburg, Grant must have been extremely frustrated considering the recent disappointments of his three-pronged campaign. With General Smith failing to take Petersburg and General Hunter abandoning the valley to the Confederates, Grant felt he must act decisively, without hesitation.

Bypassing the Washington red tape, Grant selected cavalry commander Gen. Philip H. Sheridan, then at Harpers Ferry, to command a new army, the Army of the Shenandoah. Sheridan, a five-foot, five-inch son of Irish immigrants, was to rout General Early from the Shenandoah and lay waste the many farms proliferating there, as well as their capacity to continue supporting the Southern war effort.

To Union military strategists, the Shenandoah Valley was a tremendous asset to the Confederacy, more so than to the North. As an immensely fertile region supplying the Rebel armies with vegetables, livestock and grains, the valley could also be used by the Southern forces as a superhighway to invade Maryland and Pennsylvania. Configured in a southwest to northeast direction, and conveniently hidden between the Blue Ridge and Allegheny Mountains, its natural line gave the Rebel forces an excellent path to their Northern objectives, particularly Washington. On the other hand, the Yankee forces marching south through the valley were carried away from their

Southern targets in Virginia, especially Richmond. Speaking of Grant's plan to devastate the valley, Gen. Wesley Merritt wrote that, "the advantage would be with us, who did not want it as a source of supplies, nor a place of arms, and against the Confederates, who wanted it for both."

An indication of Grant's frustration was evident in the tone of his instructions to Sheridan. Addressing his new commander, Grant ordered him to pursue Early "and to follow him to the death." As for destroying the Southern farmlands, Grant's position was equally resolute. In clear terms, Sheridan was told that by the time his men had finished with the valley, crows flying over the region for the rest of the season should have to carry their own rations with them.

Sheridan's new command, the Army of the Shenandoah, had some 37,000 men. It was formed by combining the 6th Corps, borrowed from the Army of the Potomac, under Gen. Horatio G. Wright, with two divisions from the 19th Corps led by Gen. William H. Emery, and two divisions from Hunter's old command. The force came to a total of seven infantry divisions, in addition to a considerable artillery force, and a cavalry arm of two divisions commanded by Gen. Alfred T. Torbert.

Sheridan's enemy, a much smaller army of about 15,000 soldiers, consisted of three infantry divisions commanded by Gens. John B. Gordon, Stephen D. Ramseur, and Robert E. Rodes. In addition, two divisions led by Kershaw and Wharton were sent from Anderson's corps of the Army of Northern Virginia. Early also commanded two divisions of cavalry, one brigade of artillery, and could still count on support from the forces under General Breckinridge.

On the morning of August 10, the Army of the Shenandoah set out from Halltown, West Virginia, near Harpers Ferry, in pursuit of the Confederate agitator in the valley. Earlier, as Sheridan was preparing his army for its first operation as a newly organized unit, the authorities in Washington had advised Sheridan on the scope of his campaign, at least from their perspective. In several months, the presidential election between Lincoln and the Democratic candidate, former Union general and Lincoln's old antagonizer George B. McClellan, would be decided. The administration feared that if the rebellion dragged on without significant Union gains, the war-weary voters could decide to reject the president, in favor of the "peace" candidate, McClellan. By the time the briefing was over, Sheridan was fully impressed with the notion that if his army was not successful, the Democrats might lose the White House, which event, Sheridan wrote, "would at least retard the progress of the war, if, indeed it did not lead to the complete abandonment of all coercive measures."

Whether this briefing had any impact on Sheridan's campaign strategy remains a matter of conjecture. For about the next six weeks, the Army of the Shenandoah got off to a very slow start indeed. Sheridan moved his army very carefully and with more caution then would normally be expected from a general of his stature. Playing a game of hit and run, the two armies sparred and wove, fighting minor but bloody skirmishes, mostly between Berryville and Winchester. The only significant incident occurred when Tolbert's cavalry rounded up all the cattle and livestock in that vicinity and burned all the grain from Cedar Creek to Berryville.

Despite his dire circumstances at Petersburg, General Lee had previously sent the Kershaw and Wharton divisions from Anderson's corps 25 pieces of artillery and a number of cavalrymen to help reinforce Early against Sheridan's forces. At Winchester, Early received a dispatch ordering one of the divisions back to the Confederate lines at Petersburg. Taking advantage of Lee's weaker defenses, Grant had cut one of Lee's supply lines by capturing the Weldon Railroad. This act forced Lee to depend on wagons to carry his supplies on a longer route which now required more men to protect the wagons.

From an informant living in Winchester, Sheridan learned that Kershaw's division had been called back to Petersburg on September 14, and that Early had taken Gordon and Rodes' divisions north to Martinsburg to destroy the Baltimore and Ohio Railroad. This left only Ramseur and Wharton at Winchester. With the rest of the army too far away to help, Sheridan seized this opportunity to strike with his entire force, and was confident that he would crush the two Confederate divisions defending Winchester.

Battle plans were quickly drawn up, positions assigned and orders issued. The Battle of Winchester, or Opequon Creek, was set for September 19. The Union offensive began in the moonlight of the early morning hours when Union cavalrymen attacked a small contingent of Rebel defenders covering the passage over Opequon Creek. The entrenched Confederates were no match for the Union horsemen and were quickly driven off, opening the way for the corps of Wright and Emery to ford the creek safely. An unexpected misfortune occurred when Emery's command became tangled among the guns and trains of Wright's corps. This confusion forced Emery to stand aside and wait until the way was clear to move. This unfortunate delay gave General Early enough time to march the divisions of Gordon and Rodes back to Winchester before Sheridan's troops commenced their fire, with Breckinridge arriving later that afternoon.

Finally, by 11:30 A.M., when Union tempers were composed and the cursing had subsided, the lines were once again organized. The Union bluecoats began their attack. Sheridan took full advantage of his superior artillery support as his guns blasted the resilient Southerners with shell and canister. Fighting in the open, both sides suffered heavily with mounting casualties. The fighting raged on all day, but as dusk approached, concerted attacks by two Union cavalry divisions, sporting rapid-firing carbines, and the entire Union infantry, drove the Confederates from the field. General Early took his army limping south down the valley, 20 miles to Fisher's Hill, with the Union victors close behind them on the main valley pike.

Even though Early was able to regroup his forces at Winchester, Sheridan's overwhelming manpower was too much for the Southerners to handle. When the dust finally settled, both sides reported casualties of over 4,000 men killed, wounded or missing. Among the Confederate casualties was Gen. Robert E. Rodes, veteran of Chancellorsville, Gettysburg and the Wilderness, killed in a fight along the Berryville Road. Although the Battle of Winchester was a resounding victory for Sheridan, it may have been a hollow victory considering that the main objective of his original plan had been to destroy nearly half of Early's army.

With the defeat of Early's forces at Winchester and the Confederate retreat to Fisher's Hill, Sheridan and his Army of the Shenandoah now held the Shenandoah Valley from Strasburg to the Potomac, much to the relief of the Northern border states as well as the national capital.

Early's retreat to Fisher's Hill was his most logical move to establish a serious defense against the pursuing Yankees. Just south of Strasburg, Fisher's Hill was protected by the Massanutten Mountains and a fork of the Shenandoah River. It was more significant that at that point the valley narrowed to only four or five miles, affording the Confederates a considerable degree of security.

On September 22, the Battle of Fisher's Hill was quick and decisive in favor of the Union forces. As a result of Sheridan's reconnaissance several days before, a frontal assault on Early's strong position had been ruled out. Instead, Sheridan would attack the Confederates where they were most vulnerable, their left flank at Little North Mountain. Accordingly, under the cover of darkness, General George Crooks' command marched close to the Confederate stronghold and hid in the nearby woods. Suddenly, while James Ricketts' division created a diversion, Crooks' men burst from the woods and completely surprised the unsuspecting Rebels. Quickly joined by the entire Union infantry, the fast-moving charge swept the stunned Confederates back. With little time to form a line of defense, the Confederate soldiers faced a choice of certain capture or a hasty retreat. Wasting little time to decide, Early abandoned his camp and ordered an immediate general retreat, which eventually turned into a complete rout. Fleeing down the Shenandoah Valley, the Confederate army marched 15 miles to Woodstock. As darkness fell, Sheridan's men gave up their chase and went into camp, as did Early's men a short distance away.

The following day Early continued his withdrawal, this time moving farther on to Waynesboro. At this point, Early took a sudden easterly route for the vicinity of Port Republic to await reinforcements coming through Brown's Gap. The Confederate reinforcements were the men of Kershaw's division, who were on their way back to Petersburg. Learning of Early's defeat at Winchester and the subsequent rout, General Lee ordered Kershaw, camped at Culpeper, back to help in Early's defense.

When Early broke off the main road and went east, Sheridan assumed that the Confederates were beaten and retreating from the valley through the Blue Ridge. In this context, Sheridan let down his guard, relaxed his security and began the second phase of his mission, to lay waste the Southern breadbasket, after which he intended to return to Petersburg.

In Washington, President Lincoln was monitoring Sheridan's movements with much trepidation. Concerned over a possible Union defeat, Lincoln worried over the repercussions a loss would have on his election and the future of the rebellion.

Over the next few weeks, Sheridan's men began their deeds of destruction. They destroyed the harvest, rounded up the livestock and ravaged the land. Elsewhere, Tolbert's cavalry demolished huge quantities of supplies at Staunton, pulled up railroad tracks and burned all the bridges in the surrounding area.

Sheridan's earlier assessment of Early's maneuver to the east was wrong. Early was not retreating from the Valley. With their reinforcements back, the Confederate army was now about 20,000 strong; when informed of the devastation to their farmland, the Rebels seethed with anger and swore revenge.

Allowing that Sheridan was the field commander, Grant permitted his general the option of driving Early into eastern Virginia or returning to the Army of the Potomac. Still considering his mission essentially over, Sheridan chose the second option and began his withdrawal from the Shenandoah Valley on October 6. General Grant did not favor this decision. On October 16, Sheridan was called to Washington to meet with Secretary of War Stanton to discuss the future of his operation.

Following their pursuit of Early down the Shenandoah Pike, the Union army settled down on the north side of Cedar Creek, 20 miles south of Winchester. Secure in their knowledge that the Confederate forces were whipped, Sheridan's men took on an air of relaxed complacency. Their attitude was in error. With Sheridan away from his army and General Wright in temporary command, the Confederates were more than eager to strike.

On October 19, early on a dark and chilly fall morning, Early's troops, once again on Fisher's Hill, secretly filed down from their camp, only six miles from the Union bivouac. Then, with only the moonlight to guide them, the Confederates silently snaked their way across the Shenandoah River, and by dawn, still undetected, were quickly positioned in battle formations. With their muskets primed and loaded, Early's men were ready to begin the Battle of Cedar Creek.

At a given signal, thousands of Rebel-yelling Southern soldiers exploded into the Union camp and surprised the sleeping soldiers and officers of the 6th and 19th Corps. Catapulted into a sudden state of panic, the Union troops rushed from their tents incredulous over this new turn of events. Trying desperately to form a battle line to fight off the Confederate invaders proved a futile exercise, and the spooked Union troops fled for their lives. Thousands of Federals were killed, wounded or captured without raising their weapons, and in one hour the Union camp fell.

Southern forces were exhilarated over the success of their surprise attack and pursued the shattered enemy with a newfound energy. As General Gordon prepared to apply the coup de grace to the outnumbered Union 6th Corps, General Early rode up and called off the attack, simply explaining, "No use, they will all go directly." Dumbfounded over this lost opportunity, Gordon could not believe his ears, and would later call Early "the evil genius of the South."

On the Northern side, by sheer coincidence, General Sheridan had returned to the front that morning and witnessed with disbelieving eyes his disorganized army abandoning the field. When Sheridan's men saw their commander riding into their midst, rousing cheers filled the air and almost instantly the mood reversed. As word of Sheridan's return spreads, the stragglers stopped their retreat and, newly inspired, returned to the fight. Galloping through the front, waving his hat and calling his men, Sheridan rallied his troops for a counterattack. "About face, boys! We're going back to our camps! We're going to lick them out of their boots!"

By mid-afternoon, while Gen. George A. Custer, commander of the 3d Cavalry, kept the Confederates occupied, the Union lines of the 6th and 19th Corps were again reorganized, and at 4 P.M., a forward movement was ordered. As one witness later described the scene, "To one who had seen the rout and panic and loss of the morning, it seemed impossible that this was the same army."

As the two infantry forces clashed in a din of shot, shell, canister and musketry, the Union cavalry was ordered into action. Charging into both Confederate flanks through the smoke and fire, the Union horsemen broke the Rebel line as the Yankee infantry advanced headlong into the center. Amazingly, the vanquished were now the victors as the stunned Confederates themselves were repulsed in a wild rout.

The Confederate army, broken and dejected, retreated to New Market, relentlessly hunted by General Custer's cavalrymen. Early's army was finished, and would soon be called back to Richmond.

General Sheridan's campaign was a huge success. The Army of the Shenandoah left the Southern farmland a desolate landscape of destruction. As testimony to this effort, Sheridan left a written record bearing witness to the scope of his accomplishment. The buildings and materials destroyed or seized included 1,200 barns, 71 flour mills, eight sawmills, seven furnaces, four tanneries, three saltpeter works, a woolen mill with 1,165 pounds of cotton yarn, a powder mill, a railroad depot, and 974 miles of rail. The livestock taken included 15,000 swine, 12,000 sheep, 10,918 cattle, 3,772 horses, 545 mules, and 250 calves, with 435,802 bushels of wheat, 77,176 bushels of corn, 20,397 tons of hay, 500 tons of fodder, 450 tons of straw, 12,000 pounds of bacon, 10,000 pounds of tobacco, and 874 barrels of flour.

Sheridan's victory was pivotal. This staggering amount of destruction and confiscation at the hands of his army assured, without a doubt, that the Shenandoah Valley would be useless to the Confederate army and to the South for some time. Without the Shenandoah Valley, Lee's critical supplies were cut off. Without supplies, the end was indeed in sight for the Confederacy. The Republican administration in Washington could breathe easier now, knowing Lincoln's reelection was imminent. With their mission completed, the Army of the Shenandoah returned to Petersburg.

XVI
Sherman's March to the Sea
(October–December 1864)

Having occupied Atlanta since early September, General Sherman was growing impatient and eager to move on. Now nearly a month later, his enemy, Confederate Gen. John Bell Hood, took the initiative ahead of the Union army by breaking camp at Palmetto, Georgia, and crossing the Chattahoochee River on September 29. At this moment, Hood was marching 45,000 troops toward Lost Mountain and the Western and Atlantic Railroad in Sherman's rear.

The Rebel general was under a presidential order to break up the Western and Atlantic, which connected Chattanooga to Atlanta. It was from a huge supply depot in Chattanooga that the Western and Atlanic line delivered food and materials to Sherman's army in Atlanta. Consequently, Hood's march toward Sherman's supply line was not a random maneuver but part of a comprehensive Southern strategy to cut Sherman off from the supplies he needed to continue fighting. President Jefferson Davis apparently believed that if the South cut off Sherman's food supply, the Union troops would become so weak from starvation that General Hood's forces could easily destroy them, or Sherman would have to retreat in disgrace. Whatever Sherman decided, President Davis assured the Southern people, the Confederate army would be victorious. To support this strategy, Davis also had cavalry Gen. Nathan B. Forrest and his forces, as well as cavalry commander

Gen. Joseph Wheeler's troopers, destroying railroads and depots in Tennessee and Kentucky.

To keep an eye on Hood, who was expected to continue his march north, General Sherman dispatched General Thomas and the Army of the Cumberland back to Chattanooga and from there to Nashville. As an extra measure of strength, General Schofield and his 12,000-man Army of the Ohio were also ordered to report to General Thomas, with the 4th Corps under Gen. David S. Stanley, two infantry divisions under A.J. Smith, and 16,000 cavalrymen. This gave General Thomas about 70,000 troops to cover Tennessee and Kentucky as well as for challenging General Hood. Grant also arranged for Thomas to receive all new recruits sent forward from the northwest.

With the Army of the Cumberland and the Army of the Ohio on their way to General Thomas, Sherman reorganized the remaining forces of the Army of the Tennessee into two wings. The right wing, consisting of the 15th and 17th Corps with Gens. Peter J. Osterhaus and Francis P. Blair commanding, was under the leadership of Gen. O.O. Howard. The left wing, commanded by Gen. Henry W. Slocum, was composed of the 14th and 20th Corps under Jefferson C. Davis and Alpheus S. Williams. (The 20th Corps had been formed by consolidating the 11th and 12th Corps.) Including two divisions of cavalry, Sherman's army was about 60,000 strong.

Leaving his 20th Corps behind to guard Atlanta, Sherman pursued Hood's army, driving them even farther north, but not before the Confederate troops wreaked havoc on Sherman's railroad lines. Moving to Allatoona Pass on October 5, Hood attacked a small garrison of Union troops guarding a large cache of federal stores. Although heavily outnumbered, Union reinforcements commanded by Gen. John M. Corse held the Rebels off and forced Hood to retire from the field. Undeterred, Hood continued his advance north, destroying Union-held railroads and capturing 1,000 Union soldiers. Meanwhile, Sherman's men chased Hood, pursuing him to Resaca on October 12, then to Gaylesville, Alabama, on October 21. Hood was travelling with a much smaller army, and was less encumbered in his march north than was the Northern army. Consequently, Hood's lead over the Army of the Tennessee grew. At this point, on November 10, Sherman quit the chase and returned to Atlanta with a plan that he thought would better serve the Union cause.

During his march back to Atlanta, Sherman posed a new and

somewhat radical strategy for Grant to consider. Since he had assumed overall command, Grant's strategic philosophy on the conduct of the war had been rather straightforward. The Confederate army was the enemy, and the army would be followed and attacked. The cities and the non-combatants would be spared. Now Sherman wanted to ignore the enemy's army and attack the morale, the will, and the heart of the Confederacy itself by bringing the war directly to the Southern people and their capacity to support its cause. Sherman wanted to march his army to Savannah, Georgia, and along the way destroy the railroads, depots, farms, plantations, crops, factories, and anything else that would be of value to the Southern people or would assist the Southern forces. As he explained to General Halleck, "If the people raise a howl against my barbarity and cruelty, I will answer that war is war, and not popularity seeking. If they want peace, they and their relatives must stop the war."

Sherman's idea was a hard proposition to sell. Breaking away from Hood's army to cut a swath of destruction from Atlanta to Savannah was an idea that President Lincoln had difficulty accepting. It was not well received by General Grant either, or by General Halleck. The longer Sherman talked to his old buddy about it, the more Grant relented. Finally convinced, on November 2 Grant gave his final approval and persuaded the president to agree to this singular march. Summing up his case to Grant, an elated Sherman said "I can make the march, and make Georgia howl."

Because the long, 285-mile march to Savannah would be physically demanding, the men that General Sherman took with him were all handpicked. Only the healthiest troops were selected. The weak, the disabled and the sick were sent back to Chattanooga and Nashville.

Sherman would begin his march as soon as supplies came from Chattanooga. With large sections of his rail line destroyed by Hood's Army of Tennessee, Sherman's first priority was setting his men to work repairing the damage. Sherman had another problem, too: he found it impossible to protect all of his supply lines and his communication lines because, as prime targets for Forrest, Wheeler and Hood, they were constantly subjected to attacks. As he advanced, his lines would extend farther and farther, requiring more troops to protect them. These troops would have to come from his regular army, which would reduce his troop strength and his fighting capabilities.

Sherman's solution to this problem was quite simple. The Army of the Tennessee would cut loose from its base. Sherman would take only what he needed to begin his march, and after that his men would live off the land. The wagons would carry only small rations such as coffee, hardtack, and salt pork, and enough ammunition to supply each man with 200 rounds, even though, as a participant of the march related, "our mission was not to fight but to consume and destroy." Besides his musket, each soldier would carry his tin oyster can for making coffee, and a canteen, half of which he sometimes used as a frying pan. His haversack would probably contain the ever-present coffee, sugar, salt, a piece of salt pork and a piece of hard bread. This supply was to last him ten days.

To undertake an aggressive venture such as this one with any degree of confidence in its ultimate success, the Army of the Tennessee would have to undergo a mid–19th century form of downsizing. Sherman needed to travel lightly, for speed and efficiency. With the surplus troops, all superfluous artillery, wagons, clothes, baggage, and animals were sent by train to Chattanooga.

Once the army was ready to break camp, the railroad and bridges were destroyed. Severed from his base, Sherman cut the telegraph lines, effectively severing contact with the outside world. "There was something intensely exciting in this perfect isolation," wrote one Union captain from the 2d Massachusetts Volunteers. It was to be a great adventure, and every one of Sherman's troops looked forward to it.

Before leaving Atlanta, General Sherman ordered the entire population to evacuate the city. Over 1,600 whites and scores of blacks, the young and the old, the sick and the fit, carried off whatever possessions their wagons could hold as they abandoned their homes and their property. The army was then ordered to torch all public buildings, supply depots, machine shops, warehouses, arsenals, and any other building judged to be of value to the Confederates. To the mayor of Atlanta, Sherman explained, "War is cruelty and you cannot refine it. We cannot change the hearts of those people of the South, but we can make war so terrible ... [and] make them so sick of war that generations would pass away before they would again appeal to it."

The citizens of Atlanta saw Sherman's destruction quite differently, as the editor of the *Richmond Examiner* lamented: "The next morning Sherman's army moved from a scene of desolation such as had occurred in no modern picture of civilized war. From 4,000 to 5,000 houses were reduced to ruins; 400 left standing were the melancholy remnant of Atlanta. Nearly all the shade trees in the park and city had been destroyed, and the suburbs, stripped of timber, presented to the eye one vast, naked, ruined, deserted camp."

Sherman's campaign provided a new term to the lexicon of military studies: "total war." His philosophy was to use military force not only against the enemy armies but also against its people. In this way, the civilians as well as the troops would be so demoralized that he hoped to destroy the South's will to fight.

The March to the Sea began on the morning of November 15. Travelling with the 60,000 men were over 30,000 horses, mules and cattle, and approximately 3,200 wagons. Tagging along at a discreet distance were the ever-present freed slaves, who were always willing to do menial jobs or any other work in hopes of getting something to eat or an article of someone's discarded clothing. "[The slaves followed the army] like a sable cloud in the sky before a thunderstorm," a Union officer wrote. "They thought it was freedom now or never."

It was a strange development. The two armies that had been fighting and killing each other for the past three years were now marching away from each other in opposite directions.

As he marched from Atlanta in three columns, Sherman's orders were to cover about 15 miles a day. Each wing had a front line extending 30 to 36 miles wide, and travelled over different but parallel routes, with a rendezvous planned for Milledgeville, the state capital at that time. The right wing and the cavalry moved through Jonesboro, Gordon and Irwinton; Sherman was with the left wing as they travelled through Covington and Eatonton to Milledgeville.

Every brigade had a company responsible for fanning out into the surrounding farms and rich plantations each day to search for provisions. Called "bummers," the scavenger-soldiers were specifically selected from each regiment for their intelligence and daring. Proud of what they did and efficient at it, the Union foragers found abundant quantities of hams, sweet potatoes, corn meal, chickens, hogs, vegetables, bacon, turkeys, and other edibles. Their booty was always more than enough to keep the Union wagons well stocked and Sherman's men well fed. They became so adept at scrounging from the land that at one point, President Davis tried to persuade the Southern people to destroy the food themselves to prevent Sherman's troops from taking it for their own use. This scheme failed because everyone thought that their own farm would be missed by the Union foragers.

Sherman's March Through the South

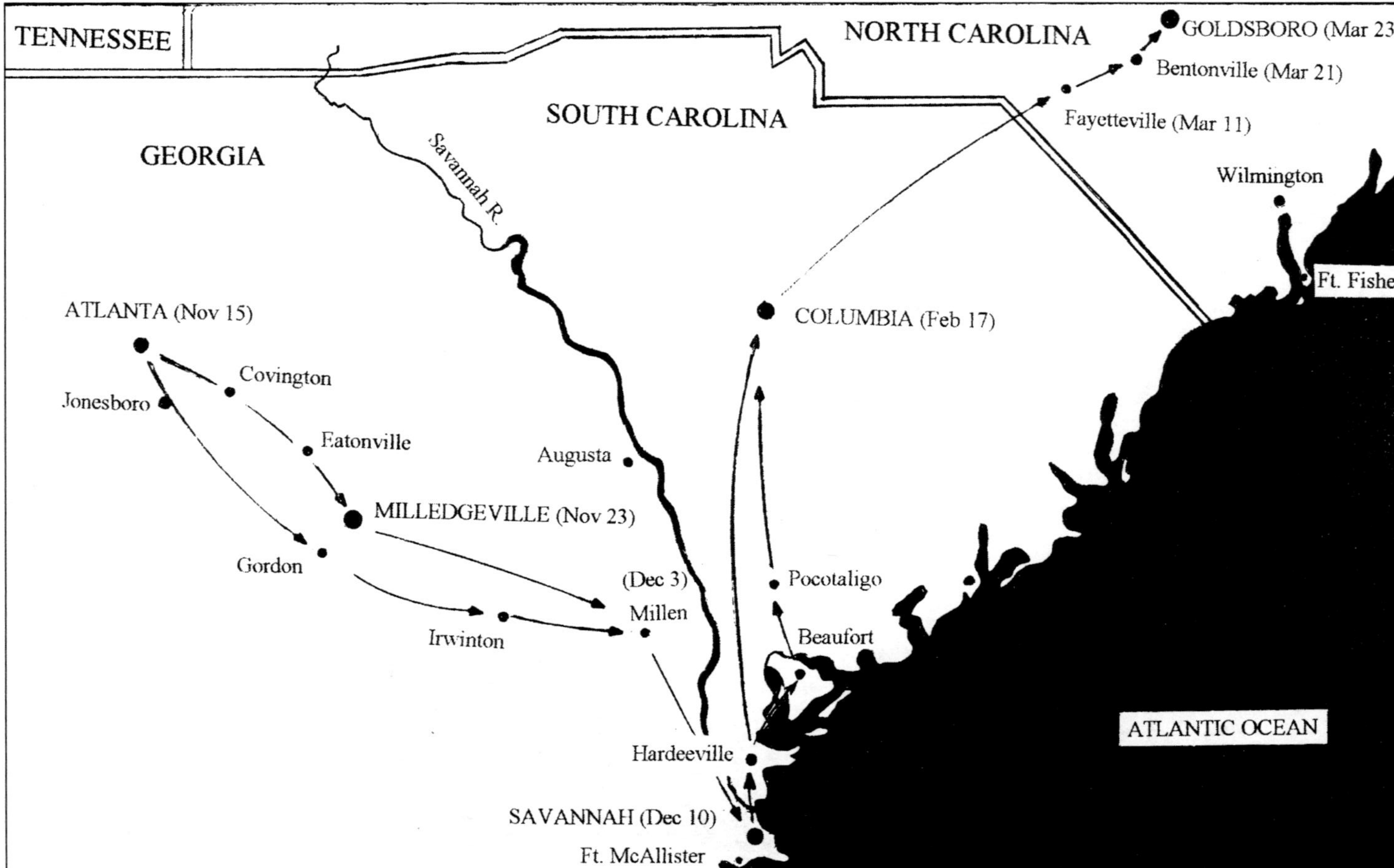

As Sherman's army approached Milledgeville on November 23, Governor Brown and the entire legislature abandoned the city to the Union troops. Staying only a day to rest, Sherman used the governor's mansion for his headquarters, and his men found fun and relaxation by taking over the state house and conducting mock legislative debates. Early the next morning, Sherman's troops set fire to the prison and the railroad depot before continuing their march. Leaving Milledgeville on the 24th, the left wing headed for the town of Millen, about 100 miles away, where they rendezvoused with the right wing on December 3.

To this point, Confederate resistance to the Union march had been minimal. With the exception of the Georgia militia, which was certainly no serious threat, owing to its composition of old men and boys not over 15, the only real opposition came from the Confederate cavalry under Gen. Joseph Wheeler. Overpowered by the Union cavalry, Wheeler's 3,500 men were no match and were easily repulsed with no significant losses to the Union army.

Sherman's men cheerfully marched along the railroad lines, destroying the tracks as they went using the same technique previously mastered near Atlanta. Men heated the rails over burning railroad ties until red-hot and then twisted them into "Sherman's neckties" around tree trunks. At the same time, the railway depots were burned down and all the train cars were blown up, leaving nothing behind but charred reminders and piles of scrap metal. In the towns, the Union soldiers razed most public buildings and factories and stripped the farms clean. Even buried goods were found by the Union bummers, who quickly learned to probe suspicious looking loose soil with long iron rods. The *Richmond Examiner* reported, "Even crockery, bedcovering, or clothes were fair spoils.... Furniture was smashed to pieces, music was pounded out of 400-dollar pianos with the ends of muskets. Rich cushions and carpets were carried off to adorn teams and war steeds." Sherman's army left behind a path of unparalleled destruction 60 miles wide. While all three columns had a hand in the damage, it was the primary duty of the center, while the columns on each flank assured its safety.

Easily approachable, Sherman was known for his preference for wearing low shoes and only one spur. Called "Uncle Billy" by some, the Union general was extremely well liked by his officers as well as by his front-line privates. Sherman's intimate knowledge of each officer's capabilities and his personal relationship with them made any one of them feel important and appreciated, and gave each one a sense that the commander was paying special attention to him.

On December 10, all four corps reached the outskirts of Savannah and found the city garrisoned by some 15,000 Confederate troops under the command of Gen. William J. Hardee. Discovering torpedoes (land mines) buried in his front, Sherman marched a tightly formed group of Confederate prisoners forward through the area to either locate or explode the torpedoes. Although none were detonated, a reconnaissance of the surrounding area convinced Sherman that the marshy lowlands around Savannah were not conducive to a successful attack. Sherman rejected a frontal assault and ordered his troops to place Savannah under siege.

While his troops prepared their lines for the siege, Sherman and a sufficient force of troops marched to the coast to contact the federal fleet in Ossabaw Sound, just south of Savannah. The Union commander needed to establish a line of communications with the Union Navy anchored there in hopes of getting their gunboats to assist in capturing Savannah, and to bring back some badly needed supplies. With his contingent of troops, Sherman followed the Ogeechee River, which terminates directly into the sound. Only 15 miles from Savannah, on December 13, the Union troops came to Fort McAllister, a small Confederate outpost on the south bank of the river. Finding it necessary to take out the fort first, Sherman ordered Gen. William B. Hazen and his division across the river to make the assault. Within 15 minutes, Hazen's division captured the Confederate fortification and Sherman continued his march to the coast.

Waiting in the sound was a Union steamer previously dispatched by General Grant with an accumulation of mail for Sherman's troops and a load of supplies. There to meet Sherman was Gen. John G. Foster, commander of all Union troops on the East Coast south of North Carolina, with headquarters at Hilton Head. Following a friendly and relaxed meeting, General Foster agreed to supply the Union army with siege guns, hardtack, clothing, and other supplies.

Arriving back at the Union camp on December 15, Sherman learned that with the exception of one open road, the combination of Union military forces and the low swamplands had General Hardee practically surrounded. Sherman and General Foster arranged to close off the only remaining road, Hardee's only line of communications with the outside, and the Confederates withdrew from Savannah. Crossing a hastily built pontoon bridge over the Savannah River on the night of December 21, General Hardee and his garrison abandoned Savannah to the Union forces.

Elated over this turn of events, Sherman wired President Lincoln, "I beg to present you as a Christmas gift the city of Savannah, with one hundred and fifty guns and plenty of ammunition, also about twenty five thousand bales of cotton."

XVII
The Final Battles for Tennessee (November–December 1864)

While Sherman's forces cut a path of destruction from Atlanta to Savannah, Georgia, General Hood was far from sitting idle in his Confederate camp. Back on November 10, when General Sherman had abandoned his pursuit of the Army of Tennessee, General Hood was bivouacked at Florence, Alabama, having arrived there from Decatur to replenish supplies. Apprised of Sherman's departure for Atlanta, General Hood boldly set his sights on taking Nashville, the state capital. The city had been occupied by Union forces since Fort Donelson had surrendered in February, 1862. General Thomas was now strongly entrenched there with about 60,000 Union troops.

Calculating that Hood would continue his march north, Thomas had previously dispatched General Schofield 75 miles south of Nashville with the 4th and 23rd Corps, and three brigades of cavalry to keep an eye on Hood's movements. Camped at Pulaski, Tennessee, with his 30,000 troops, Schofield had received orders to keep Hood's army under surveillance, but under no circumstances was he to engage. If Hood made a move toward Nashville, Schofield was to return immediately for reinforcements from Thomas.

The Army of Tennessee at this time had about 35,000 troops in three infantry corps, commanded by Gens. Stephen D. Lee, Alexander P.

Stewart, and Benjamin F. Cheatham, as well as Hood's cavalry under Gen. Nathan B. Forrest. Hood marched his infantry into Tennessee on November 17. His advance across the border triggered Schofield into withdrawing his forces to Nashville, passing through Columbia on November 21. Marching along the Columbia to Franklin Pike, the Union army quickly headed toward Nashville as General Thomas had ordered.

General Hood then changed his priorities. His immediate goal was to intercept Schofield's forces by placing his army squarely across the pike between the Union bluecoats and Franklin. By accomplishing this, Hood hoped to destroy Schofield's army before it reached Nashville. Once Schofield was defeated, Hood could expect to confront a much smaller force under General Thomas. Hood was now more confident then ever that he would easily retake Nashville for the Confederacy and then march east to help Lee defeat Grant and Sherman. The key to Hood's success was to defeat General Schofield first.

Late in the afternoon of November 29, Hood's army was 12 miles from the village of Spring Hill and in sight of the pike, only two miles away. More important, the Union army was also in sight proceeding north along the pike, the advance forces passing through Spring Hill. A reconnaissance disclosed to Hood that only a line of skirmishes guarded the huge wagon train and could be easily taken. In fact, two Union divisions were present to escort the wagons.

Eager to launch his attack, Hood ordered General Cheatham to take the pike just south of Spring Hill with a sweeping flank attack while General Forrest attacked the Union advance forces head-on north of Spring Hill. To counter Hood's maneuver, Schofield shifted Wagner's division of Stanley's 4th Corps to the front of the train, north of Spring Hill, to challenge Forrest. Forming a defensive semicircle north of the village, the Union troops handily beat back the Confederate cavalry attack. On the pike, south of Spring Hill, Cheatham inexplicably lost his nerve, and to the surprise of his own men, ordered a halt to the advance. After failing to take possession of the Pike, Cheatham explained later to an utterly exasperated Hood that "the [Union] line looked a little too long for him." Whether Hood or Cheatham or someone else bungled the attack, as far as Hood was concerned, a golden opportunity to cut off and defeat Schofield's army had been lost. By this time, darkness had settled on the field and the Confederate soldiers were ordered into camp for the night. Barely visible in the moonlight,

THE FINAL BATTLES FOR TENNESSEE

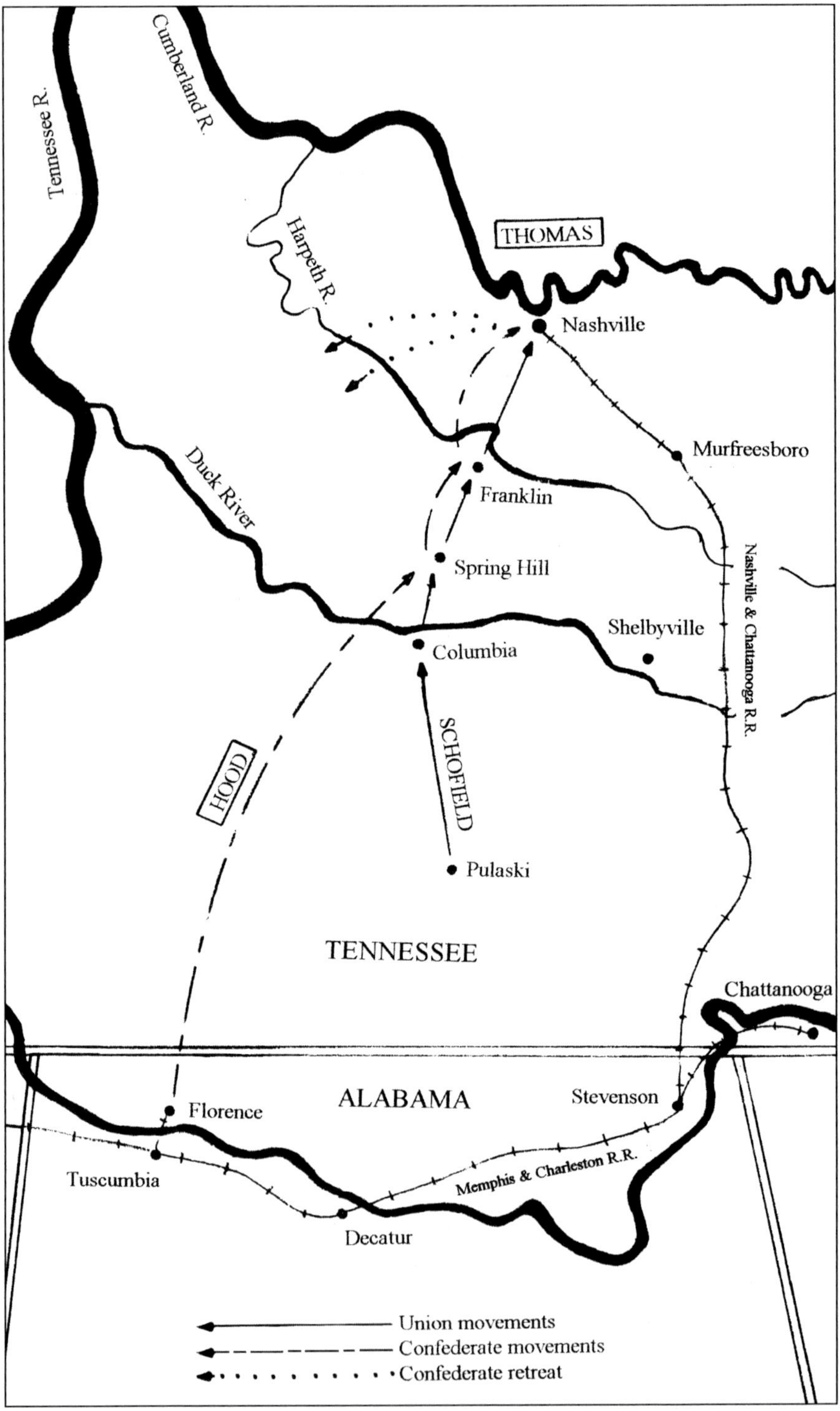

Schofield's wagon train doggedly continued its journey through Spring Hill to Franklin.

Learning that the Union army was still on the move, Hood again relied on General Cheatham to attack the Union forces. The Confederate objective this time was to stall Schofield's forward movement before an all-out, concentrated attack on the Union army in the morning. Again, as a totally frustrated Hood would lament, "Nothing was done." Strangely enough, in camp the Confederates built fires and cooked their meals, all within gunshot range and within sight of the Union wagon train. Without orders to the contrary, the Confederate soldiers bedded down for the night as Schofield's huge wagon train passed the Rebel camp less then a half-mile away.

On the morning of November 30, General Hood awakened to find the Union trains gone from his front, just as he had expected. Exasperated that his once-in-a-lifetime opportunity was quickly slipping away, Hood was still unable to believe the events of the day before: that on two occasions the Union army had been his for the taking, and both times his commanders had failed to carry out his orders, twice permitting Schofield to slip away. To the Confederate troops, the blame for the previous day's fiasco rested squarely on the shoulders of their commander. As one soldier later wrote, "Every soldier mistrusted General Hood's judgment. I remember when passing by Hood how feeble and decrepit he looked, with an arm in a sling and a crutch in the other hand, trying to guide and control his horse. I prayed in my heart that day for General Hood. Poor fellow!" (Hood had an arm disabled at Gettysburg and lost a leg at Chickamauga.) Although Hood had a reputation for reckless attacks and was prone to impulsive decisions, many of his soldiers thought his mind was severely influenced by the medication he took for his fight against the racking pain he experienced each day. As a result of this growing distrust, a corresponding rise in Confederate desertions from the Army of Tennessee was cause for concern.

As the Confederates broke camp, Schofield was about 18 miles north of Spring Hill, on the southern outskirts of Franklin. Once by Franklin, the Union army would cross the Harpeth River and march 15 miles into Nashville. Immediately putting the Rebel army into pursuit, Hood hoped to catch Schofield's army before they reached the river.

Marching at a double-quick pace, Hood's army caught the Union forces about three miles from Franklin on November 30. Although Hood's troops made remarkable time marching from Spring Hill, the Army of Tennessee arrived without its artillery and without the infantry corps commanded by Gen. S.D. Lee.

When the Confederate army, still shorthanded, approached within sight of their enemy, the Union troops withdrew within the confines of Franklin. Quickly constructing makeshift breastworks within the perimeter of the town, Schofield's men prepared to defend themselves against an assault expected to be fierce and bloody. The defensive positions built by the Union soldiers were, however, strong and secure, and would no doubt test the fighting spirit of Hood's men.

Considering that Franklin was surrounded by open fields which had to be crossed in carrying out their assault, the Confederate commanders objected to Hood's attack orders. Citing it suicidal for their men to charge across open fields against an army using artillery support of grape and canister, when they had no such armaments for protective cover, Hood's commanders adamantly opposed his order to attack, but to no avail.

As the late-afternoon sun cast its long shadows across the landscape, the Confederate lines charged over the open expanse. Amid the burst of artillery and musketry, Hood's troops moved toward the town with seemingly reckless abandon. Raging violently on into the cool November night, the battle was a bloody exchange of death and carnage, with Hood's forces taking the brunt of the losses. At one point, the Confederates broke through the lines of two brigades under General Wagner, and severely threatened the entire Union defensive structure. The threat was only temporary. Responding to this sudden breach in the Union defenses, Col. Emerson Opdycke rallied his brigade to the fractured line and drove the invading Confederates back, reclaiming the lost Yankee breastworks and saving Schofield's army from a certain rout.

The statistics from the Battle of Franklin tell a grim story. The Confederate casualties were over 7,000 killed, wounded, and missing. More Confederate troops were lost at Franklin than the Union lost at Cold Harbor, or even in all the Seven Days' battles combined. Included in these casualty figures were 12 Confederate generals, six of whom died in that one bloody battle. Union losses were moderate in comparison, with 189 killed, about 1,000 wounded, and 1,100 captured.

Never one to give up easily, Hood was determined to fight for a victory he had been repeatedly denied. With Schofield in Nashville, on December 2, Hood ordered his 23,000 troops to entrench four miles in front of the city. There, the Army of Tennessee would wait for Thomas to attack.

General Thomas anticipated Hood's advance to the outskirts of Nashville and had prepared his troops for the upcoming battle, which he scheduled for December 8. On the morning of the appointed day, the weather conditions were so bad that Thomas called off the attack. A fast-moving storm blanketed the area with freezing sleet and snow and immobilized both armies.

In Washington, Thomas was severely criticized for "allowing" Hood to entrench around Nashville with hardly a token of Union resistance. Even worse, both the Lincoln war department and General Grant were highly disturbed over Thomas' decision to postpone the attack merely because of inclement weather. Their concern was that Hood would find a way to elude Thomas, despite the terrible weather conditions, and get north of the Cumberland River. In that eventuality, additional troops from the east would have been required to head the Confederate army off at the Ohio River. The officials in Washington feared that by Thomas' inaction, a highly undesirable incursion into Northern territory, similar to Jubal Early's, was quite possible.

Grant repeatedly urged Thomas to attack Hood's works. Seven messages were wired to Thomas from City Point between December 2 and the 15th. Grant's imploring tone was readily discernible in one of his dispatches of December 8: "Now is one of the finest opportunities ever presented of destroying one of the three armies of the enemy. If destroyed he never can replace it. Use the means at your command, and you can do this and cause a rejoicing that will resound from one end of the land to the other." The pleading was to no avail. Thomas told Grant he would move only when he could. Grant had little choice but to relieve the "Rock of Chickamauga" from his command. He dispatched Gen. John A. Logan to Nashville to replace Thomas. Before leaving City Point, General Logan was instructed to disregard these orders if Thomas carried out the attack before he arrived in Nashville. That is what occurred while Logan, en route to Nashville, was in Louisville.

On the morning of December 15, the Battle of Nashville finally opened. With the snow and ice now melted, General Thomas ordered his troops to break camp for the long-awaited advance on the Army of Tennessee, dug in only a few miles away. The battle would last all day until darkness obscured the battlefront. Although the fighting raged on in a bloody struggle for superiority, it ended with a modest gain of only two miles for the Federals. Even though the Union forces had the advantage in numbers that could easily overwhelm the Rebel army, Hood's men poured an endless rain of musketry, shot and shell from their protection of strong fortifications and on a battlefield of their choosing. Feeling the loss of General Forrest and his cavalry, who were at Murfreesboro, 30 miles away, the Confederate soldiers held their own but were near collapse.

Recovered somewhat from the previous day's fight, in the afternoon of the 16th the Union army opened a concentrated artillery attack on a carefully chosen section of Hood's front line at Shy's Hill. Immediately following this bombardment, the long blue lines of Union soldiers charged headlong through the deadly Confederate musket fire, and up and over the enemy's works. Once breached, within a short time the entire Confederate line was broken and Hood's men ran for their lives. The Rebel army abandoned the field in wild disorder, leaving behind 13,000 prisoners, their dead and wounded, their artillery and large quantities of small arms. General Hood and the few Rebel commanders still alive tried in vain to stem the rout. Failing to rally their men, even the officers joined the dash to the Confederate rear. One Confederate soldier, a witness to the rout, described what he saw that afternoon: "The whole army had broken and were running in every direction. Such a scene I never saw. The woods everywhere were full of running soldiers. The once proud Army of Tennessee had degenerated into a mob. Our country was gone, our cause lost." With no control over their men, Confederate officers ordered a general retreat to the Tennessee River under the cover of General Forrest and his cavalry troops, who had arrived at the front after learning of Hood's plight.

A pursuit of Hood's army was attempted in a drenching rain by the Union cavalry, but Hood's men had a huge head start. The Union cavalrymen were fighting dismounted that day, and by the time their horses arrived, Hood's army had substantially increased the distance between the two forces. When the Army of Tennessee reached the Duck River on December 18, they destroyed all the bridges and effectively forced the Union to abandon its chase.

Now less than half their original strength, the Army of Tennessee was no longer a fighting force. The shattered and demoralized remains of Hood's army gathered at Tupelo, Mississippi, on December 29 for the last time. The ragged, barefooted and starving remnants of a once-proud army were called east to join General Johnston's fight against Sherman's march through the Carolinas. Gen. John Bell Hood, their proud and dedicated commander, had lost the confidence of his men and his officers. He resigned from the Confederate service on January 13.

XVIII
Sherman's March Through the Carolinas (January–March 1865)

With Union forces in Savannah preparing to head north, General Grant initiated a flurry of troop movements designed to support Sherman's march through the Carolinas. His original plan was to ferry Sherman's men from Savannah up the coastline on a number of transports to the James River. At the time, this manner of conveying Sherman's troops and artillery north was considered much preferable to marching overland. The winter rains, from a record-breaking wet season, had turned the roads into muddy quagmires that many Southerners thought would save the Carolinians from Sherman's wrath. Gen. Joseph E. Johnston thought so too, writing, "My engineers reported that it was absolutely impossible for an army to march across the lower portion of the State in winter." To collect all the ships would take too much time, however, and Sherman's nature was not one that accepted idle waiting. Consequently, he chose to confront the challenges and march overland instead.

General Grant considered the march to Savannah an outstanding success because it wiped out many sources of food and materials the Confederates depended on from the west. Grant felt Sherman's march through the Carolinas would benefit the Union if it accomplished the same results. The Confederate army would then be limited to only a small section of Virginia for acquiring supplies via blockade runners. Based on this prospect, Grant gave the go-ahead for Sherman's foray through South and North Carolina. Then, while Grant held Lee in check at Petersburg with the Army of the Potomac, Sherman's army would come up on Lee's rear, effectively trapping the Army of Northern Virginia between the two Union pincers.

One of Grant's immediate concerns was to prevent the Confederate troops in the West from moving east to interfere with Sherman's campaign. This concern triggered a flurry of activity involving seven generals moving armies through six different states.

Gen. Edward R.S. Canby, commander of the Army of the Gulf at New Orleans with 18,000 troops, was ordered on January 18 to advance from the Gulf Coast to Mobile, Montgomery, and Selma, Alabama, to destroy railroads, warehouses, machine shops, and other targets. In addition, Grant put Gen. Benjamin Grierson in command of Canby's cavalry with instructions to advance into Mississippi to occupy the Rebel cavalry under Nathan B. Forrest. As for General Thomas, the "Rock of Chickamauga" apparently slipped out of favor with Grant because of his sluggishness in pursuing Hood from Tennessee, and more recently, on February 20, when he failed to carry out Grant's order to send his cavalry on raids in Mississippi. As a result, Thomas' forces were split, a portion going to reinforce Canby and a portion going to Gen. Alfred Terry's Army of the James. (On January 8, Grant had relieved General Butler from command of the Army of the James and had put Terry in charge.) Thomas and the remainder of his forces were to head for Lynchburg, Virginia, while his cavalry under Gen. George Stoneman carried out raids through the northwest corner of South Carolina. Also directed to Lynchburg was Gen. Philip H. Sheridan. With his cavalry troopers, Sheridan was to destroy the Virginia and Tennessee Railroad and the James River Canal just west of Richmond. General Schofield was ordered to send his 4th Corps under Gen. David S. Stanley to Bull Gap, Tennessee, while Schofield and the balance of his command arrived in Annapolis, Maryland, around the end of January. From there Schofield's 21,000 troops were transported to the mouth of Cape Fear River. Their mission was to capture the Wilmington and Charlotte Railroad, take the city of Wilmington, North Carolina, and rendezvous with Sherman's troops at Goldsboro.

With his wagons fully loaded, Sherman was ready to move out of Savannah. In contrast to his preparations for the march across Georgia, this time Sherman had to take along an abundant amount of supplies and rations. The Carolina area was cleaned out and would not be able to sustain the Union army no matter how ingenious the "bummers" proved. On January 10, the Army of the Tennessee broke camp and marched out in two columns. One column, the right wing, under Gen. O.O. Howard, was composed of the 15th Corps, now under General John A. Logan, and the 17th Corps. Howard's wing marched 25 miles to Pototaligo, via Beaufort. The cavalry would threaten Charleston while the left wing, the 14th and 20th Corps, commanded by Gen. Henry W. Slocum, moved north along the Savannah River from Hardeeville.

Sherman's initial destination was the state capital, Columbia, South Carolina. From there his army would travel to Fayetteville, North Carolina, and finally to Goldsboro, a distance of 425 miles from Savannah. While his army moved through South Carolina, Sherman admitted he would not be able to guarantee the behavior of his men. To a man, they held South Carolina fully responsible for starting the war and for causing all the problems both sides had suffered over the past four years. For that they aimed to punish the South Carolinians dearly. As General Sherman would disclose to Lincoln's chief of staff, Gen. Henry W. Halleck, "The whole army is burning with insatiable desire to wreak vengeance upon South Carolina. I almost tremble at her fate, but feel that she deserves all that seems to be in store for her."

On January 15, Fort Fisher, a Confederate fortification guarding the mouth of the Cape Fear River and the port city of Wilmington, was captured with its commander, Col. William Lamb, and a garrison of 2,000 troops. The massive L-shaped fort was built of sand over a log frame, with huge traverses covered with sods of coarse marsh grass to protect the gun emplacements. With walls 25 feet thick, the grass sods and sand absorbed the incoming shells instead of being disintegrated into rubble by the impact, as more conventional fortifications would have been. Nevertheless, Fort Fisher was taken by Gen. Alfred Terry commanding an infantry force of 8,000 men and reinforced by Adm. David D. Porter's fleet of gunboats, the North Atlantic Blockading Squadron.

This was the second attempt to take the fort. The first assault had been launched on Christmas Eve of 1864, and had proved a huge fiasco. Before invading the Confederate bulwark with his infantry, Gen. Benjamin Butler, commander of the Army of the James, had attempted to inflict heavy damage to the fort by detonating a nearby ship loaded with 215 tons of gunpowder. The ship had exploded without a hitch, but the fort had sustained practically no damage. To make matters worse, Admiral Porter's supporting gunboats, a huge fleet of 60 warships, had blasted Fort Fisher with the heaviest shelling of the Civil War, but had inflicted minimal damage. Butler had called off the invasion when he had discovered the approaches to the fort laced with land mines.

Now that the presidential election was over, Butler, a politically appointed general, could no longer exert the same political influence over his job security that he had once enjoyed. As a result, on January 8, Grant had used this opportunity to dismiss Butler and to appoint General Terry to the command of the Army of the James. With his new command, General Terry had received orders for a second assault on Fort Fisher.

Admiral Porter's fleet of gunboats still provided the heavy artillery support for the second invasion, but this time Porter's guns devastated the fort's gun batteries and also destroyed the detonating wires to the now-harmless land mines.

The fall of Fort Fisher sent shock waves through the Confederate government in Richmond, and forced the resignation of Secretary of War James A. Seddon. Even members of the Confederate congress were stunned and voiced their fear that the end was rapidly approaching. With wringing hands and trembling voices, some congressmen called for the government to make terms with the enemy, on the basis of the old Union.

On February 3, three peace commissioners met with President Lincoln on board the steamer *River Queen* at Hampton Roads, Virginia. They were Alexander H. Stephens, the Confederate vice-president; Judge John A. Campbell, the assistant secretary of war; and Sen. R.M.T. Hunter. The four hours of discussions dealt with such issues as the Emancipation Proclamation, monetary compensation to slave holders, and the Thirteenth Amendment passed on January 31. Lincoln refused to discuss an armistice, reiterating his position that serious negotiations could not be entertained unless the commissioners agreed on two points: that the Union must be restored under a federal authority, and that slavery in the South must be abolished. Hearing those terms, the commissioners abruptly left the ship and returned to Richmond.

Receiving the commissioners' report, Confederate President

Jefferson Davis was extremely upset and vowed never to surrender, but to fight until the Yankees "petition us for peace on our own terms."

Sherman's forces reached Columbia on February 17. According to Union reports, as the Federals occupied the city, bales of cotton were found stacked in the street burning out of control. Arriving on the scene, Union soldiers tried to extinguish the flames, but the high winds caused the fire to spread to nearby wooden buildings. By the next morning, an entire city block had been reduced to ashes before the flames were finally put out. In that block were the state house, several churches and public buildings, some homes and a convent. Those responsible for setting the fire never admitted their role. The Union blamed Gen. Wade Hampton for allowing his cavalrymen to set the blaze before they withdrew from the city. General Hampton vigorously denied that he, his men or the citizens of Columbia had anything to do with the fire. Hampton placed the blame entirely on the vengeance of the Union army. Some time later, Sherman set the record straight with his exact sentiments: "Though I never ordered it, and never wished it, I have never shed any tears over the event, because I believe that it hastened what we all fought for, the end of the war."

By this time, Columbia had degenerated into a lawless city. Even the implementation of martial law by Union forces failed to stem the pillage, robbery and murder of citizens and blacks by soldiers of both camps. William G. Simms, a resident of Columbia and one of the South's leading literary men, related what he saw that day: "Hardly had the troops reached the head of Main Street, when the work of pillage was begun. Stores were broken open within the first hour after their arrival, and gold, silver, jewels and liquors, eagerly sought. The authorities, officers, soldiers, all seemed to consider it a matter of course. And woe to him who carried a watch with a gold pendant; or who wore a choice hat, or overcoat, or boots or shoes. He was stripped in the twinkling of an eye."

On February 20, three days after the city of Charleston had been evacuated, the right wing marched out of Columbia and resumed its trek north, toward Cheraw, South Carolina. The march through the Carolinas was not the same stroll in the park Sherman's men had experienced marching through Georgia. Winter rains had swollen the rivers, transforming the surrounding country into long ribbons of swampland. The troops had to cut their way through a waterlogged landscape of timbers, vines and thickets. Bridges had to be constructed or rebuilt and many miles of roads corduroyed. It was slow and tedious work and employed teams of entire brigades or regiments for lifting wagons and caissons out of the axle-deep mud or for cutting miles of woods to make new roads.

In Washington, March 4 was a cold and raw setting for President Lincoln's second inauguration. Taking the oath of office before the recently completed Capitol building, Lincoln appeared tired and aged. The war had clearly taken its toll on the president, who later said, "I am a tired man. Sometimes I think I am the tiredest man on earth."

When Sherman's men had passed through Georgia, most of the private homes had been left untouched, but along Sherman's path in South Carolina, a home left standing was a rare sight indeed. In South Carolina, Sherman's men made it a point to leave behind their signature devastation of destroyed railroads, "Sherman bow ties," and razed public buildings. Because South Carolina was considered by the Union soldiers the seat of the Confederacy, the citizens were also victims of Sherman's "total war." Their homes, personal property, livestock and food were all subject to the whims of Sherman's troops. This intense destruction of private property ended at the border as one Union officer reported a few days later from North Carolina. "Not a single column of the fire or smoke which a few days ago marked the positions of heads of column, can be seen on the horizon. Not a house was burned, and the army gave to the people more than it took from them." In some places, the Confederate troops themselves caused more destruction and misery for the Southern people than did the Yankees.

Throughout this havoc, the backroads of the South were filled with refugees attempting to escape from the Union armies. Southerners by the thousands, on foot, on horseback or in wagons, fled their homes from Baton Rouge, Louisiana, to Richmond, Virginia.

Passing through Cheraw without incident, Sherman's army crossed the Peedee on March 6 and headed directly for Fayetteville, North Carolina.

To this point, Sherman's army had yet to encounter any serious Confederate resistance, although occasionally the cavalry drove off a battery or a small line of skirmishers. To be sure, the Confederates were there and would attack in force, but the commander waited for an opportune time and for the battlefield of his choice. General Hardee, General Wheeler and General Hampton had a combined force of about 15,000 men lurking in Sherman's vicinity to impede his forward movement. There were also the 16,000 men that General Lee had previously dispatched from Petersburg to reinforce Fort Fisher. Just before the fort was captured they had been withdrawn and combined with the approximately 9,000 men left from General Hood's army, into what was now called the Army of the South. On February 22, these 25,000 men came under the command of old Gen. Joseph E. Johnston, who had been restored to command at the recommendation of General Lee, who was himself elevated to commander of all Confederate forces.

The Union army marched into Fayetteville on March 11. After averaging about 10 miles a day, the weary bluecoats welcomed this opportunity to relax in camp, have a good meal and perhaps write a letter home. Always considering the welfare of his men, General Sherman had dispatched a letter before their arrival to General Terry at Wilmington, asking him to send a steamer up the Cape Fear River with supplies, rations, mail and clothing. One of Sherman's first priorities at Fayetteville was to rid his army of the vast crowd of refugees, black and white, which followed it incessantly, and which Sherman called "20,000 to 30,000 useless mouths." Stopping at Fayetteville also gave Sherman the chance to purge all of his sick animals from the wagon train and replace them with fresh animals taken from the local citizens. On March 15, the Union camp was dismantled and once again the long blue line snaked its way north, but not before the public and government buildings were destroyed, an act which Sherman considered his military duty.

The next day, Sherman's men had their first encounter with Confederate resistance outside the small town of Averasboro, North Carolina. In more of a delaying action than a fight, the 20th Corps was challenged by General Hardee's troops, who were quickly driven off toward Raleigh.

Following Hardee's withdrawal, Sherman was positive that his last 30 miles to Goldsboro would be free and clear of Confederate forces. There was nothing Sherman wanted more than to reach Goldsboro, and as soon as possible to rendezvous with Grant against the Army of Northern Virginia. Sherman's excess confidence seemed to override his military instincts, because waiting to pounce on Sherman's left wing at the small village of Bentonville was Sherman's old rival, Joe Johnston.

At Bentonville, General Johnston's Confederate army attacked

Slocum's left wing on March 19. The attack was a last-ditch effort by Rebel forces to prevent Sherman from reaching Goldsboro. Johnston's men were poised on the right flank and to the front of two divisions of the 14th Corps, who were on the road between Averasboro and Goldsboro. The Confederate troops were fighting from strong breastworks and backed up by several batteries of artillery. Slocum's men pushed forward, but in the face of Confederate musketry and artillery, the Union troops were forced to retreat with severe losses. As the Union men fell back, line after line of Confederate troops were spotted advancing across the fields, firing as they pressed forward. Soon two brigades of the 20th Corps arrived and were ordered into action against the approaching Rebels. The sudden Union counterattack caught Johnston's troops off guard and drove them back to their works, where they regrouped for another attack. The Confederate attack was anticipated and met with deadly rounds of canister from Union artillery support and concentrated fire from the Union infantry. The next morning, the remaining half of Slocum's wing came to reinforce the 14th Corps, and by March 21, Sherman's entire army was near Bentonville. True to form, General Johnston, now heavily outnumbered, withdrew on the night of the 21st to Smithfield, 15 miles to the north. In this last engagement with Johnston, Sherman lost 1,600 men killed, wounded and missing.

On March 23, General Sherman and his road-weary but victorious men finally marched into Goldsboro. Sherman was now a national hero for his marches through Georgia and the Carolinas. There to greet him were General Schofield and General Terry, who with their commands had recently arrived from Wilmington and New Bern. Two days later, an ecstatic Sherman boarded a train for City Point to meet with General Grant to discuss their rendezvous in Richmond.

XIX
The Evacuation of Petersburg and Richmond
(March–April 1865)

The winter of 1864 to 1865 was unusually rainy. Torrential downpours occurred practically on a daily basis, and the roads became rivers of thick, sticky mud useless for moving the wagons, the animals and the artillery. To some extent, even the cavalry found its mobility limited. At his headquarters in City Point, General Grant grew impatient and eager to begin his spring campaign, confident that his attack on Lee's forces in Petersburg would be the final drive of the rebellion. The country was becoming extremely tired of the war, which had dragged on now for nearly four years. In this regard, Grant was committed, more than ever, to stop the bloodshed, the killing and the suffering. "I mean to end the business here," he told his cavalry chief. One of Grant's gnawing fears was that while he waited for the roads to dry, he would discover some morning that Lee and the Army of Northern Virginia had withdrawn from Petersburg to join Johnston.

Lee certainly had the means to leave. The Confederate army, smaller and travelling lighter, could easily get the jump on Grant and once on the move south could combine forces with General Johnston's 20,000-man army near Raleigh and overwhelm Sherman. They could then march north to challenge Grant. Lee had every intention of following this plan. The Confederate general knew his position at Petersburg was growing more and more unstable. In a few weeks, the roads would be dry. If his troops had not escaped before then, he expected to be surrounded by the combined armies of Grant and Sherman, and all would be lost. Just as the bad weather hampered the North and delayed its efforts to close the noose around Lee's army, it also prevented Lee from pulling out of Petersburg. Both armies therefore bided their time until the roads were dry enough for one of them to make the first move.

In the Southern camp, desertions were still reducing the Army of Northern Virginia to levels that jeopardized the very existence of the Confederacy. Desperate for more troops, Lee found himself doing what under normal circumstances would have been unthinkable. With no recruits or reinforcements available to replenish his diminishing army, Lee recommended that slaves be armed to help fight in the rebellion. Surprisingly, the Confederacy authorized the establishment of two black companies within only a few days of Lee's suggestion. This decision created quite a stir in the South, but as a Richmond newspaper lamented, "The country will not deny General Lee anything he may ask for."

If Lee's sudden evacuation of Petersburg or the conditions of the roads were not enough to fret over, Grant had another matter to worry about before he could launch his spring offensive. That was the timely return of General Sheridan and his 10,000 cavalrymen from their raids between Lynchburg and Richmond. Sheridan had successfully carried out his mission to destroy the railroads and the James River Canal, and as of March 19, his forces were known to be at White House Landing, Virginia. Grant's plan called for the cavalry to play a key role in the spring offensive. Consequently, the Union commander was compelled to wait for Sheridan to return.

For the Army of Northern Virginia to escape from Petersburg, they first had to reach the Weldon Railroad. To get there, the 50,000 Confederate troops would have to pass between Fort Stedman and a commanding battery position, both under Union control. Lee planned to seize these two points and force Grant to contract his lines, thereby widening the Confederate escape route, thus giving the Army of Northern Virginia more room to maneuver and increase their chances of reaching the railroad with a minimum of casualties.

On March 24, Lee attacked. The Confederate assault was under the orders of Gen. John B. Gordon, commander of the 2d Corps, whose strategy was to send a number of Rebel troops into the Union picket lines pretending to surrender. When taken in by the Union troops, the Rebels would seize the unsuspecting Yanks and take over the Union works, only 50 yards from the fort. The Confederate ploy worked well. Completely fooling the credulous Union pickets, Gordon's men continued their charge and swarmed into Fort Stedman, capturing the sleeping garrison as well as three adjacent artillery batteries.

Early on the 25th, a Union counterattack was ordered by Burnside's replacement, Gen. John G. Parke of the 9th Infantry Corps. Parke's men retook the batteries and drove the onrushing Southerners back, some into Fort Stedman and the rest to the Union entrenchments previously captured.

Quickly surrounding the fort with artillery, General Parke ordered a continuous barrage of shelling until the Confederates, unable to retreat, were forced to surrender. Another charge by Union forces then retook the picket fortifications.

For his attempt to escape from Petersburg, Lee suffered over 5,000 casualties and only exacerbated the desertion problem plaguing the Southern army. As the situation became more and more apparent, Southern troops by the thousands were leaving the ranks. Some returned to their homes concerned over the plights of their families, while others went north to wait out the war there. The once-fierce Army of Northern Virginia was down to 35,000 worn-out and ragged skeletons. Fighting against 125,000 well-fed soldiers, Lee had to do something to save his army. In Richmond, the Davis administration was also beginning to consider the days of the Confederacy numbered and quietly planned for a possible evacuation from the capital city.

Two days later, on the James River outside City Point, a meeting took place between President Lincoln, General Grant, General Sherman and Admiral Porter on board the *River Queen*, Grant's headquarters boat. Held on March 27 and 28, the summit was designed to coordinate the campaigns of the Army and the Navy in the final days of the war. To Grant, the president specifically expressed his desire for a quick end to the war, and wished no reprisals against the Confederates.

One overriding consideration of Sherman's participation in the final offensive was the long distance his army would have to travel to reach Richmond. Marching through hostile territory, devoid of forage for the "bummers" to plunder, meant Sherman's army would have to carry all of their rations, supplies and materials with them. As a consequence, Sherman's army would have to sit tight at Goldsboro until sufficient quantities of stores were transported to their camp. After taking all this into consideration, April 14 was the date scheduled for Sherman to leave Goldsboro. Judging by General Sherman's behavior, he may have been somewhat disappointed that by mid–April his army would still be in North Carolina. He knew Grant was planning to break camp as soon as the roads were passable, in early April, and he wanted very badly to have Grant wait for his army to arrive, to "make a sure thing of it." In deference to his old friend, Grant included Sherman's forces in his plans to destroy Lee's army, but all the while, Grant knew the war was over for General Sherman.

The Union front line was configured in a 40-mile arc extending from a point opposite Richmond around to the southwest of Petersburg. The Army of the Potomac, 125,000 strong, consisted of the 2d, 5th, 6th and 9th Corps, commanded by Gens. Andrew A. Humphreys, Gouverneur K. Warren, Horatio G. Wright, and John G. Parke. Also on hand were the 24th and 25th Corps of the Army of the James, under Gen. Edward O. Ord, who had been transferred from north of the James on March 27 to help Humphreys and Warren extend the Union line as far as possible to the left.

Refusing to attack Lee's fortifications head-on, Grant took advantage of his superior manpower by gradually extending his line to the left during the winter months, compelling his adversary to stretch his own lines likewise. In the process, the Confederate lines became mere defensive skeletons. Dangerously thin, Lee's works were highly susceptible to Union penetration.

On March 29, with General Sheridan back from the Shenandoah Valley, and considering the roads reasonably dry, Grant gave the long-awaited order for the Army of the Potomac to move out. Marching toward the southwest of Petersburg, the Union men were excited and anticipated capturing the Army of Northern Virginia and ending the war. At the same time, Sheridan's 12,000-man cavalry was dispatched to the extreme right of the Confederate line, then at the road junction of Five Forks, 15 miles west of Petersburg. Sheridan's orders were to turn Lee's right and to get in on his rear. Grant planned to provoke Lee into further weakening his center in order to protect his critical right flank. At that point, General Wright's corps, in position and waiting for the command, would charge directly into the Confederate center. Once Wright's corps penetrated Lee's line, the Union forces

The Final Drive to Appomattox

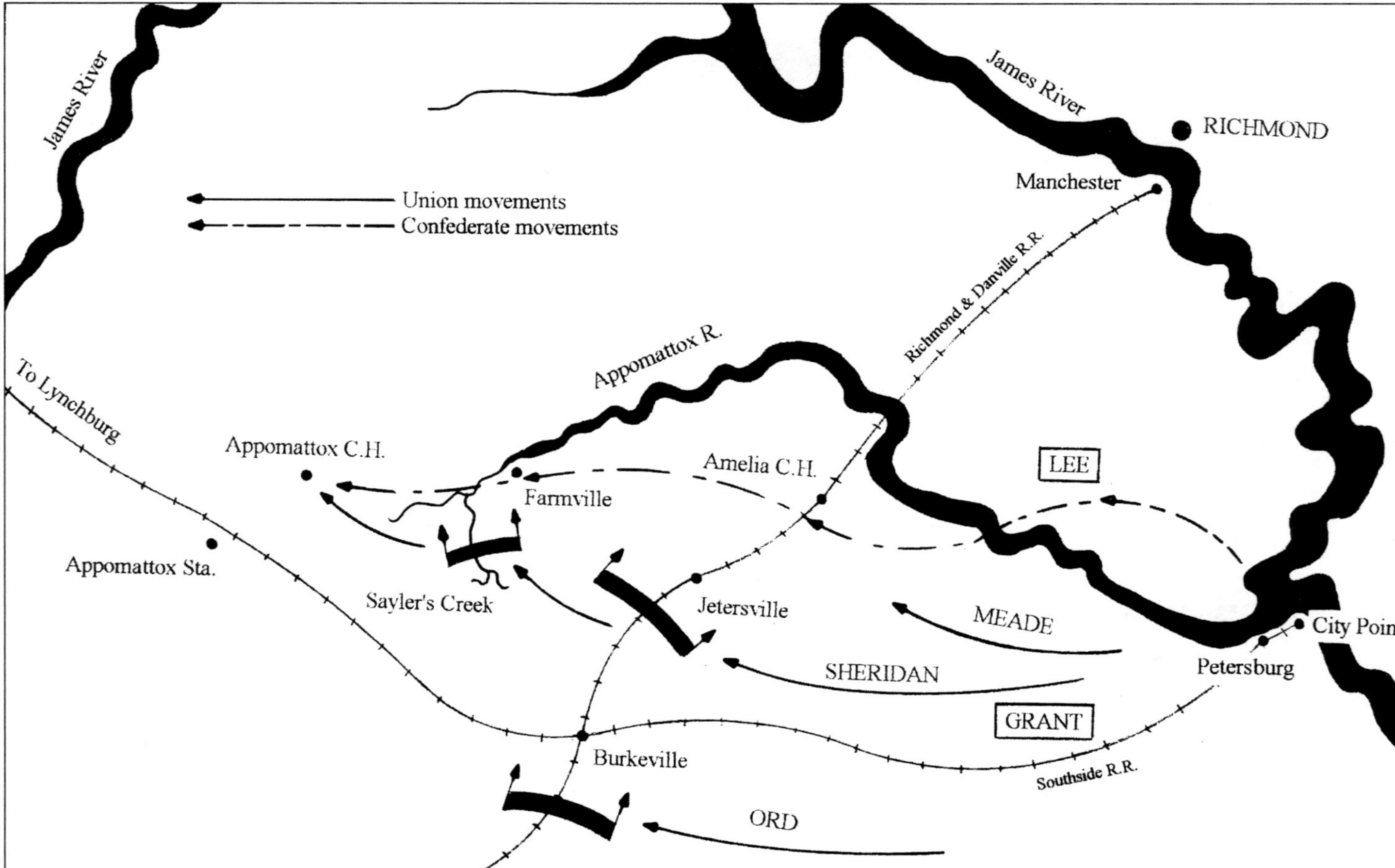

would go directly for the Southside and the Weldon railroads, the only roads still supplying Lee, and critical for his escape.

Another rainstorm moved in on March 30 while Sheridan advanced along the road leading to Five Forks. During the storm, the Union cavalry, without supporting artillery or reinforcements, confronted their Confederate counterparts, commanded by Lee's nephew, Gen. W.H. Fitzhugh Lee. In spite of the terrible weather, Sheridan's troopers drove the enemy horsemen back, but near Five Forks they came under heavy fire from Confederate infantry forces. Without support, Sheridan had no choice but to order his men to retreat to Dinwiddie Court House.

During his retreat to Dinwiddie, Sheridan notified Grant of his plight and requested infantry reinforcements before he made another attempt to breach the Rebel right flank.

In the meantime, General Lee, well aware of Grant's move to attack his right flank, sent Gen. George E. Pickett and his command of two infantry divisions to reinforce the five or so brigades at Five Forks. This sector was so critical to Lee that he rode to Five Forks to supervise personally the defense of his flank.

In response to Sheridan's request for reinforcements, the 5th Infantry Corps, under the command of General Warren, was dispatched to Sheridan's forces to conduct a joint strike on Five Forks. The severe rainstorm had flooded the Gravelly Run, however, causing the river to overflow its banks and preventing Warren's corps, with the exception of one division, from reaching Sheridan in time. By the afternoon of April 1, Sheridan was in position to attack Five Forks, but could not wait much longer for Warren. After repeated attempts by Sheridan's staff to locate Warren proved unsuccessful, the highly irate cavalry chief, with the authorization of Grant, relieved Warren of his command and appointed Gen. Charles Griffin, commander of the 1st Division of the 5th Corps, to replace him. The 5th Corps was then brought up, and Sheridan commenced his assault about dusk. Leading a concentrated attack on Pickett's front line and flank, the combined forces of Sheridan's cavalry and the 5th Corps decimated the Confederate defenders and caused the Rebel line to collapse. Over 5,000 Confederate soldiers, about one half of Pickett's men, quickly surrendered, while the remainder of Pickett's army scattered to the rear in a wild rout. When word of Sheridan's success at Five Forks reached General Grant, the order was immediately given for Wright, with the support of General Parke's corps, to prepare for the next day's attack on the Confederate center.

"The great day had arrived," wrote Gen. Regis de Trobriand.

On April 2, row after row of long blue lines, containing many thousands of Union soldiers, stepped off at 5 A.M. Their advance was a spirited one, filled with the banter and laugher that reflected the supreme confidence expected from this grand Army of the Potomac. Charging against a barrage of musketry and artillery, the Union aggressors breached the Confederate abatis and marched directly into the Rebel lines. Driving back the outmatched Southerners, Wright, pressing from the left side, moved toward Hatcher's Run, where his 5th Corps destroyed the South Side Railroad and took over 3,000 prisoners. A.P. Hill, Confederate general and veteran of the Peninsula Campaign, Cedar Mountain, Antietam, Gettysburg and the Wilderness, was killed in this action. General Parke, advancing steadily on the right, easily overwhelmed the Confederate defenders, and took possession of the outer lines of works in his sector. In the meantime, the troops of Humphreys and Ord, under instructions to commence an assault when the opportunity came, captured the outer picket lines and proceeded to take the outer Confederate entrenchments around Petersburg. To further confound General Lee, Sheridan's cavalry, following up on the past day's victory, penetrated the Rebel line at several points and now possessed the Weldon Railroad.

Recognizing his need for more troops to shore up his right flank, Lee called for General Longstreet, now recovered from his wounds suffered in the Wilderness, to march his 1st Corps over from the north side of the James River. To counter this concentration of Southern forces on Lee's right, Grant ordered Gen. Godfrey Weitzel, commanding the remaining troops of the Army of the James, at Bermuda Hundred, to bring in his troops in order "to keep up close to the enemy," thus tightening the encirclement of the Southern army.

As nightfall crept in and closed a long day, the Union lines nearly surrounded Petersburg from the Appomattox River above the city to the same river below. With Lee on the ropes, Grant planned his knockout punch for the morning, an artillery bombardment to soften the Rebels up a bit, followed by a general assault along the entire front.

With the Southside and the Weldon railroads lost, his outer works in Union hands, his army surrounded by Union forces, and with no food to feed his starving troops, the Confederate commander had run out of options. During the night of April 2, General Lee and his scattered Army of Northern Virginia evacuated Petersburg to assemble at Amelia Court House. "It has happened as I told them in Richmond it would happen," remarked Lee. "The line has been stretched until it is broken."

Earlier, on the morning of April 2, as the Yankee noose was slowly closing around the Confederate army, Lee had sent an urgent telegram to President Davis. It was a Sunday, and Davis was found attending ten o'clock services at St. Paul's Episcopal Church, in Richmond. Reading the message, Davis learned that Lee's lines were broken in three places and that he could no longer hold Petersburg, and that the army would begin to evacuate Petersburg and Richmond that very evening. The congregation's attention was fixed on the Confederate president. They could not help notice his ashen pallor after reading Lee's recommendation for Davis to give up Richmond. Davis and his party left the church, and by nightfall Davis and his cabinet had abandoned Richmond for Danville, 140 miles to the south.

The most striking feature of this departure was that Davis and his government entourage left Richmond aboard a freight train, with each car clearly identifying a different cabinet department. The Confederate government was now on wheels and under the circumstances, forced to be mobile.

That night, after the government and most of the Confederate soldiers left Richmond, rowdy mobs took over the city. Looting was rampant. The shops, mills, warehouses, factories and even homes were ravaged by the citizens of Richmond. Hungry and destitute, their months of suffering culminated in a wild orgy of lawlessness. Drinking plundered whiskey exacerbated the excited crowds' madness. Fires were started, and before long the shifting winds carried hot embers over the entire city. Soon, Richmond was a blazing inferno, out of control. Over 900 buildings were destroyed. All the while, within this chaos and madness, the city's black residents were screaming with joy and dancing in the streets. In the Navy yard, the new ironclad, *Virginia,* was scuttled in a tremendous explosion along with several steamers and gunboats. Adding to this grotesque spectacle, the military arsenal, also in flames, lighted the night sky as magazines and boxes of ammunition were consumed in the blaze.

A Confederate colonel evacuating the fallen capital described his impressions looking back on the dense pall of smoke hanging over

Richmond: "The old war-scarred city seems to prefer annihilation to conquest—a useless sacrifice, however much it may have added to the grandeur of the closing act."

On May 3, General Grant received word from General Weitzel that Richmond had been evacuated and that he was in possession of the city. At 8 A.M., the Stars and Stripes were hoisted above the capitol building.

After maintaining a siege for ten months, General Grant and General Meade finally entered the city of Petersburg. From a house they occupied that morning, Grant and Meade watched as Confederate troops filled the streets some distance away and escaped across a bridge over the Appomattox River. Gazing at the demoralized men fleeing from the city, Grant refused to fire on the ragged and starved remnants of the once-proud army. As the general would explain, "I had not the heart to turn the artillery on such a mass of defeated and fleeing men, and I hoped to capture them soon."

Despite the arrangements for Sherman and his western army to participate in Lee's demise, Grant had secretly planned for some time to have the Army of the Potomac the sole victors in the eastern theater. In Grant's opinion, the western armies were already successful from the Mississippi River to North Carolina. On the other hand, the Army of Northern Virginia was the sole enemy of the eastern forces, who had for so long attempted to subdue them. It was only fitting, therefore, that the Army of the Potomac would receive full credit for Lee's downfall.

When told of the evacuation of Richmond, Lincoln was at City Point waiting for news about Grant's attack. Elated over this glorious information, Lincoln said, "Thank God, that I have lived to see this! It seems to me that I have been dreaming a horrid nightmare for four years, and now the nightmare is over. I want to see Richmond."

At Richmond, the president was welcomed as the Messiah and great Emancipator. The black residents, still inhabiting the burned out and otherwise-deserted city flocked around Lincoln singing and weeping. Beaming with joy, they struggled to touch him to see if he was indeed real. Following a visit to Davis' home and the state house, Lincoln started back for Washington, somewhat depressed and saddened over the terrible scenes of despair and destruction that he had observed.

XX
Lee Surrenders at Appomattox
(April 1865)

The Army of Northern Virginia, finally flushed out into the open, was in full retreat toward the small village of Amelia Court House, some 35 miles west of Petersburg. In a scene reminiscent of an English foxhunt, the Union forces quickly sprang into action to chase and trap Lee's fleeing army.

The Confederate soldiers were exhausted, hungry and totally demoralized. Fed up after this latest turn of events, many threw their weapons away to search the surrounding area for something to eat, only to be captured by the Union armies lurking nearby. Others, too weak to continue, simply fell out of the ranks and sat by the road, while some merely trudged out to the Union lines and surrendered. Not believing his eyes over the sight of his diminishing army, Lee exclaimed, "My God, has the army dissolved?"

Sometime previously, Lee had sent off a dispatch to Danville for 200,000 rations to be delivered by rail to Amelia Court House. Consequently, after evacuating Petersburg on April 2, the Confederate army marched west, crossing the Appomattox River at Goode's Bridge to reach the Danville Railroad. Once in possession of the rations, Lee intended to follow the rails south for seven miles to Jetersville, and then go another 13 miles to Burkesville, where a waiting train would transport his troops to General Johnston's army in

North Carolina. Lee's plan was simple enough, but first he had to reach Burkesville.

General Grant suspected Lee's intentions. From his headquarters in City Point, Grant fired off orders directing Meade to pursue Lee from Petersburg. He also ordered Sheridan to post an infantry corps across the Danville Railroad line at Jetersville to prevent Lee's army from reaching Burkesville, and to hold this position until the rest of the army arrived. At the same time, the Army of the James, under General Ord, marching west along the Southside Railroad, was directed to take possession of Burkesville.

Skirmishing with the Union cavalry during the day and marching during the night, the exhausted and road-weary Rebels reached Amelia Court House on April 5. Little did Lee know that on that very day, the Union cavalry and the corps of Gens. Wright and Humphreys had arrived at Jetersville, only seven miles away, to join forces with Sheridan's 18,000 men now entrenched there. Even General Grant was in Jetersville, having moved his headquarters from City Point to be on hand for the final victory. Also arriving on the 5th was the Army of the James, with General Parke's 9th Corps, marching into Burkesville that night. As the troops filed into the Union camp, Sheridan extended his lines farther and farther to the northwest, gradually enclosing Lee's diminishing forces.

At Amelia Court House, Lee suffered yet another setback. His promised rations were not to be found. Lee's order, found by Sheridan's troopers, had never left the telegraph office in Jetersville. Desperate for food, Lee's men fanned out into the surrounding area foraging for whatever they could find to eat. After spending 24 hours searching for food in an area affording very little in the way of edibles, their diet for some time would be kernels of corn meant for the horses to eat, parched in the coals, mixed with salt, and eaten on the road. This "meal" was so tough to chew that "It made the jaws ache, and the gums so sore as to cause almost unendurable pain."

Finding the road to Burkesville blocked by Union infantry, Lee was forced to revise his escape route to the southwest, toward Farmville, a small, obscure village on the south side of the Appomattox River.

In hot pursuit, General Sheridan's command, now including Wright's 6th Corps, met the Confederate army on April 6 at Sayler's Creek, a tiny tributary flowing north into the Appomattox. Sheridan's adversary at Sayler's Creek was Gen. Richard S. Ewell, veteran of both Bull Runs, the Shenandoah campaign, Antietam, Gettysburg and the Wilderness campaign. Ewell's corps of 4,200 men was sent to reinforce Pickett's division, now dreadfully reduced to a mere 800 troops. The Union forces, commanding the high ground, had the advantage of position and manpower. Utilizing their superiority to the fullest, Sheridan's deadly artillery found its mark and drove the Southerners to the rear. In the heavy fighting, Pickett's division broke, never to be reformed again. Despite their hardships, the remaining Confederate soldiers did not give up. Fighting with the same tenacity that the Army of Northern Virginia had always been known for, however, proved inadequate now. Overwhelmed by sheer numbers, General Ewell was captured, with most of his command. By the time darkness crept over the field, over 7,000 Confederate prisoners were brought into the Union side. The fighting at Sayler's Creek was Lee's last major battle of the war, and according to Gen. Regis de Trobriand, "the coup de grace to Lee's army."

Union forces marched into Farmville on the morning of April 7 as the Confederate troops crossed to the northern side of the Appomattox, destroying the bridge behind them.

After his capture, General Ewell admitted to a Union officer, a relative of his, that the Southern cause was lost. He also expressed his hope for Lee to surrender because, as he saw it, from now on the killing would be nothing short of murder, and both generals would have to live with the blood on their hands. When this conversation was conveyed to the general-in-chief, it pressured Grant into considering anew the tremendous disparity of the opposing armies and the inevitable results expected. This compelled Grant to question the morality of causing further bloodshed and death. Now foremost in Grant's mind was the belief that the responsibility for the useless waste of human lives must not be his. On April 7, from the hotel serving as his headquarters in Farmville, the Union general communicated a message to General Lee, requesting that he surrender the Army of Northern Virginia. The message read:

> General R.E. Lee, Commanding C.S.A.: April 7, 1865
>
> The results of the last week must convince you of the hopelessness of further resistance on the part of the Army of Northern Virginia in this struggle. I feel that it is so, and regard it as my duty to shift from myself the responsibility of any further effusion of blood, by asking of you the

> surrender of that portion of the Confederate States army known as the Army of Northern Virginia.
>
> *U.S. Grant, Lieutenant-General*

That same evening, April 7, General Lee responded to Grant's request for surrender:

> General: I have received your note of this day. Though not entertaining the opinion you express on the hopelessness of further resistance on the part of the Army of Northern Virginia, I reciprocate your desire to avoid useless effusion of blood, and therefore before considering your proposition, ask the terms you will offer on condition of the surrender.
>
> *R.E. Lee, General*

The following day, General Grant penned this reply:

> General R.E. Lee, Commanding C.S.A.: April 8, 1865
>
> Your note of last evening in reply to mine of same date, asking the conditions on which I will accept the surrender of the Army of Northern Virginia is just received. In reply I would say that, peace being my great desire, there is but one condition I would insist upon, namely: that the men and officers surrendered shall be disqualified for taking up arms again against the Government of the United States until properly exchanged. I will meet you, or will designate officers to meet any officers you may name for the same purpose, at any point agreeable to you, for the purpose of arranging definitely the terms upon which the surrender of the Army of Northern Virginia will be received.
>
> *U.S. Grant, Lieutenant-General*

Grant's letters were delivered to General Humphreys' front, that being the closest to Lee's army, from which they were sent into Confederate lines. Lee's letters to Grant were routed along the same channels but from the opposite direction.

Suffering terribly from a severe tension headache, General Grant was aroused from his sleep on the night of April 8. Handed another letter from Lee, Grant read,

> General: I received at a late hour your note of to-day. In mine of yesterday I did not intend to propose the surrender of the Army of Northern Virginia, but to ask the terms of your proposition. To be frank, I do not think the emergency has arisen to call for the surrender of this army, but, as the restoration of peace should be the sole object of all, I desired to know whether your proposals would lead to that end. I cannot,

> therefore, meet you with a view to surrender the Army of Northern Virginia; but as far as your proposal may affect the Confederate States forces under my command, and tend to the restoration of peace, I should be pleased to meet you at 10 A.M. to-morrow on the stage road to Richmond, between the picket-lines of the two armies.
>
> *R.E. Lee, General*

After reading Lee's letter, Grant conferred with General Meade about Lee's insistence on discussing peace but not the surrender of his army. On April 9 the Union commander-in-chief wrote the following:

> General: Your note of yesterday is received. I have no authority to treat on the subject of peace. The meeting proposed for 10 A.M. to-day could lead to no good. I will state, however, that I am equally desirous for peace with yourself, and the whole North entertains the same feeling. The terms upon which peace can be had are well understood. By the South laying down their arms, they would hasten that most desirable event, save thousands of lives, and hundreds of millions of property not yet destroyed. Seriously hoping that all our difficulties may be settled without the loss of another life, I subscribe myself, etc.
>
> *U.S. Grant, Lieutenant-General*

Pursued by the corps of Gens. Wright and Humphreys, Lee continued his retreat, now toward Appomattox Station after learning that four Confederate supply trains were there for the taking. General Sheridan was also aware of the provisions at Appomattox, and his cavalry arrived first, immediately taking possession of the much sought-after provisions.

That night, near Appomattox Court House, Lee and his commanders, sitting around a bivouac fire, held their last council of war. In the flickering glow of the fire, General Lee informed the group, Longstreet, Gordon and Fitzhugh Lee, of his communications with Grant, and of the proposal to surrender. After the discussions, they agreed that surrender was the final option and that one last attempt should be made to break through the Union lines and head for Lynchburg. When the meeting was over, Lee remarked, "I will strike that man a blow in the morning."

On the morning of April 9, Palm Sunday, Lee's 1,600 advance troops under the command of Gen. John B. Gordon were surprised to find Gen. George A. Custer and his cavalrymen holding the rations needed so badly by the starving Rebels. Soon, however, the rest of Lee's army arrived as well as the Union's 5th Corps and three divisions of the Army of the James. The Union troops sensed that four years of fighting would end here, on this day, at this hour. Motivated by this new rush of pride in themselves and their army, the Union soldiers fought with unparalleled aggressiveness. Outmatched, outgunned, and too weak to continue, General Gordon's men, on the verge of collapse, were about to break. The last charge of the war for the Army of Northern Virginia had failed.

Gordon's troops were near collapse, Longstreet's corps were heavily engaged and struggling with the Union 6th and 2d Corps, as well as being outnumbered four to one. Lee finally relented to the futility of further resistance, saying, "There is nothing left but to go and see General Grant, and I had rather die a thousand deaths." Shortly before noon, Lee ordered a white flag hoisted and a halt to the firing until terms of surrender were fixed.

That night, in the Confederate camp, the dejected troops saw visible evidence of their defeat. They saw the glowing night sky, lighted by the thousands of Union campfires nearly surrounding their tiny enclave.

On the morning of April 9, General Grant was about three miles from Appomattox Court House when a Confederate officer and his escort delivered a letter from General Lee which read,

> General: I received your note of this morning on the picket-line whither I had come to meet you and ascertain definitely what terms were embraced in your proposal of yesterday with reference to the surrender of this army. I now request an interview in accordance with the offer contained in your letter of yesterday for that purpose.

After reading Lee's letter, Grant's headache seemed to disappear. At last the day had come and Grant gladly wrote a reply,

> General R.E. Lee, Commanding C.S. Army: April 9, 1865
>
> Your note of this date is but this moment (11:50 A.M.) received, in consequence of my having passed from the Richmond and Lynchburg road to the Farmville and Lynchburg road. I am at this writing about four miles west of Walker's Church and will push forward to the front for the purpose of meeting you. Notice sent to me on this road where you wish the interview to take place will meet me.
>
> *U.S. Grant, Lieutenant-General*

Soon after Grant dispatched this letter to General Lee, around 1 P.M., he mounted his horse, Cincinnati, and accompanied by his aide, Gen. Horace Porter, started for Appomattox Court House.

Grant's message was delivered to Lee by Col. Orville E. Babcock, a member of Grant's military staff. Babcock found Lee resting under an apple tree by the road. Lee and his secretary, Col. Charles Marshall, began their ride to Appomattox, followed by Marshall's orderly and Colonel Babcock. Riding into Appomattox, which was nothing more than a handful of houses and only one road, Lee's party hailed a resident standing out on the street. They asked the resident, Mr. Wilmer McClean, if he could direct them to adequate accommodations for General Lee. When the visitors were not entirely satisfied with the room they were shown, McClean offered the use of his own home for the occasion. Here, sitting in Mr. McClean's parlor, General Lee and Colonel Marshall waited for Grant's arrival.

When Grant and Porter reached Appomattox, a small group of Union officers were seen by the road. Among them were General Ord and General Sheridan, who pointed out the McClean home and escorted Grant and Porter to the residence.

Dismounting in the front yard, the four Union officers were greeted by Colonel Babcock's orderly, who ushered General Grant into the McClean house. The house, a brick dwelling with a large porch, consisted of two comfortable-sized rooms separated by a central hall running down the middle of the house. A few minutes later, Colonel Marshall came to the porch and beckoned the officers standing outside to enter the sparsely furnished room. The Union officers filed into the room and quietly positioned themselves along the walls at the sides of the room, "very much as people enter a sick-chamber when they expect to find the patient dangerously ill," reported Gen. Horace Porter. The mood was somber and formal. General Lee and General Grant sat by separate small tables, politely discussing their service in the Mexican War. At this point, Lee abruptly turned Grant's attention to the proposed terms of the surrender, and requested that Grant put them in writing, "so that they may be formally acted on."

Following his reading of Grant's penciled draft, Lee informed Grant that many of his men owned their own horses, and asked if they would be permitted to keep them. Although not specifically written in the terms, Grant agreed to allow it, ordering that any Confederate soldier claiming to own a horse or mule would be allowed to take the animal home with him. This concession was made because Grant thought that the soldiers returning home would need the animals to work their farms again. The draft documents were handed to a member of Grant's staff, Col. Ely S. Parker, a full-blooded Indian and chief of the Six Nations. Having the best handwriting of those present, Parker rewrote the formal document outlining the terms of surrender in ink, as follows:

> APPOMATTOX Ct. H., Va., April 9, 1865
>
> General R.E. Lee, Commanding C.S.A.
>
> General: In accordance with the substance of my letter to you of the 8th inst., I propose to receive the surrender of the Army of Northern Virginia on the following terms, to wit: Rolls of all the officers and men to be made in duplicate, one copy to be given to an officer to be designated by me, the other to be retained by such officer or officers as you may designate. The officers to give their individual paroles not to take up arms against the Government of the United States until properly exchanged, and each company or regimental commander to sign a like parole for the men of their commands. The arms, artillery, and public property to be parked, and stacked, and turned over to the officers, nor their private horses or baggage. This done, each officer and man will be allowed to return to his home, not to be disturbed by the United States authorities so long as they observe their paroles, and the laws in force where they may reside.
>
> Very Respectfully,
>
> *U.S. GRANT, Lieutenant-General*

Meanwhile, Colonel Marshall, at the behest of General Lee, was writing a formal letter of acceptance for the terms of surrender. After much editing by General Lee, the letter read:

> HEADQUARTERS, ARMY OF NORTHERN VIRGINIA, April 9, 1865
>
> General: I received your letter of this date containing the terms of the surrender of the Army of Northern Virginia as proposed by you. As they are substantially the same as those expressed in your letter of the 8th inst., they are accepted. I will proceed to designate the proper officers to carry the stipulations into effect.
>
> *R.E. Lee, General*

As the documents were being copied, General Grant introduced Lee to the Union officers standing around the room. At this point, General Lee informed Grant that, without rations, his men had been living on parched corn. The discussion then turned to the distribution of rations for Lee's hungry troops. Estimating Lee's army at about 25,000 men, Grant issued orders to furnish all of them with the provisions they so desperately needed.

Not wearing a sidearm himself, Grant found his attention drawn to General Lee's magnificent sword, presented to him by the state of Virginia. Following several minutes of idle conversation between the two generals about Lee's sword, the two documents were signed and sealed at 4 P.M. Then, with a handshake and a bow, General Lee mounted his large, gray horse, Traveller, and rode toward the Confederate lines to deliver the unhappy news to his troops.

Watching General Lee from the steps of the front porch, Grant later wrote, "I felt ... sad and depressed at the downfall of a foe who had fought so long and valiantly, and had suffered so much for a cause, though that cause was, I believe, one of the worst for which a people ever fought."

As word of Lee's surrender spread through the Union camp, wild and joyous celebrations took place, with batteries firing off 100-gun salutes. Hearing the demonstrations while riding back to his headquarters, Grant sent out orders for the celebrations to stop, saying, "The war is over, the rebels are our countrymen again, and the best sign of rejoicing after the victory will be to abstain from all demonstrations in the field."

On April 10, before leaving his troops, General Lee issued his last order to his men:

> After four years of arduous service, marked by unsurpassed courage and fortitude, the Army of Northern Virginia has been compelled to yield to overwhelming numbers and resources. I need not tell the survivors of so many hard-fought battles, who have remained steadfast to the last, that I have consented to this result from no distrust of them, but, feeling that valor and devotion could accomplish nothing that could compensate for the loss that would have attended the continuation of the contest, I have determined to avoid the useless sacrifice of those whose past services have endeared them to their countrymen.
>
> By the terms of the agreement, officers and men can return to their homes, and remain there until exchanged. You will take with you the satisfaction that proceeds from the consciousness of duty faithfully performed; and I earnestly pray that a merciful God will extend to you his blessing and protection.
>
> With an increasing admiration for your constancy and devotion to your country, and a grateful remembrance of your kind and generous consideration of myself, I bid you an affectionate farewell.
>
> *R.E. Lee, General*

At the McClean house that morning, General Grant spent several hours greeting many Confederate officers who were old friends of his and had come to see him and to pay their respects. Then, about noon, with Gens. John Gibbons, Wesley Merritt, and Charles Griffin in charge of paroling Lee's troops, General Grant and his staff left for Washington.

Epilogue

On April 12, the formal ceremony accepting the surrender of the Army of Northern Virginia was conducted without pomp and circumstance but with a sense of respect and solemnity. For the many Union soldiers staring wide-eyed at the proceedings, it was a sad spectacle indeed to witness the ragged, emaciated and dispirited remnants of the once-mighty Confederate army march into their camp. The Union bands were quiet. There were no gun salutes. Nobody was cheering, and nobody was celebrating. A strange stillness prevailed, punctuated by an occasional command, loud and sharp, and the clatter of weapons being stacked as 28,231 Southern soldiers lay down their arms and furled their colors. It marked the end of a four-year struggle, a struggle that had left the country battered and bleeding, but somewhat wiser then it had been four years earlier.

In charge of the ceremony was Gen. Joshua L. Chamberlain, the hero and Medal of Honor winner for his gallant efforts on Little Round Top at Gettysburg. Leading the Southerners as they marched toward Chamberlain's brigades was John B. Gordon, one of Lee's most aggressive fighters, wounded five times, once through the face, and who now commanded Stonewall Jackson's old corps. First in line behind him marched the Stonewall Brigade, five regiments containing the last 210 ragged survivors of four years of battle. As General Gordon led his men by the Union troops, standing proudly erect in formation, Gordon's downcast gaze reflected this most painful and crushing moment in his life. At that point Chamberlain gave a sharp command from order arms to carry arms, a salute of honor. "At the sound of that machine-like snap of arms," Chamberlain wrote, "General Gordon started ... [then] wheeled his horse facing me, touching him gently with the spur so that the animal slightly reared, and as he wheeled, horse and rider made one motion, the horse's head swung down with a graceful bow, and General Gordon dropped his sword-point to his toe in salutation." Gordon in turn ordered his own men to carry arms. The adversaries of four bloody years ended the war not with humiliation on one side and triumph on the other but with soldiers' mutual salutes and farewells.

Two days later, President Lincoln was assassinated by a single gunshot to the temple while he and his wife enjoyed a stage play at Ford's Theater in Washington. His assassin, John Wilkes Booth, an actor and Southern sympathizer, wrote, "Our country owed all her troubles to him, and God simply made me the instrument of His Punishment." After an intensive manhunt, Booth was cornered in a burning barn on April 26 and shot to death. Eight other people were convicted of complicity in Lincoln's assassination. Four were sentenced to prison terms ranging from six years to life. The remaining four, three men and one woman, judged to be more actively involved in the plot, were hanged on July 7 on the grounds of the Old Penitentiary Building.

In a dilapidated little house near Durham Station, North Carolina, Gen. Joseph E. Johnston capitulated and surrendered the Army of Tennessee on April 26. Initially, Sherman had offered conditional terms that included the United States' recognition of existing state governments and a general amnesty. With these terms quickly rejected by an angry President Andrew Johnson and Secretary Stanton, Sherman revised them to reflect those given to Lee at Appomattox.

The two remaining active armies, those of Gen. Richard Taylor and Gen. E. Kirby Smith, surrendered on May 4 and May 26, respectively, both to Union Gen. Edward R.S. Canby, commander of the Army of the Gulf. Taylor surrendered at Citronelle, Alabama, near Mobile, and Smith at New Orleans.

In human terms, the cost of the war had been catastrophic. Over 640,000 men had died in the four years of fighting. More American lives were lost in the Civil War than in the total from all the other wars the U.S. ever fought, including World War I and World War II. For the North, 380,000 troops never returned home; 258,000 Southerners died for a losing cause. Sickness and disease were the biggest killers of all, accounting for more deaths than battlefield casualties, 60 percent of the Northern deaths, 64 percent of the South's.

In lost property, the cost exceeded four billion dollars. When the dust finally settled, five major Southern cities lay in ruins: Richmond, Charleston, Atlanta, Mobile and Vicksburg.

Jefferson Davis, defiant in his belief that the Confederacy would be reborn, fled west, toward Texas. Davis was located by the Union cavalry in Irwinville, Georgia, captured in his tent on the night of May 10, and brought back east and incarcerated at Fort Monroe. Two years later, he was released on bail without standing trial.

In Washington, a grand review was held to honor the main Northern armies on May 23 and 24, 1865. The 200,000 troops of Meade's and Sherman's armies marched from the Capitol to the Treasury Building in columns of companies. The spectacular parade was witnessed by thousands of people lining the streets, watching from every window and from the Washington rooftops. On Pennsylvania Avenue, the procession passed a reviewing stand containing such dignitaries as the new president, Andrew Johnson; Generals Grant, Meade and Sherman, as well as Johnson's cabinet.

At the end of the march, the soldiers gathered for a final handshake and a sad farewell. With their hearts full and their fate unknown, the victorious Union troops headed for home.

Postwar Notes on Major Figures

Robert Anderson was forced to resign in 1863 from poor health. After Lee's surrender, Anderson returned to Fort Sumter on April 14, 1865, to raise the same American flag he had lowered four years earlier. Anderson died while traveling to France in 1871 and was buried at the United States Military Academy at West Point, New York.

Pierre G.T. Beauregard returned to his home state of Louisiana after declining offers to command the Romanian and the Egyptian armies. He served as president of the New Orleans, Jackson & Mississippi Railroad for five years, managed the Louisiana state lottery, and was commissioner of public works in New Orleans in 1888. He died in New Orleans in 1893.

Braxton Bragg became the chief civil engineer for the state of Alabama, supervising the improvements of Mobile harbor. He was later appointed commissioner of public works. He died suddenly at Galveston, Texas, in 1876.

Ambrose E. Burnside was a director of the Illinois Central Railroad in 1864, after which he became president of several other railroad companies. Burnside was elected governor of Rhode Island from 1866 to 1868 and as its U.S. senator in 1874, serving until his death in Bristol, Rhode Island, in 1881.

Joshua L. Chamberlain entered politics and was elected governor of Maine for four terms. Appointed president of Bowdoin College in 1871, Chamberlain died from an old war wound in Portland, Maine, in 1914.

Jubal A. Early traveled to Mexico and Canada following the war. Finally returning to the United States in 1869, he resumed his old law practice and for a time ran the Louisiana state lottery. He died in Lynchburg, Virginia, in 1894.

Richard S. Ewell was released from a Union prison three months after the end of the war. Following his discharge, Ewell took up residence on a farm in Spring Hill, Tennessee, where he died of pneumonia in 1872.

Ulysses S. Grant went on to serve two terms as the eighteenth president of the United States. Following his stay in the White House, he and his wife embarked on an around-the-world tour, after which he established a residence in New York City. Associated with a Wall Street brokerage firm that went bankrupt, Grant lost everything. Diagnosed with throat cancer in 1885, he moved to the Adirondacks to write his memoirs in order to provide for his family. Unable to eat or speak, Grant died one week after finishing his immensely successful book, in 1885, at the age of 63.

John B. Hood moved to Texas, his adopted home, and became a successful entrepreneur. Taking up residence in New Orleans, Hood was reduced to poverty after several unwise business ventures. He died in 1879 during the yellow fever epidemic with his wife and oldest daughter.

Joseph Hooker was placed in command of the Department of the East in New York City in July 1865, and the Department of the Lakes at Detroit in 1866. Hooker retired in 1868, incapacitated from paralysis, and died in Garden City, New York, in 1879.

Joseph E. Johnston became an insurance agent in Savannah, Georgia, and Richmond, Virginia. While in Richmond, Johnston was elected to Congress for one term in 1878 and was appointed federal commissioner of railroads in 1885. Living in Washington, D.C., Johnston died in 1891 after coming down with pneumonia from standing in the rain during the funeral of his old respected foe, William T. Sherman.

Robert E. Lee became president of Washington College in Lexington, Virginia, now known as Washington and Lee University, where he spent the remainder of his years. At the age of 63, Lee died of a heart attack on October 12, 1870. The postwar Congress refused to restore Lee's citizenship. By a special act of the U.S. Congress, Lee's citizenship was restored posthumously, in 1975.

James C. Longstreet became the head of an insurance firm, but after joining the Republican Party he entered the world of politics. Following his tenure as U.S. minister to Turkey in the Grant administration, Longstreet spent some time as a U.S. marshal in Georgia and as U.S. railroad commissioner. He died in Gainesville, Texas, in 1904.

George B. McClellan lost to Lincoln in the presidential election of 1864 and chose to stay in Europe for the next three years. Returning to the U.S., McClellan participated in several large engineering projects, after which he reentered politics. In 1878, he won the election for governor of New Jersey, and served one three-year term. McClellan died of coronary problems in New Jersey in 1885.

George G. Meade remained in the Army commanding the Military Department of the Atlantic and the Department of the East. In 1868, Meade was transferred to Atlanta, Georgia, to take over the third military district of the Department of the South, and in 1869 he took command of the Military Department of the Atlantic in Philadelphia, a post in which he served until his death in 1872 at the age of 57. Meade died in Philadelphia from pneumonia, a complication resulting from an old wound received in the war.

George E. Pickett turned down a commission as general in the Egyptian army, as well as President Grant's offer of a U.S. marshal's position in Virginia, becoming an insurance agent instead. He died in Norfolk, Virginia, in 1875, and was buried in Richmond.

Philip H. Sheridan was assigned to command American forces on the Mexican border and to fight the Indians from 1865 to 1867, when he was appointed military governor of Texas and Louisiana. After only a few months, Sheridan's policies were considered too extreme, and he was transferred to the command of the Department of Missouri. In 1884, he succeeded Sherman as general-in-chief and died while in Nonquitt, Massachusetts, in 1888 as a full general.

William Tecumseh Sherman was commissioned a lieutenant general in 1866, and following Grant's election to the presidency was promoted to general-in-chief and honored with the rank of full general. Sherman retired in 1883, but remained active as a speaker and writer until his death in 1891 in New York City. His body was interred with full military honors in St. Louis, Missouri.

George H. Thomas was honored by Congress for his service at Nashville and took on a new sobriquet, "Sledge of Nashville." Remaining as commander of the Army of the Tennessee, Thomas refused to accept a promotion to lieutenant general because of its connection to Reconstruction politics. In 1869, Thomas took over the command of the Military Department of the Pacific, but died in San Francisco a year later.

Bibliography

Bradford, Ned, ed. *Battles and Leaders of the Civil War.* 1887. N.p.: Meridian, 1984.
Cannan, John. *The Antietam Campaign.* New York: Gallery Books, 1990.
Catton, Bruce. *The American Heritage Picture of the Civil War.* 1960. New York: Bonanza, 1982.
Davis, William C., and Bell Irvin Wiley, ed. *The Civil War Times Illustrated Photographic History of the Civil War.* 1981. 2 vols. New York: Black Dog and Leventhal, 1994.
Eisenschiml, Otto, and Ralph Newman, ed. *The Civil War: The American Iliad, As Told by Those Who Lived It.* 1947. New York: Mallard, 1991.
Hunt, Harrison. *Heroes of the Civil War.* New York: Military Press, 1990.
Kolchin, Peter. *American Slavery 1619—1877.* New York: Hill and Wang, 1993.
Kunhardt, Dorothy M., and Philip B. Kunhardt. *Twenty Days: A Narrative in Text and Pictures of the Assassination of Abraham Lincoln and the Twenty Days and Nights That Followed— The Nation in Mourning, the Long Trip Home to Springfield.* New York: Castle Books, 1965.
Kunhardt, Philip B., Jr., Philip B. Kunhardt III, and Peter W. Kunhardt. *Lincoln, An Illustrated Biography.* New York: Knopf, 1992.
McPherson, James M. *Battle Cry of Freedom: The Civil War Era.* 1988. New York: Ballantine, 1989.
Nofi, Albert A., ed. *The Bloody Struggle: The Civil War Era.* 1862. New York: Gallery, 1988.
_____, ed. *Opening Guns: Fort Sumter to Bull Run, 1861.* New York: Gallery, 1988.
Reynolds, Clark G. *The Civil War.* New York: Mallard, 1991.
Stiles, T.J., ed. *Civil War Commanders.* New York: Berkley, 1995.
Ward, Geoffrey C. *The Civil War: An Illustrated History.* New York: Knopf, 1990.
Welsh, Douglas. *The Complete Military History of the Civil War.* N.p.: Dorset, 1990.

Index